AFTER OEDIPUS

AFTER OEDIPUS

SHAKESPEARE IN PSYCHOANALYSIS

Julia Reinhard Lupton
and Kenneth Reinhard

Cornell University Press

ITHACA AND LONDON

International Standard Book Number 0–8014–2407–0 (cloth)
International Standard Book Number 0–8014–9687-x (paper)
Library of Congress Catalog Card Number 92–54975
Printed in the United States of America
Librarians: Library of Congress cataloging information appears
on the last page of the book.

For our parents and step-parents

Contents

Acknowledgments   ix
A Note on Citations   xi
Introduction   1

PART ONE: *HAMLET* IN PSYCHOANALYSIS

1   "Shapes of Grief": *Hamlet,* Freud, and Mourning   11
2   The *Trauerspiel* of Criticism   34
3   *Hamlet*'s Flesh: Lacan and the Desire of the Mother   60
4   *Hamlet*'s "Ursceneca"   89

INTER-SECTION   119

PART TWO: THE *LEAR* REAL

5   The Motif of the Three Caskets   145
6   The Lacanian Thing   163
7   The Tragedy of Foreclosure   190

AFTER-WORD   230

Works Cited   248
Index   263

Acknowledgments

The writing of this book over the last several years has brought us into contact with many people whose learning, advice, and interests have variously shaped our thinking about this project. Special thanks are due to Thomas Greene at Yale and Neil Hertz and John Irwin at Johns Hopkins. Other teachers who influenced our thinking and who advised us on the book at various points include Judith Butler, Jonathan Crewe, John Guillory, Ruth Leys, Rainer Nägele, and Peter Sacks. Bruce Fink has probably guided our thinking about Lacan more than anyone else. As a teacher at the Paris Lacan Workshop, as leader of the Lacan Reading Group at The University of California–Irvine, and as a reader of the manuscript in its many avatars, Bruce has generously shared his time, his knowledge, and, along with Héloïse Fink, his friendship with us. Vincent Pecora, Lowell Gallagher, Robert Watson, and the other participants in the UCLA Critical Studies and the Human Sciences seminar provided cogent criticisms of Chapter 7. The Organized Research Initiative on Women and the Image at the University of California–Irvine provided research assistance. At Irvine, Michael Clark, Alex Gelley, Juliet Flower Mac-Cannell, Jane Newman, and John Smith have offered advice and support. At other institutions, we would also like to thank Harry Berger, Jr., Daniel Buccino, Cynthia Chase, Marjorie Garber, Russell Grigg, Natasha Korda, Timothy Murray, Eric

Nicholson, Jahan Ramazani, Avital Ronell, and Jacqueline Rose for their useful readings and interest. We thank Rabbi Elie Spitz for providing intellectual and personal guidance of another order.

Our students have been invaluable sounding boards as well as astute critics. Jacques Duvoisin, Philip Leider, Tracy McNulty, and Timothy Murphy were excellent research assistants and readers of the manuscript. The participants in our graduate courses on Seneca and *Lear* at Irvine and melancholia and psychosis at UCLA from 1990 to 1992 were always stimulating and patient interlocuters.

Bruce Fink has advised us on our translations of Lacan, and Ellen Lupton designed the graphs, which are modified versions of Lacan's. Bernhard Kendler, Andrew Lewis, Joanne Hindman, and the readers for Cornell University Press have provided useful criticism on the many drafts of this book. Victor Burgin generously allowed us to reprint his photograph from *The Bridge* for the dust jacket of this book.

A version of Chapter 1 appeared in *Genders* 4 (1989); we thank *Genders* and its publisher, the University of Texas Press, both for permission to reprint and for editorial comments.

Finally we thank our families. Frank Reinhard and Rosalind Reinhard have been ever generous with their love, their support, and their confidence in the value of our vocation. Mary Jane Lupton and Kenneth Baldwin have combined their deep affection and interest with occasional reminders that Freud came before Lacan. William Lupton and Shirley Landon Lupton have continually shown us that intellectuals need not be academics. We thank Ellen Lupton for agreeing to give her twin away in marriage, and Jerry Abbott Miller for taking such good care of the remaining half.

JULIA REINHARD LUPTON and KENNETH REINHARD
Irvine and Los Angeles, California

A Note on Citations

Works by Freud are cited from *The Standard Edition* (*SE*) and the *Studienausgabe* (*SA*), unless noted otherwise.

Works by Lacan are cited from *Écrits* (E = English edition, F = French edition) and from the seminars, unless noted otherwise. We used published translations when available, modified as indicated. When published translations were not available, we used our own, unless noted otherwise. Unpublished seminars are cited by date of session as well as page number of typescripts.

Editions used in different languages are abbreviated as follows: E = English; F = French; G = German.

We have used the Arden editions of *Hamlet* and *Lear* and the Riverside edition of all other plays by Shakespeare.

AFTER OEDIPUS

INTRODUCTION

"A little more than kin, and less than kind": Hamlet's first line in the play diagnoses in advance the relationship between Shakespeare and psychoanalysis as a bad pun that renders discursive filiations overdetermined and unchaste, "too much in the sun." It is not so much that Shakespeare and psychoanalysis are of different kinds—tragedy versus theory—but rather that their very proximity renders them "less than kind," prone to sibling rivalry and other children's games, from "playing doctor" to the Hegelian "struggle for pure prestige." If the first game describes the sexual research of psychoanalysis as an infantile theory applied to literature, the latter marks the "mirror up to philosophy" in which the structuralist and poststructuralist Shakespeares fruitlessly multiply.

In relation to Oedipal tragedy, *Hamlet* is "less than kind"; that is, *Hamlet* remains within the classical genre of *Oedipus Rex* but only as its Baroque falling off. Psychoanalysis, however, is "more than kin" to both *Oedipus Rex* and *Hamlet*, fashioning out of the one play an incestuous namesake ("Incest, thy name is Oedipus"), and out of the other, a hermeneutic copy machine that unkindly reproduces "more" of Oedipus everywhere. This intersection of deficit and excess marks Shakespeare and psychoanalysis as kindred discourses that fall "after Oedipus," both "in the manner of, according to Oedipus" (as a painting might be "after" Raphael), and as logically consequent and chron-

1

ologically subsequent to, as the addendum, revision, or *Nachtrag* of, Oedipus. Moreover, it is precisely in its engagement with Shakespeare, we argue, that psychoanalysis comes up against the limits of Oedipal narrative, both its pre-Oedipal origination and its post-Oedipal denouement. Finally, if "After Oedipus" sounds elegiac, it is only fitting that mourning be the theoretical and intertextual apparatus that both constructs and dissolves the Oedipus complex, leaving in its wake what Lacan calls the "scraps and fragments" of Oedipal tragedy.

The sexual and linguistic economy of Hamlet's line compels us to think the relationship between Shakespeare and psychoanalysis in a conceptual framework other than those of influence, anticipation, or exemplification. Shakespeare is "more than kin," more than a passive literary source for psychoanalysis, and therefore "less than kind," refusing to serve as a convenient poetic prediction and confirmation of theory. Although the Shakespearean text may offer figures of psychoanalytic theory, it does so actively—as an intertextual participant in the leaps, lags, and lapses of psychoanalysis as a discourse. The mode of this encounter is not simply one of "influence," in either its passive or active senses: as we suggest further on, Shakespeare is both an object *in* psychoanalysis—imagined and shaped by it—and an object as *cause* of psychoanalysis, which, like a rock in a stream or a knot in wood, silently reorients the discourse that closes around it.

The Shakespeare that has informed and been formed by psychoanalysis includes not only Shakespeare as a set of themes or character types, but also Shakespeare as a process of signification: patterns of intertextual transformation that migrate between Shakespeare, classical drama, and modern theory. Furthermore, this shift from "Shakespeare the man" to "Shakespeare the text"—from the proper name as it authorizes an imaginary set of meanings to the metonymy of a symbolic set of relations and mutations—must be thought in conjunction with "Shakespeare the signifier," the improper noun that marks the nonidentity of both man and work. Thus Hamlet's quip poses a riddle about the signifier: what's more than "kin" is, of course, the "d" of "kind," the letter that makes the difference upon which the pun depends. As a pun about punning, about linguistic and sexual similarity and difference, the line enacts the structural incest between literal incest and incest of the letter. As signifier, "Shakespeare" is the killing letter substituted in the night by Hamlet and delivered to the Anglo-America of literary criticism by way of the France and Austria of psychoanalysis, which, to modify Freud's phrase, has unwittingly "brought the pla(y)gue" of Shakespeare to both criticism and itself.

The history and logic of psychoanalytic criticism can be mapped according to the shifting conceptualization of the object in Lacanian discourse: the object *of* desire, the object *in* desire, and the object as *cause* of desire. This first moment of Freudian criticism, dominated by the techniques of psychobiography and character analysis, applied theory to literature considered as an exemplary object to be mastered by science and philosophy. Facilitating the introduction of Lacan into American literary criticism, Shoshana Felman's incisive prolegomenon, "To Open the Question," opposed the procedures of such "application" to the structural discourse of "implication": "The interpreter's role would here be, not to *apply* to the text an acquired science, a preconceived knowledge, but to act as a go-between, to *generate implications* between literature and psychoanalysis—to explore, bring to light and articulate the various (indirect) ways in which the two domains do indeed *implicate each other,* each one finding itself enlightened, informed, but also affected, displaced, by the other" (8–9). Taking the symbolization of the imaginary as its structuring imperative, this second moment of "implicating" literature and psychoanalysis is supported by Lacan's insistence that the object *of* desire is always rather an object *in* desire, constituted by rather than anterior to the displacements of representation. And whereas "application," in casting the literary object as the discrete, autonomous, and passive other of interpretive activity, ends up projecting literature as its self-confirming mirror, "implication" traces the retroactive production of the object in critical analysis, whose philosophical reflections are in turn refracted by the literary significations they purport to analyze. As such, the "implication" of literature and theory in large part entails the study of the symbolic conditions and consequences of theory's imaginary application.

Whereas the wave of innovative criticism announced by Felman's work has been informed by the structuralist dialectic of the imaginary and symbolic in the early Lacan, the current state of the Freudian field is oriented by the attempt to accommodate the category of the "real," which is approached with increasing urgency in Lacan's later seminars. Conceptualizing the real occasioned Lacan's rethinking of the object as the *cause* of desire, the *objet a*. As a fragment of unsymbolized reality, the cause of desire is a "thing" more than an object, at once the material origin and the detritus of symbolic exchange. Slavoj Zizek has termed it "the sublime object," the pure quantity in excess of quantification that materializes the "Id" in "ideology." The notion of the object as the cause of desire demands a criticism of the residual: both a criticism that tracks the obdurate remainders of dialectical symbolization in the structures of culture, history, and tradition, and criticism *as* precisely the remainder of those literary and linguistic operations. In this third moment, the model for the relation between literature and psychoanalysis is not implication so much as what Lacan and Jacques-Alain Miller have called *extimité:* the intimate exteriority of the material letter, the mute signifier intransigently lodged through primal repression, incorporation, or foreclosure in the significations that it sets into motion (Miller "Extimité").

These three moments determine a certain historical trajectory within psychoanalytic criticism. They also demarcate a logic and ethics of reading whose repeated traversals may inflect the elements of imaginary application, symbolic implication, and real *extimité* differently, but can never fully isolate or disengage any one from the rest. Thus the imaginary moment of character analysis constitutes a necessary error whose insights and intuitions can be qualified or redirected but never fully avoided by other modes of criticism. The frequently voiced claim to have transcended character criticism usually amounts to no more than a repression or disavowal—and hence a sur-reptitious renewal—of the powerfully specular identificatory tendencies put into motion by the application of psychoanalytic theory.

So, too, the critical encounter with the "litter" in literature—the real fragments, holes, and waste products, the broken let-ters, of dominant traditions—cannot be elaborated apart from the literary and critical discourses they exceed. Unlike an "anti-Oedipal" schizocriticism that, however affirmatively, would de-nounce the law of psychoanalysis, we locate such a denunciation both "before the law," as its primal excessive instance, and hence within the law, as the ongoing cause of its perverse au-thority. Thus the *denunciation* of Oedipus has always been its founding *enunciation*. Accordingly, our reading of psychosis locates foreclosure at the ex-centric heart of the Oedipal drama. So, too, our discussion of incorporation, although influenced by the work of Nicolas Abraham and Maria Torok, embeds the concept within the normative paradigm of mourning as elab-orated according to the textual imperatives of the Lacanian return to Freud. Our aim is not merely to reveal the symbolic beneath the imaginary or the real beneath the symbolic, but rather, following Lacan, to express the inextricable entwining, at once normative and extraordinary, of the three orders.

Our project is neither simply to theorize nor to exemplify these interlocking modes, but instead to trace their articulation in the constitutive engagement of psychoanalysis with Shake-speare. If *Hamlet* is the literary object *in* psychoanalysis—its topic, thematic, and self-image —*King Lear* holds the position of its "Thing": the text at the limit of Oedipal interpretation, the play that casts and casts *out* femininity as the cause (the *causa* or *chose*) of radical loss, foreclosure, and psychosis. Across each discourse, the coupling of *Hamlet* and *Lear* is infolded within and counterpointed by the tri-logic of Sophocles' *Oedipus* trilogy. *Hamlet,* consistently paired by Freud with *Oedipus Rex,* constitutes the "model object" of neurotic desire and interpre-tation that informs psychoanalytic discourse. Hence the inau-gural position of *Hamlet* as a second Oedipus in *The Interpretation of Dreams* is reworked in Lacan's "Seminar VI," subtitled "Desire

and Its Interpretation," which implicitly translates the key
terms of Freud's foundational work.

From Freud's letters to Wilhelm Fliess to his essay "The
Theme of the Three Caskets," however, the Oedipal *Hamlet* is
countered by a *Lear* "extimate" to the representational and
dramatic space of Oedipus. So, too, the transition between Lacan's sixth and seventh seminars repeats the implicit contrast
and conjunction of *Hamlet* and *Lear* in Freud. In "Seminar VI,"
Lacan's reading of *Hamlet* narrates the origin of mourning in
a "hole in the real," a narrative replayed and recovered through
the dissolution of the Oedipus complex. In *Seminar VII: The
Ethics of Psychoanalysis,* taking *Antigone, Oedipus at Colonus,* and
King Lear as his specimen tragedies, Lacan reformulates this
"hole in the real" as *das Ding* or *la Chose,* the Thing of primordial
loss that marks the vanishing point or navel at which the real,
symbolic, and imaginary converge. If *Hamlet* exemplifies the
"Shakespeare effect" in psychoanalysis, the text whose "effec-
tive history" in Hans-Georg Gadamer's sense has permeated
Freudian conceptions and narratives, *King Lear* functions, or
malfunctions, as a "Shakespearean cause," the depository or
casket of what psychoanalysis symbolizes as nonsymbolizable.

In both parts of *After Oedipus* we stage the knotting of the
object and the thing in the formations of psychoanalysis and
tragedy. In Part One we focus on the melancholic passage of
Hamlet into psychoanalysis, and more broadly, of tragedy into
theory. In Part Two we examine the psychotic exclusions that
riddle that passage with pockets of traumatic loss and *jouissance.*
In the first part, then, we emphasize the psychoanalytic work
of interpretation and mourning, which we combine and extend
here into a principle of retroactive intertextuality through our
reading of Walter Benjamin's *Origin of German Tragic Drama*
(see Chapter 2). This intertextual emphasis encompasses both
our reading of *Hamlet* in Freud and Lacan (Chapters 1 and 3),
and our reading of Seneca in *Hamlet* (Chapter 4).

In the second part of the book we turn from psychoanalytic interpretation to psychoanalytic *construction,* which Freud
presents as the analyst's therapeutic equivalent of paranoid
delusion. The analyst's construction, like the psychotic's

hallucination, involves a piece of repudiated, nonhistoricized reality intransigently lodged rather than rhetorically refigured within a fictional, yet efficacious, delusion. In literary terms, "construction" displaces the question of intertextual genealogy with that of canon construction, which entails the "writing" of Shakespeare's plays through their placement in the tradition of tragedy. Thus we read *Hamlet* through Senecan drama and its afterlife in Baroque *Trauerspiel,* but we read *Lear* across Sophocles, who became the paradigm of tragedy only after the Renaissance. If the interpretation of *Hamlet* emblematizes the *retroaction of signification,* the construction of *Lear* by and around *Antigone* indicates the *retroaction of the cause,* as that which, in traumatically exceeding signification, puts it into play—and insistent replay. In Chapter 6 we read Freud's "The Theme of the Three Caskets" as an allegory of the imaginary, symbolic, and real. In Chapter 7 we locate the rhythm of refinding that precipitates the real thing in Lacan's unfolding account of the object. In Chapter 8 we connect the ethics of psychoanalysis with the Lacanian logic of psychosis in order to establish the plot of foreclosure and the foreclosure of plot in *King Lear.* The two halves of the book are punctuated by two anatomies that predict and recapitulate the overall argument. The "Inter-Section" and the "*After*-Word" map the trajectory of the book through an interpretation and reconstruction of a series of Lacanian diagrams that graphically materialize the temporal and logical relations of *Hamlet* and *Lear* in psychoanalysis.

PART ONE

HAMLET IN
PSYCHOANALYSIS

CHAPTER ONE

"Shapes of Grief":
Hamlet, Freud, and Mourning

Consistently paired in Freud's early writing, together *Oedipus Rex* and *Hamlet* have come to stand for the vicissitudes of the Oedipal in psychoanalytic literary criticism, whether as a master key to meaning, a reductive allegoresis, or a weathered milestone on the royal roads to post-Freudian truth. And although recent critics have rededicated psychoanalysis in the name of Hamlet by diagnosing his melancholy, this mournful Hamlet is already at play throughout Freud's texts. Hamlet is a double emblem of grief and patricide that informs Freud's autobiographically enunciated theories of the Oedipus complex and mourning, implicating them within a legacy of melancholic self-reflection. Moreover, the tension in Freud's writings between pre-Oedipal and Oedipal readings of *Hamlet* implicates mourning in the gendering as well as engendering of subject, object, and other. Feminist discussions of psychoanalysis too often oppose the pre-Oedipal mother of object-relations theory and the castrating father of the Oedipus complex associated with certain versions of Freud and Lacan. This is, we would argue, a false polarity, since Freud's writings already enact and articulate the movement between a dyadic relationship emblematized by the lost breast and the triangular family romance inaugurated in the shadow of the phallus. Both the Oedipal and the pre-Oedipal, however, are myths, in the sense of ideal narratives constructed retroactively in individual and discursive history, and not chronologically discrete, observable stages.

In this chapter we map Hamlet's "forms, moods, shapes of grief" as they conjoin Shakespeare, mourning, and autobiography in Freud's letters to Fliess, *The Interpretation of Dreams*, "Mourning and Melancholia," and *Beyond the Pleasure Principle*. In these texts, the processes of "projection" and "introjection"—aligned by Lacan with the dialectic of the imaginary and symbolic orders—simultaneously articulate and interfold inside and outside, subject and object, and presence and absence in the faulty act of accommodating loss. In Freud's writing, *Hamlet* marks the convergence of mourning, allegory, and the Oedipus complex; as both histrionic avenger and melancholy introvert, Hamlet defines the subject *as* mourner for literature and psychoanalysis.[1]

Mourning "in My Own Case"

In a May 1897 draft to Fliess, written seven months after the death of his father, Freud associates the self-reproach experienced at the death of parents with hostile impulses toward them. During bereavement,

> it is a manifestation of mourning to reproach oneself for their death (so called melancholia) or to punish oneself in a hysterical fashion, through the medium of the idea of retribution, with the same states [of illness] that they have had. The identification

1. The mournful Hamlet has become increasingly prominent in recent psychoanalytic theory and criticism. Jacques Lacan, in his 1959 seminar on *Hamlet*, remarks magisterially, "from one end of *Hamlet* to the other, all anyone talks about is mourning" ("Desire" 39). Nicolas Abraham, certainly the most rich and strange post-Freudian theorist of mourning, has written a "Sixth Act" to *Hamlet* based on his theory of intergenerational "phantoms" or unconsciously transmitted secrets. Abraham and Maria Torok have continued and transformed a tradition of mourning theory, including works by Sandor Ferenczi, Karl Abraham, and Melanie Klein. In literary studies, Jonathan Crewe, Marjorie Garber, Rainer Nägele, Jahan Ramazani, Jacqueline Rose, and Peter Sacks have variously read *Hamlet*'s melancholy and its place in psychoanalytic discourse.

which occurs here is, as can be seen, nothing other than a mode of thinking and does not make the search for the motive superfluous.

Freud then anticipates one side of the Oedipus complex: "It seems as though this death wish is directed in sons against their fathers and in daughters against their mothers." He concludes with a scenario of three: "A maidservant makes a transference from this by wishing her mistress to die so that her master can marry her" (*Complete Letters* 250). The passage begins with mourning and ends by staging a scene of domestic and social romance that prefigures the full Oedipus complex.

Thus Freud first articulates the Oedipus complex under the melancholic sign of Saturn.[2] He initially enunciates mourning as *pathological*, that is, as melancholia, rather than melancholia as an unhealthy version of mourning. Furthermore, he presents mourning in adulthood as the repetition or "transference" (as in the case of Freud's maidservant) of infantile experiences that are available to interpretation only in their belated, secondary form. Thus the passage itself both reflects and reflects upon the period of mourning and self-analysis in which Freud wrote it. Third, mourning appears as a kind of failed revenge tragedy, in which "the idea of retribution" is inflicted on the self. This self-punishment occurs through identification, which refigures the son or daughter in the image of the dying parent: in this sense, the mourner's mimetic symptoms constitute "a mode of thinking." Finally, the passage slides without comment from a binary, "pre-Oedipal" relation of mourning to the triadic structure of the Oedipal. These features will resurface and recombine in Freud's engagement with *Hamlet* and *Oedipus Rex*.

In the famous letter to Fliess of 15 October 1897, Freud

2. See Raymond Klibansky, Fritz Saxl, and Erwin Panofsky, *Saturn and Melancholy*. The editors of the *Standard Edition* describe Draft N as "one of the most significant instances of Freud's pre-vision" in anticipating the 1915 "Mourning and Melancholia." They also note that the draft is "incidentally the one in which Freud first foreshadowed the Oedipus complex" (*SE* 14:240). For the full text of Draft N, see *SE* 1:254–57.

works from love of the mother and jealousy of the father "in
my own case" to *Oedipus* and *Hamlet,* in such a way that autobiography, psychological theory, and literary criticism converge
and reconfigure as psychoanalysis.[3] This constellation reappears in *The Interpretation of Dreams* (1900), in which Freud
presents Hamlet as a repressed and belated Oedipus:

> Another of the great creations of tragic poetry, Shakespeare's
> *Hamlet,* has its roots in the same soil as *Oedipus Rex.* But the
> changed treatment of the same material reveals the whole dif-
> ference in the mental life of these two widely separated epochs
> of civilization: the secular advance of repression in the emotional
> life of mankind. In the *Oedipus* the child's wishful phantasy that
> underlies it is brought into the open and realized as it would be
> in a dream. In *Hamlet* it remains repressed; and—just as in the
> case of a neurosis—we only learn of its existence from its in-
> hibiting consequences.
>
> (*SE* 4:264)

Here, history proceeds from transparent, mythic representations of every man's wish to inhibited, disfigured narratives in
which wishes remain unconscious and unfulfilled. In a final,
privileged position stands the psychoanalytic interpreter, who
translates Hamlet's symptom into Oedipus's desire: "Here I
have translated into conscious terms what was bound to remain
unconscious in Hamlet's mind" (*SE* 4:265). In this typological
model of history, the Freudian reader finds the Oedipal scenario, the autobiographical nexus of ancient myth and modern
theory, in the distorted narratives of literature and life.

The insight animating this historical model tends to collapse
beneath the critical objections it now raises: above all, the self-
gratulatory reductiveness of translating, in a brutally appro-
priative allegoresis, one text (*Hamlet,* the conscious surface) into
another (*Oedipus,* the unconscious meaning). This relationship,
however, invites rereading. If *Hamlet* is the "translation" of

---

3. On the relation between autobiography, narrative, and theory in Freud,
see Shoshana Felman, "Beyond Oedipus" 101.

Oedipus, it is also a *translatio* in the sense of metaphor.[4] That is, *Hamlet*, in its very figurative distortion, points back to a structure only retroactively "prior," rather than being the secondary text that merely confirms the authoritative meaning of its archetype. As Jonathan Crewe argues, "The hermeneutic of discovery as well as the concurrent dynamic of appropriation would indeed seem to make *Hamlet* rather than *Oedipus Rex* the crucial 'Freudian' work, since it is in relation to it rather than the Greek play that the *discovery* of the oedipal structure of unconscious desire can be (re)effected" ("Naught So Damned" 41). Furthermore, *Hamlet*'s scenes of imperfect mourning, which prevent Aristotelian closure and preclude reductive Oedipal readings, are precisely what render it a "problem play" demanding interpretation: *Hamlet*'s excessive mourning both resists and enables the Oedipal reading as such.

In *The Interpretation of Dreams*, Freud directly links mourning, autobiography, and *Hamlet*'s Oedipal drama:

> For it can of course only be the poet's own mind which confronts us in Hamlet. I observe in a book on Shakespeare by George Brandes (1896) a statement that *Hamlet* was written immediately after the death of Shakespeare's father (in 1601), that is, under the immediate impact of his bereavement and, as we may well assume, while his childhood feelings about his father had been freshly revived. It is known, too, that Shakespeare's own son who died at an early age bore the name of 'Hamnet', which is identical with 'Hamlet'.
>
> (*SE* 4:265–66)

Freud presents Hamlet as the autobiographical mask of Shakespeare. He specifically locates Shakespeare's self-representation in the experience of bereavement, which once more appears as the theater of memory in which a repressed Oedipal drama

4. Freud's *Hamlet* is also a translation of *Oedipus* in the sense of psychoanalytic transference; the patient's repetition of childhood conflicts would later become the shared drama interpreted by the analyst and analysand. In *The Interpretation of Dreams*, Freud, in a Shakespearean mood, terms these transferential repetitions *revenants* or ghosts (*SE* 5:424).

is replayed or "revived."[5] According to Freud, Shakespeare
figures himself in Hamlet as mourner; at the same time, in
naming the hero after his son Hamnet, Shakespeare, who according to legend played the Ghost, also takes the position of
the dead father.[6] This ambivalent identification with both father and son divides and constitutes the subject by turning
Oedipal rage against itself. Thus in Freud's later essay "Mourning and Melancholia" it is Hamlet who displays the melancholic's self-reproach (*SE* 14:246).[7] Furthermore, in naming his
play after his dead son, Freud's Shakespeare makes the drama
into an epitaph. The play is a Shakespearean "will," a legacy
of mournful identification to be revived and repeated by
posterity.

Freud's reading of Hamlet as an autobiographical figure for
Shakespeare occurs in the context of his self-analysis, paralleling the movement in the letter to Fliess from "my own case"
to *Oedipus* and *Hamlet*. In the second preface (1908) to *The
Interpretation of Dreams,* Freud presents the text as the working
through of his father's death: "For this book has a further
subjective significance for me personally—a significance which
I only grasped after I had completed it. It was, I found, a
portion of my own self-analysis, my reaction to my father's
death—that is to say, to the most important event, the most
poignant loss, of a man's life. Having discovered that this was
so, I felt unable to obliterate the traces of the experience" (*SE*
4:xxvi). In the retrospection afforded by this later preface,
Freud traces his theoretical discoveries in an autobiography of
mourning. He inherits and transforms the Romantic tendency
to read *Hamlet* as doubly autobiographical: Hamlet is Shakespeare, and Shakespeare's modern reader (Goethe, Coleridge,

5. Here, *Wiederbelebung,* literally, brought to life again; cf. Freud's "revenants" mentioned at note 4.
6. For an example of the legend of Shakespeare playing the ghost, see
George Bernard Shaw's *Dark Lady of the Sonnets* (1910).
7. See also Draft N (*SE* 1:254–57). As Freud says of Hamlet in *The Interpretation of Dreams,* "The loathing which should drive him on to revenge is
replaced in him by self-reproaches, by scruples of conscience, which remind
him that he himself is literally no better than the sinner whom he is to punish"
(*SE* 4:265).

Freud...) is Hamlet. This reduplication of autobiography leads not to the transparent, self-confirming identity of reader, text, and author, but to an allegorical splitting that infects interpreting subject, literary object, and authorial ground. Hamlet's legacy is a layered identification with the grieving son who has himself infolded the murdered father. How does Freud the son take on—or rather, take *in*—the lost parent?

The letter of 15 October, the first full interpretation of *Oedipus* and *Hamlet*, begins with the story of another loss. Freud produces childhood material concerning a nurse whom his elder brother had arrested for theft, a crime in which the young Sigmund had been a complicit victim. Freud recalls standing before a wardrobe looking for his mother:

> My mother was nowhere to be found; I was crying in despair. My brother Philipp (twenty years older than I) unlocked a wardrobe [*Kasten*] for me, and when I did not find my mother inside it either, I cried even more until, slender and beautiful, she came in through the door.
>
> (*Complete Letters* 271)

The young Freud feared that his mother had been locked or boxed up (*eingekastelt*) by Philipp just as the nurse had been, and had asked his older brother to let her out. In Freud's letter, a narrative of parental loss and restoration, already within a nascent Oedipal triangle, directly precedes the reading of *Hamlet* and *Oedipus*. As Stephan Bröser argues in his essay, "Kästchen, Kasten, Kastration," the letter splits into two, the first half presenting a tenuous, fantastic relation to the mother, the second announcing the inaugural account of the Oedipus complex.[8]

In an associated dream discussed in the same letter, Freud algebraically identifies himself with the arrested nurse: "The correct interpretation is: I = she." In the *Kasten* memory, this

8. For related readings of the mother in the cupboard, see Jim Swan, "*Mater* and Nannie: Freud's Two Mothers and the Discovery of the Oedipus Complex" and William Warner, *Chance and the Text of Experience* 102.

identification with the lost maternal figure becomes a complex image of enclosure. That is, the child experiences the mother's absence as a sealed box or casket (*Kasten*), an image of interiorization, at once womb and tomb, commemorating the lost mother by preserving her as lost. The *Kasten* is both an image of Freud's desire to interiorize his mother and a hollowed-out symbol of her: thus, in the service of re-presenting the mother, the *Kasten* becomes a specular self-representation (I = *Kasten*).[9] Finally, the mother's entry into the room refigures the act of introjection represented in the image of the casket: "I cried even more until, slender and beautiful, she came in through the door." The memory is structured like a dream in which the mother's reentry represents a fantastic resolution, a wish-fulfillment of introjection as full, perfect restoration. Yet, as a crossing from outside to inside, it is a compromise-formation that continues to manifest the more difficult, divisive process of introjection, which can do no more than interiorize emptiness in the effort to make the absent present. Philipp's coinage *einkasteln*, to lock up or in (*ein*), encloses the deadlier connotation of entombing in a *Kasten*. This narrative of loss followed by imperfect restoration through introjection will return in the mechanics of mourning later theorized by Freud.

Thus Freud, like his Hamlet, takes in the one he mourns. Note, however, that the letter to Fliess moves from loss of the mother to the enunciation of Oedipal hostility toward the father. Similarly, in a 1924 footnote to the same material in *The Psychopathology of Everyday Life*, Freud subordinates his earlier emphasis on the mother to the Oedipal conflict with his older brother Philipp, whom the child suspects of having impregnated his recently "confined" mother. Freud reads the memory as displacing anxiety from the "deeper" conflict with the father-figure to the more "superficial" fear of losing his mother: "The affect of disappointment when the cupboard was found to be empty derived, therefore, from the superficial motivation for

9. In a late footnote to the same material in *The Psychopathology of Everyday Life*, Freud connects the memory to the birth of his sister: "The wardrobe or cupboard was a symbol for him of his mother's inside" (*SE* 6:51).

the child's demand. As regards the *deeper* trend of thought, the affect was in the wrong place" (*SE* 6:51–52). Both passages shift from mourning the mother to conflict with the father, with the tendency for the loss of the mother itself to be lost. The absent mother is once more "boxed up," *eingekastelt*, now within the full-blown Oedipus complex. So, too, the screen memory of maternal loss already takes place in the court of paternal law; pre-Oedipal catastrophe is both imagined and effaced from the symbolic retrospection of the Oedipal triangle.

A pattern emerges. The repeated association of *Hamlet* and *Oedipus* finds a parallel in the contiguity between mourning the mother and uncovering the Oedipal scenario. Freud's presentation of *Hamlet* as a secondary, inhibited *Oedipus* resembles his lapsed attention to mourning in the process of inflecting the Oedipal, and the accompanying displacement from the lost mother to the hostile father. Freud's early enunciations of the Oedipus complex bear within them the ellipses of objects emptied by loss. In Freud's early representations of mourning, the mourner enfolds the lost object in an embedded identification or "introjection" through a masochistic turning of loss into the self. *Hamlet* is the death mask worn by Shakespeare as son and father, a mask he bequeaths to Freud and ourselves.

The Shadow of the Object

Freud's "Mourning and Melancholia," quoted in almost literary, epigrammatic fashion by later theorists of mourning, is a kind of "specimen text," in the psychoanalytic discourse on mourning a metapsychological equivalent to *Hamlet*. Freud's writings on mourning trace and manifest the interplay between "introjection" and "projection": the articulation and interfolding of inside and outside, subject and object, presence and absence, around an experience of loss.

"In mourning it is the world which has become poor and empty; in melancholia it is the ego itself" (*SE* 14:246). Here Freud founds the distinction between mourning and melancholia on the assumedly prior division between self and world.

The essay in general distinguishes the egoism of the melancholic's narcissistic self-reproach and ambivalent love from the mourner's unconflicted absorption in the lost object. Yet the crucial distinction between self and world breaks down—and is constituted in—the melancholic's alternation between introjection and projection. Thus Hamlet enters as an exemplar of melancholic self-reproach, yet speaks the language of a misanthrope: " 'Use every man after his desert, and who shall scape whipping?' " (*SE* 14:246). Hamlet's world has become "a sterile promontory" (II.ii.299), because he has fashioned it in the image of his own ego.

This construction of an outside world through the projection of an interior state is not peculiar to the melancholic, but is central to the process of subject-formation.[10] Thus in "Mourning and Melancholia," Freud defines melancholic narcissism as regression to an infantile stage of object-choice in which the ego is constructed out of the carcasses of its sadistically devoured loved ones: "The ego wants to incorporate this object into itself, and, in accordance with the oral or cannibalistic phase of libidinal development in which it is, it wants to do so by devouring it" (249–50).[11] In "Instincts and Their Vicissitudes," Freud presents introjection and projection as the processes, at once interpretive and constructive, that create self out of world and world out of self. A postulated "primary" stage of bodily and psychic equilibrium is disrupted by an upsurge of unpleasure, initially experienced as neither inside nor outside, but as foreign and hostile. This trauma results in the institution of the pleasure principle, dividing the world into pleasurable interior and painful exterior: "In so far as the objects which are presented to it [the ego] are sources of pleasure,

10. Freud argues this point in *The Ego and the Id* (1923) and "Negation" (1925); see *SE* 19:28 and passim.
11. See Karl Abraham's letter to Freud, 31 March 1915, in which he suggests the cannibalistic aspects of melancholia (217). Incorporation, as a primitive oral relation to objects, is the prototype of, though not identical to, introjection. Nicolas Abraham and Maria Torok develop a different notion of incorporation based on Ferenczi's writings in "Deuil *ou* melancholie," in *L'écorce et le noyau*, translated as "Introjection—Incorporation; Mourning *or* Melancholy."

it takes them into itself, 'introjects' them (to use Ferenczi's [1909] term); and, on the other hand, it expels whatever within it becomes a cause of unpleasure" (*SE* 14:136).[12] Freud describes the melancholic's desire to devour the lost object as a regression to an earlier narcissistic object-choice; it is also a regression to an early object-*loss*, to an infantile experience of mourning. A feeling of unpleasure is projected as external, to be refigured, as Melanie Klein will argue, as the absent, lost mother.[13] "Unpleasure" becomes "loss" through a process of expulsive projection that will eventually personify the painful tension of hunger as the absent or "bad" mother.[14] Moreover, projection, as expulsion, enacts the process of loss, which enables "personification," that is, the formation of self and other.

Projection institutes above all a relation between the child and its maternal object.[15] The reference in "Mourning and Melancholia" to a "narcissistic oral phase" (250), implying the most primitive libidinal organization and a dual, specular relationship, is coordinate with what Freud and others would later call the pre-Oedipal. Whether projection involves the idealizing, specular extension of the ego into the world, or the disruptive expulsion of pain, it is fundamentally narcissistic in nature, insofar as self- and world-representations circulate in

12. See Sandor Ferenczi, "Introjection and Transference," which Freud refers to here. In Freud's 1925 essay "Negation" (*Die Verneinung*), introjection and projection are the processes by which the subject constructs the notions of inside and outside and tests the reality of a thing based on the distinction, by rediscovering it as an object.

13. Melanie Klein, in "Mourning and Its Relation to Manic-Depressive States," sees the prototype of all mourning in the infantile "depressive position," "a melancholia in *statu nascendi*," which is the model for Oedipal loss (*Writings of Melanie Klein* 1:345 and passim).

14. This is, of course, a simplification of Freudian and later theory. For example, pleasure can be projected outward in an idealization of the mother, but pain can be retained to form a "bad" self. See Joseph Smith, "On the Work of Mourning."

15. Julia Kristeva, in *Powers of Horror: An Essay on Abjection*, terms this its maternal "abject," which she defines as "the violence of mourning for an 'object' that has always already been lost" (15). Kristeva's notion of abjection derives from Lacan's discussion of *das Ding* in *Seminar VII* and elsewhere.

a closed economy of two.[16] Moreover, this conjunction of narcissism, projection, and melancholy bridges psychoanalytic and
literary discourses. The "pathetic fallacy," for example, diagnoses the rhetorical projection of human emotions onto nature;
John Ruskin, who coined the phrase, gives "reason unhinged
by grief" as one of its occasions (Rosenberg 65).[17] This formulation illuminates pastoral elegy's weeping landscapes and
the mournful personae they mirror. Elegiac prosopopoeia, the
trope (akin to personification) of making the absent present,
also functions in the matrix of projection, narcissism, and
melancholy.

If projection defines subject and object around the trauma
later narrated as the "primary" loss of the mother, introjection
returns that defining loss onto the self. Freud, like Moses de-
scending from Mount Sinai, describes the birth of law out of
mourning:

> Thus the shadow of the object fell upon the ego, and the latter
> could henceforth be judged by a special agency, as though it
> were an object, the forsaken object. In this way an object-loss
> was transformed into an ego-loss and the conflict between the
> ego and the loved person into a cleavage [*Zwiespalt*] between the
> critical activity of the ego and the ego as altered by identification.
>
> (*SE* 14:249; *SA* 3:203)[18]

Whereas projection determines the self in narcissistic relation
to an image of the mother, introjection, in dividing the subject,
configures a relation of three: the object, the ego, and its new
critical "special agency." In this triangle, the object, identified
by Melanie Klein as the breast, is a figure of inaugural loss,

16. Cf. Jean Laplanche and J.-B. Pontalis's distinction between "cinema-
tographic" projection as "not wishing to know" (*méconnaissance*) and expulsive
projection as "not wishing to be" (*The Language of Psychoanalysis* 354).
17. We thank Charles Dove for this reference.
18. The passage's opening aphorism recurs throughout psychoanalytic
writings on mourning. Thus Melanie Klein cites Karl Abraham: " 'We have
only to reverse [Freud's] statement that "the shadow of the lost love-object falls
upon the ego" and say that in this case it was not the shadow but the bright
radiance of his loved mother which was shed upon her son' " (*Writings of Melanie
Klein* 1:355).

consumed in that "narcissistic oral phase" dominated by the voracious grief of the nascent ego. The critical agency antici- pates Freud's notion of the superego, the introjected nay-saying father.[19] Between the two stands the ego, narcissistically iden- tifying with both positions at the threshold of diacritically de- fined sexual difference. The Oedipal structure emerging out of introjection subsumes specular, dyadic losses into its symbolic familial order. At the same time, this triangle is constructed out of the very binary relations that it reconfigures.[20]

At this point in Freud's writing, the critical agency is not a preexisting masculine other, but rather is gendered (and en- gendered) through introjection as a structural process. In the emerging asymmetry between projection of the mother and introjection of the father, "mother" and "father" represent structural positions rather than sexually fixed objects or tem- porally distinct stages. Maternally oriented projection, con- structing an "other" out of a simultaneously produced "self," operates outside of gender relations in a specular union of two. Introjection, insofar as it produces a relation of three by in- troducing difference into the ego, anticipates the sexual posi- tions of the Oedipal triangle. Retroactively, from the vantage point of the Oedipus complex in decline, these positions be- come gendered as the subject attempts to accede to one of them. At the same time, loss, associated with the breast, is retroped and becomes meaningful as lack of the phallus (the phallus as lack) under the threat of castration.[21] Recall the transition from

19. See *The Ego and the Id* (1923) and "The Dissolution of the Oedipus Complex" (1924) in *SE* 19:179.
20. Nicolas Abraham argues that the introjection of the mother-child "dual unity" splits the self by redoubling a binary opposition, in the process creating the duplicitous condition of language. See *L'écorce et le noyau* 126 and passim.
21. See Laplanche and Pontalis on "deferred action" or *Nachträglichkeit:* "Experiences, impressions and memory-traces may be revised at a later date to fit in with fresh experiences or with the attainment of a new stage of de- velopment. They may in that event be endowed not only with a new meaning but also with psychical effectiveness" (111). They point to an early formulation of this principle in *Studies on Hysteria* in the context of a scene of mourning that (as the editors of the *Standard Edition* point out) anticipates *Trauerarbeit* (*SE* 2:162). Thus *Nachträglichkeit* and *Trauerarbeit*, both models of psychic de- velopment as a process of retrospective interpretation, are linked in Freud's

the mother in her *Kasten* to the dead fathers of Oedipus and Hamlet in Freud's letter to Fliess: the object of loss has slipped from maternal to paternal in the theoretical and autobiographical "working through" of the Oedipus complex. Our analysis stems from Lacan's rereading of Klein's famous case of "Little Dick" in *Seminar I* and from Shoshana Felman's glossing of Lacan. Felman points out that for Lacan, projection and introjection are not symmetrical. Projection is associated with the narcissistic, dual order of the *Imaginary*, and introjection with the Oedipal triangle of the *Symbolic:* "Thus, while projection is always in Lacan's conception the displacement of an image from the 'inside' to the 'outside,' that is, a displacement of any one given object with respect to the ego, introjection is ... always a *linguistic* introjection, in that it is always *the introjection of a relation*" ("Beyond Oedipus" 115). Similarly, we have aligned projection with the lost mother in a world differentiated from the self, and introjection with the inclusion of the linguistic father into a split ego. The lost mother is a projection in the cinematic sense, an "image" of difference, a specular other painfully created out of the psyche it defines. Introjection introduces a principle of splitting, a "relation" of difference attached to the culturally shared, external structure of language, a process that in turn sets the stage for the family romance. Thus introjection does not so much take in "the father" as masculine object but rather institutes gender as a relation of linguistic difference.

The asymmetry between projection and introjection, which Felman rightly emphasizes, brings with it, however, a problematic tendency to separate the pre-Oedipal and Oedipal, the imaginary and symbolic, into distinct stages of development. The Freudian passages we have been reading suggest the structural imbrication of the two modes.[22] In "Mourning and Mel-

---

early writings. *Nachträglichkeit* informs the process of mourning that reinscribes the lost breast as the lost phallus. See *The Language of Psychoanalysis* 111–14.

22. Kristeva locates the appearance of the "imaginary father" in an "already ternary structuration with a different articulation from the Ego-object-Other triangle that is put together in the shadow of the Oedipus complex" (*Tales of Love* 23).

ancholia" 's epitaphic phrase, "the shadow of the object fell upon the ego" (249), it is not the object but its shadow that darkens the ego, a projection or representation of the object *as lost* which is then introjected. Moreover, this effect of interiority is produced as a purely surface phenomenon—a shadow *on* the ego rather than within it. Introjection imposes relations of difference onto the ego only when it infolds a projection, insofar as projection demarcates the difference between self and other. In *Hamlet*, the paternal ghost visits the sins of the mother on the son, dividing him from himself: in this sense, "the shadow of the object" has fallen on Hamlet.[23]

Whereas the melancholic shadow on the ego is the introjection of a projection, Freud's *Kasten* memory is, in the asymmetry hidden in chiasmus, the projection of an introjection. The memory condenses two reactions to loss: projection of the object as lost in an image outside the body envelope, and the fantasy of introjection represented by the *Kasten*. Of the two, projection here is the dominant movement, a simultaneous differentiation and equation of self and other. Recall that Freud's interpretation of the memory shifted from a maternal to a paternal orientation; "the affect," he wrote in 1924, "was in the wrong place." The phrase evokes the spatially contiguous and infolded rather than temporally distinct relation of the pre-Oedipal and Oedipal while exemplifying the interpretive tendency for the former to disappear into the latter. Indeed, affect, one could say, is always in the wrong place, insofar as interpretation, as *Oedipal* interpretation, necessarily cancels and reorganizes the impossible affectivity of the maternal. This is not, however, to elegize the "loss of emotion" in symbolization, but to suggest that it is the condition of affect to be displaced and misplaced.

---

23. Éric Laurent distinguishes two strands of the theorization of melancholia in Freud's work through his double figures for loss and self-division: the "shadow of the object" of "Mourning and Melancholia," and the dead father of *The Ego and the Id*. Laurent associates the "shadow of the object" with Lacan's *Ding*, related to maternal loss, and suggests that the pre-Oedipal Thing and the decisively Oedipal father are two sides of the same structure of melancholia ("Mélancolie, douleur d'exister, lâcheté morale").

The place of *Hamlet* in Freud's writings recapitulates this inter-implication of introjection and projection. Hamlet is textually internalized in the letter to Fliess and *The Interpretation of Dreams*, in which he functions as an allegorical emblem of parental mourning. Yet this autobiographical reading of *Hamlet* is literally undercut in *The Interpretation of Dreams* by a 1930 footnote denying Shakespeare's authorship: "Incidently, I have in the meantime ceased to believe that the author of Shakespeare's works was the man from Stratford" (*SE* 4:266n). Thus although Freud may be Hamlet, and Hamlet may be Shakespeare, Shakespeare is not Shakespeare; in Marjorie Garber's phrase, Shakespeare's plays are "ghost-written" by the authorial controversy, whose de-authorization of Shakespeare both underwrites and undermines the Shakespearean legacy of autobiographical identification. In "Mourning and Melancholia," Hamlet reappears sadistically projecting masochistic self-reproach: " 'Use every man after his desert, and who shall scape whipping?' " (*SE* 14:246). This line occurs in a footnote, both internalized and put beneath the body of the text, underlining it. Freud speaks through Hamlet, but *sotto voce*, in an "under-voice" that projects Hamlet, the philosopher of melancholy, as Freud's ghostly double. The introjection and projection illustrated by the quotation are exemplified by Freud's treatment of the quotation. He both includes *Hamlet* as an autobiographical mask and excludes it by denying Shakespeare's authorship and by ejecting the quotation into the interior exterior of the footnote. *Hamlet*, the tragedy around which mourning is theorized in psychoanalysis, itself becomes an object of textual displacement and mourning. Finally, pre-Oedipal mourning tends to disappear silently into and be restructured by the Oedipal triangle. This disappearance is repeated by Freud's subordination of *Hamlet* to *Oedipus Rex*, and, with regard to *Hamlet*, by the institutionalization of the Oedipal reading, at the expense of the melancholic.

The Undiscover'd Country

In *The Interpretation of Dreams*, the yoking of *Oedipus* and *Hamlet* appears as a literary analogy in the chapter "Dreams of the Death of Persons of Whom the Dreamer Is Fond," which at this point is merely one category of dreams among others. Freud's progressive revisions, which expand and centralize the reading of the two plays, raise *Hamlet* and *Oedipus* from casual literary examples to definitive, informing instances of Oedipal narrative. In the process, the example, "Oedipal" dreams, comes to determine and reorganize the category ("Death of Persons of Whom the Dreamer Is Fond"). Freud's retroactively programmatic reading of the two tragedies, however, is preceded by a more symptomatic allusion to *Hamlet* in *The Interpretation of Dreams:*

> To children, who, moreover, are spared the sight of the scenes of suffering [*Szenen des Leidens*] which precede death, being 'dead' means approximately the same as being 'gone' [*fort sein*]— not troubling the survivors any longer. A child makes no distinction as to how this absence is brought about: whether it is due to a journey, to a dismissal, to an estrangement, or to death. If, during a child's prehistoric epoch [*prähistorischen Jahren*], his nurse has been dismissed [*weggeschickt*], and if soon afterwards his mother has died, the two events are superimposed on each other in a single series in his memory as revealed by analysis... If their mother does actually make the journey to that 'undiscovered country, from whose bourn no traveller returns,' children seem at first to have forgotten her, and it is only later on that they begin to call their dead mother to mind [*erst nachträglich beginnen sie, sich an die Tote zu erinnern*].
> (*SE* 4:254–55; *SA* 2:259–60)

In a pattern by now familiar, mourning for the mother is enunciated through allusion to *Hamlet*. The loss of the mother, apparently originary, is, however, only remembered or *erinnert* through deferred action, *erst nachträglich;* the maternal object is taken in after the fact, constructed through and around the experience of loss. Her *Er-innerung* produces the child's effect of interiority, insofar as she is taken in *as lost*, represented by the child only in the process of gradually recognizing—and simultaneously masking—the catastrophe of maternal absence.[24] In dramatic terms, the "scenes of suffering" occur, classically, offstage, encased in the inner region of the *domos* whose episodes of life and death are off limits to the child. Uncannily echoing the *Kasten* memory, the loss of the bad nanny and the good mother are here "superimposed...in a single series" in which the "prehistoric" trauma of maternal absence is only available through its troping in other scenes.

To play on Freud's word *weggeschickt* (in the line "a nanny has been *weggeschickt,* sent away"), the pre-Oedipal scene of maternal loss is "pre-historic" in the sense of being what we would call a *Weg-Geschichte,* a "history-of-sending-away"—dismissing the nanny, but also sending away (Oedipal) history. This *Weg-Geschichte* in turn lays the groundwork for history's return, a return in and as the introjective process of *Erinnerung.* Freud's citation here of the "To be or not to be" soliloquy anticipates the definitive conjunction of *Hamlet* and *Oedipus* a few pages later, here inflected—contrary to the Shakespearean subtext—in the context of *maternal* loss. The "undiscover'd country," like the "dark continent" of feminine sexuality for Freud, figures maternal absence through a projective displacement; maternal loss, however, returns as the ghostly father and his law of lack. On the one hand, paternal law is always faulted by the maternal absence it effaces; on the other hand, that law is the means not simply of representing but also of constituting the mother for the child. The relation between mother and father and their metonymic signifiers breast and phallus is not one of antithesis or opposition, but rather of retroactive translation, a translation effected by the work of mourning.

Freud's analysis here of "being dead" as "being gone" [*fort sein*] anticipates, within Freud's most "classical" formulation and defense of the pleasure principle (*The Interpretation of Dreams*), the movement "beyond the pleasure principle" enacted in the "fort-da" game. In the *Kasten* memory, *The Interpretation of Dreams,* and *Beyond the Pleasure Principle,* the *Trauerarbeit* (or

24. To borrow a pun of Derrida's, the *Sein* of Being, figured in the maternal fullness of the *sein* or breast, is inherently displaced, not so much as *Da-Sein,* Being-There, but—in Freud's phrase—as *Fort-Sein,* Being-Gone. See Mark Taylor, *Altarity* 85.

Trauerspiel) of infantile mourning is played out in relation to
the absent mother. Ernst, Freud's grandson, had the "disturbing habit" of saying "o-o-o-o" and "da" while throwing a wooden
spool into his curtained cot and retrieving it. The child's "o-o-
o-o," his grandfather and mother agree, was no mere "*Inter-
jektion*" or expletive; indeed it was a "projection" or casting out
of the reel as a representation of the mother, insofar as the *fort*
reenacts the expulsion of unpleasure in the earliest coalescence
of subjectivity around loss.

The *fort* spatially maps the difference between self and other
in a game whose reenactment of loss resembles the mourner's
monotonous absorption in *Trauerarbeit*. Thus Freud momentarily interprets the event as "the impulse to work over [*ver-
arbeiten*] in the mind some overpowering experience so as to
make oneself master of it" (*SE* 18:16; *SA* 3:226). This language
evokes "Mourning and Melancholia," in which Freud defines
Trauerarbeit as the slow process of reality testing that ideally
ends with the detachment or decathexis of libido from the
object:

> Normally, respect for reality gains the day. Nevertheless its or-
> ders cannot be obeyed at once. They are carried out bit by bit,
> at great expense of time and cathectic energy, and in the mean-
> time the existence of the lost object is psychically prolonged
> [*fortgesetzt*]. Each single one of the memories and expectations
> in which the libido is bound to the object is brought up and
> hypercathected, and detachment of the libido is accomplished
> in respect of it ... It is remarkable that this painful unpleasure
> [*Schmerzunlust*] is taken as a matter of course by us.
>
> (*SE* 14:244–45; *SA* 3:199)

Similarly, the game of *fort* repetitively replays loss; what appears
to be a vehement detachment (decathexis) from the object at
the same time insistently continues to engage the object (hy-
percathexis). In mourning, the object is *fortgesetzt* or prolonged
in the process of being dislodged from the ego: the prefix *fort*,
meaning alternately "removal in space" and "continuation in
time," connects the game of *fort* in *Beyond the Pleasure Principle*
to both the *fortgesetzt* (prolonged, or interminable) work of

mourning in "Mourning and Melancholia" and the *fort sein* of the undiscovered mother in *The Interpretation of Dreams*.[25] The *da*, uttered with the drawing in of the spool, restores the representative of the lost object, as in introjection during mourning.[26] This introjection reinstates the object with a two-fold difference, simultaneously idealizing it in a fantastic resolution that negates loss and mortifying it in an internalization of loss as lack. In the first sense, the "joyful *da*" of return has the same structure of wish-fulfillment seen in the mother's reentry, "slender and beautiful," which closes the *Kasten* memory. In the second sense, the *da* returns the *fort* to the child, inscribing, rather than reversing, the *fort* in him. In both of its aspects, the *da* completes the *fort:* in the first, as an imaginary resolution that denies absence; in the second, as a symbolic naming of presence and absence as a relation in which the subject must take its place. *Da*, pointing to a position, has meaning only positionally: *da* means "there" in the phrase "hier und da" ["here and there"] and "here" in the phrase "da und dort" [also "here and there"].

The paternal, symbolic dimension of the introjecting *da*, as the taking in of a relation, anticipates the boy's final game. Ernst plays *fort* with his father, by telling his toys to "go to the fwont." Freud, understandably, reads the game as expressing Oedipal hostility, and the chapter following the *fort-da* game dwells upon the "tragic seriousness" ["tragischem *Ernst*," emphasis ours, *SA* 3:231] of Oedipal resolutions. We insist, however, that within and beneath the Oedipal text lies the trace of maternal mourning. Freud glosses Ernst's playful death wish against his father with a footnote on the actual death of Ernst's mother, Freud's daughter Sophie: "When this child was five

25. And the mother's *Fortgehen* or departure can also mean continuation, as Derrida notes in *The Post Card: From Socrates to Freud and Beyond* (329).

26. Hence Melanie Klein writes, echoing Karl Abraham, "the characteristic feature of normal mourning is the individual's setting up the lost loved object inside himself" (362). Cf. Freud, *The Ego and the Id* (1923), a text which in part inscribes the origin of *Beyond the Pleasure Principle* in "Mourning and Melancholia": "When it happens that a person has to give up a sexual object, there quite often ensues an alteration of his ego which can only be described as a setting up of the object inside the ego, as it occurs in melancholia" (*SE* 19:29).

and three-quarters, his mother died. Now that she was really 'gone' ('o-o-o'), the little boy showed no signs of grief" (*SE* 18:16). Here Freud ventriloquizes the hollow vocabulary of his grandson, keening the "o-o-o" of mourning. The *o*'s, reduced here to three, indicate the series of losses enacted by the *fort-da* games (mother, self, father); the parentheses bracketing the o's of loss emblematize the process of introjection.

This internalization of the *fort* through the *da* is, like the shadow of the object in "Mourning and Melancholia," the introjection of a projection. The *fort*, conversely, is the projection of an introjection; Ernst throws the spool into his curtained bed, an image of enclosure that figures both his mother and himself. As Derrida suggests in *The Post Card*, "I will not venture saying: [the curtained bed] is Sophie" (316). At the same time, the bed, the hinge of the *fort-da*, anticipates, as an "im-bedding" of the spool, the movement (in the *da*) of the object into the self; the bed embodies the entombing ego. Ernst by the curtained bed resembles young Freud in front of the *Kasten;* in both, the image of enclosure represents the lost mother as well as the mourning son. Although the *fort* pictures the projection of the mother as gone and the *da* traces the introjection of her absence, each half of the trajectory encases the other. Likewise, the passage from the pre-Oedipal to the Oedipal acted out in the *fort-da* game is not a linear progress from the imaginary to the symbolic but rather a triangle of narcissistic relations continually retraced in mourning.

In our analysis so far, as in other commentaries, the *fort-da* tends to appear as "the complete game—disappearance and return" (*SE* 18:15). Yet Ernst more often played *fort* by itself, precisely the feature that led Freud to derive the death drive from the repetition compulsion. How do these two games, *fort-da* and *fort*, represent different, perhaps incommensurate, modes of mourning? Derrida faces in his conflicted work of mourning *Memoires for Paul de Man* two inadequate alternatives: "And as concerns the other in us...where is the most unjust betrayal? Is the most distressing, or even the most deadly infidelity that of a *possible mourning* which would interiorize within us the image, idol, or ideal of the other who is dead and lives only in us? Or is it that of the impossible mourning, which, leaving the other his alterity, respecting thus his infinite remove, either refuses to take or is incapable of taking the other within oneself, as in the tomb or the vault of some narcissism?" (6) The *fort-da*, concluding in interiorization, is Derrida's "possible mourning," which betrays the object through its idealized representation in memory, or *Erinnerung*. The *fort* played by itself, refusing the closure of internalization, is Derrida's "impossible mourning," which leaves the other its otherness, in an act of sadistic, obsessive yet failed forgetting—what Derrida, following de Man's Hegelian distinction, will call *Gedächtnis* (memorization), and, following Nicolas Abraham's categories, incorporation.[27] If the "possible" mourning enacted by the *fort-da* game describes a dialectic of presence and absence, the impossible mourning of the *fort* game, its ever-present undertone, insists upon the melancholic remainder of that dialectic, refusing to distinguish, represent, or mourn. Whereas the pairing of *Hamlet* and *Oedipus* enacts the necessary rhythm of symbolization in the "fort-da," the *fort* by itself indicates the impossible mourning marked by the pre-Oedipal *Hamlet*, whose lineaments disappear into the very narrative that renders its darkness visible.

Freud's simultaneous invention of psychoanalysis and psychoanalytic literary criticism is from the beginning intertextual, since it is based not so much on individual texts (*Oedipus* or *Hamlet*) as on the relation between texts (*Oedipus* and *Hamlet*). In Freud's textual practice, the distortions and belatedness of *Hamlet*'s melancholy form the intertextual lens through which the "Oedipal" in *Oedipus* comes into—and goes out of—focus. Furthermore, Freud's writings manifest a pattern of intratextual mourning in which the scene of maternal loss is passed and bypassed within and between works; thus Freud's texts of mourning, like endlessly nested Russian dolls, are *eingekastelt* in each other. The question of legacy is in turn implicated in

27. See de Man's "Sign and Symbol in Hegel's *Aesthetics*." Derrida expands the comparison of *Gedächtnis* and *Erinnerung* to modes of mourning in the second essay in *Memoires*, "The Art of Memoires."

the explicitly autobiographical dimension of *The Interpretation of Dreams;* Freud reads *Hamlet* as Shakespeare's autobiography in the same moment that he takes Hamlet as his own mask. In reading *Hamlet* as doubly autobiographical, however, Freud reads it as an *allegorical* autobiography, in which the subject is written through the deathly, alienating texts and images of an other. Allegory is the privileged mode of mournful representation insofar as it both enacts the disjunction of signifier and signified in vehicle and tenor, and imagines their ideal reunification. Both psychoanalysis and literature narrate "allegories of mourning": representations *of* mourning that cast representation *as* mourning, as the recuperation and repetition of loss. In both literature and psychoanalysis, narratives of loss, insofar as they are stories about subjectivity, necessarily implicate and thematize autobiography as a mode; in the process, autobiography emerges not only as a conventional genre, but as a disseminated function of fiction, theory, and their "figures"— allegorical tropes within and for kinds of writing and the characters, psychological and typological, that inhabit them.

CHAPTER TWO

The *Trauerspiel* of Criticism

In his 1924 essay "The Dissolution of the Oedipus Complex," Freud chose the word *Untergang* (dissolution, passing, decline, setting) to designate the denouement of Oedipal conflict and the gendering of the child in the onset of latency. In "Le Séminaire livre VI: Le désir et son interpretation," Lacan takes the word *Untergang* to describe the work of mourning in the constitution of the object "in" desire. Moreover, according to Lacan, *Untergang* characterizes *Hamlet*'s secondary relation to Oedipus within the fin de siècle culture of psychoanalysis, for which *Hamlet* represented "a decadent form of the Oedipal situation, its decline" ("Desire" 45). Walter Benjamin's account of Baroque *Trauerspiel* as the passage of classical tragedy into modern theater and theory allows us to elaborate the psychoanalytic narrative of Oedipal dissolution in terms of generic, intertextual, and rhetorical transformations and deformations. Placing *Hamlet* after (Oedipal) tragedy both stages and disturbs the classical narratives underwriting the literary history of tragedy. By reading Freud with Benjamin, we argue that the distinction between tragedy and *Trauerspiel,* a slippage rather than an opposition, informs the Freudian drama of sexual difference, in which the boy mourns the phallus in an Oedipal tragedy, and the girl melancholically identifies with its loss in a Shakespearean *Trauerspiel.*

Benjamin's *Ursprung des deutschen Trauerspiels,* published in

1928, is, like Nietzsche's *Birth of Tragedy,* a "first book," an exercise in extravagant philology in which a moment of ostensible birth or origin in the history of tragedy serves to stage an instance of generic and cultural decline.[1] Benjamin's study organizes a history and theory of post-classical tragedy—Baroque *Trauerspiel*—around mourning as the founding trope of generic transformation. As such, Benjamin's argument reconceives Shakespearean tragic form by foregrounding genre not as a set of norms fixed in developmental narratives, but as metamorphic modalities whose shapes are only retroactively and provisionally determined. The philosophical opposition between ancient and modern tragedy inherited by Benjamin also marks Freud's historico-theoretical counterpointing of Sophocles and Shakespeare. Benjamin's elaboration of the ancient-modern dialectic in terms of mourning confirms and extends our conceptualization of the place of Shakespearean drama in the intertextual swerves of psychoanalysis. Moreover, Benjamin's study, in the process of rethinking the status of literary genre, itself constitutes a shift in the genre of philosophical criticism. *Trauerspiel,* and with it Benjamin's text, unfolds as the negative example projected by key moments in the philosophy of tragedy: the weak and irregular structures abhorred by Aristotle, the vestigial paganism of a drama always falling short of the Christian synthesis discerned by Hegel, and the Euripidean rationalism disparaged by Nietzsche. Rather than a coherent or essential form, *Trauerspiel,* as the untragic or lapsed tragic, collects around a series of discontinuous, even contradictory practices: mere rhetoric as well as artless philosophy, the brute pagan as well as the weak Christian, the all-too-theoretical as well as the simply historical.

Thus Benjamin's text neither reverses poles of value nor expands their range by canonizing underestimated works, but rather designates the necessary role of "bad tragedy" in the constitution of literary tradition and its criticism. For literary

---

1. The works we have found most useful on Benjamin's notion of *Trauerspiel* are Rainer Nägele, *Theater, Theory, Speculation* and *Benjamin's Ground;* Peter Sacks, *The English Elegy;* and Samuel Weber, "Genealogy of Modernity."

theory after Plato, *Trauerspiel* functions as both the (negative)
object, the counter example to tragedy, and the (unacknow-
ledged) model of the critical act, since tragic criticism, like
Trauerspiel, is constituted as the petrifying reflection on the classical genre it both murders and mourns. The figure of Socrates
is foundational: if, with Plato, the republic of philosophical
criticism establishes itself on the expulsion of tragedy, as a
consequence, *philosophy owes tragedy a death,* paid but not paid
off in the suicide of Socrates, the new paradigm of (post)tragedy
for, and ultimately as, philosophy. If the Socrates of the *Apology*
and the *Phaedo* marks the death of tragedy into classical philosophy, *Hamlet,* the martyr drama of the philosopher prince,
replays that transitional scene for Romanticism and psychoanalysis. Finally, the figure of Achilles, affiliated textually to both
Socrates and Hamlet, marks the tragic fold within epic that sets
each classical genre against itself, both predicting and faulting
the historical translation of tragedy into *Trauerspiel.*

Socrates, the *Ursprung* of *Trauerspiel*

In summarizing Benjamin's argument, it is tempting to oppose tragedy and *Trauerspiel* according to a self-conscious,
Brechtian, anti-Aristotelian program: as myth versus history,
as drama versus theater, as symbol versus allegory, as closed
versus open-ended, as unique versus repetitive, as the spoken
language of the logos versus the visual or graphic language of
the dumb show or pro-logos. However useful such oppositions
may be, what distinguishes Baroque *Trauerspiel* from the Brechtian aesthetics that it so clearly influenced is precisely the *absence*
of a sharply delineated, confrontational stance toward the classical models it inherited. In defining *Trauerspiel* as the other of
tragedy, Benjamin staged their relation not as a classical drama
of Oedipal or fratricidal agon but as itself a postclassical *Trauerspiel* of melancholic identification, at once mortifying and idealizing. Through Benjamin's analysis, *Trauerspiel* comes to
characterize not only a specific genre, but also the relation
between genres. This distinction between modes of distinction

requires seeing genre not only as an *object of analysis*, but also as that which informs the implied narratives of criticism itself, the "forms, moods, and shapes of grief." Part One of Benjamin's *Ursprung des deutschen Trauerspiels* is titled "Trauerspiel und Tragödie," a rubric faithfully translated as "*Trauerspiel* and Tragedy" in the English edition. The English phrase "*Trauerspiel* and Tragedy" juxtaposes a foreign German word and its familiar English *opposite*. The German title, however, couples a common German word, the vernacular *Trauerspiel*, and its erudite Greek equivalent, the foreign word *Tragödie*. The very faithfulness of the English translation fails to preserve one crucial feature of Benjamin's distinction, the foregrounding of vernacular translation itself as the process through which postclassical drama was constituted. In the vernacularization of *Tragödie* into *Trauerspiel*, moreover, translation occurs under the rubric, in the name of, mourning, *Trauer*, implicating translation as a kind of mourning that, far from entering into an Oedipal struggle with past texts, sees itself in a necromantic, recuperative, or simply (and all the more falsely) continuous relation with classical culture.

For Benjamin *Trauerspiel* begins with the death of Socrates, the key figure for the passage of tragedy into philosophy inherited from Hegel and Nietzsche. Thus Benjamin extends and distends the domain of Baroque drama—and the scope of his own project—into the textual twilight of classical Greece. In a central section of "*Trauerspiel* and Tragedy," Benjamin shifts from speculating on the modernist future of *Trauerspiel* to contemplating its Socratic prehistory:

> Here it is a question of its past. This leads us far back to a turning-point in the history of the Greek spirit itself [*Geschichte des griechischen Geistes selbst*]: the death of Socrates. The martyr-drama was born from the death of Socrates as a parody of tragedy.... Superficially, of course, the death of the philosopher resembles tragic death.... But this very similarity reveals most clearly the real significance of the agonal character of the genuinely tragic: that silent struggle, that mute flight of the hero, which, in the [Platonic] *Dialogues*, has given way to such a brilliant display of speech and consciousness. The agonal has disappeared from the

drama of Socrates—even in his philosophical struggles it is only
a question of going through the motions—and in one stroke
the death of the hero has been transformed into that of a martyr.
Like the Christian hero of the faith—which explains both the
sympathy of many a father of the Church and the hatred of
Nietzsche, who unerringly detected this—Socrates dies vol-
untarily.

(E 113–14; G 94–95)

Here Benjamin uses the death of Socrates to distinguish tragedy and *Trauerspiel:* silence versus display, the mythic agon
versus the mechanisms of philosophy, the flawed hero versus
the saintly martyr. Moreover, the disappearance of agon from
the Socratic scene affects the status of the distinctions themselves, which are revealed through *Trauerspiel*'s "very similarity"
rather than its opposition to tragic form. Finally, this parodic
transformation occurs "in one stroke," *mit einem Schlage,* not as
the consequence of a dialectical movement but as a magical,
fantasmatic metamorphosis *ex machina.*

Benjamin's reference to the death of Socrates, saturated in
the language of Hegel ("the history of the Greek spirit") and
punctuated by direct allusion to Nietzsche, locates his own text
in an overdetermined, doubly negative position in the history
and theory of tragedy. For both Hegel and Nietzsche, the death
of Socrates announces the demise of tragedy and its replace-
ment by Christianity, but, whereas for Hegel, Socrates is not
Christian enough, for Nietzsche—as Benjamin notes here—
Socrates is Christian, all too Christian.[2] Benjamin's reference
to Socrates must be read as the assumption of an intertextual
legacy, in which not only the content but also the act and mode
of citation manifest and theorize criticism as the mourning for
literature—a literature that itself, moreover, only exists qua
"literature" through its mournful commentary. In this sense,
literature is not the stable object *of* critical desire, but, in Lacan's
phrase, the object *in* desire, both constituted by and constitutive

2. George Steiner notes Benjamin's precedents in Nietzsche and Hegel
in the introduction to the English translation of *Ursprung des deutschen
Trauerspiels.*

of the critical act. If Socrates is the figure of philosophical reflection and literary cancellation, Achilles, as we shall see, emblematizes the persistence of literature within philosophy, as the moment of melancholic self-criticism that inhabits, enables, and resists reflective self-consciousness.

In his *Lectures on the History of Philosophy*, Hegel places Socrates at the border between classical tragedy and Christian redemption. For Hegel, the death of Socrates, paralleling that of Antigone, is tragic insofar as it stages the "collision" of two equally valid yet absolutely opposed rights, those of the individual and of the state. Whereas for Hegel the mythic conflict between Antigone and Creon occurs within Athenian culture, as its consummate expression, the historical tragedy of Socrates' death is staged between Athenian culture and something already on its margins—Socratic individuality, or, in Nietzsche's expression, "theoretical man." According to Hegel, in the wake of Socrates' death the Athenians internalized the Socratic principles of Oedipal innovation—"the introduction of new gods and disrespect to parents" (Paolucci and Paolucci 363); in the process, their accusations against Socrates became self-accusations, destroying the political ethos of classical tragedy. Socrates' death, Hegel writes, entails "the tragedy of Athens, the tragedy of Greece" (364): the narrative of Socrates' trial and suicide, staged through tragic conventions, cancels the discursive conditions of Athenian tragedy as such.[3] The synthesis required by this negation lies not within but beyond the limits of Greek tragedy, in the Christian narrative, which the death of Socrates anticipates but fails to realize.

The difference between Socrates and Christ—the classical feet of clay which confine the philosopher to the limbo of the virtuous pagans—is emblematized for Hegel by the figure of Achilles:

We should expect nothing else of Socrates than that he should go to meet his death in the most calm and manly fashion. Plato's

---

3. On the use of tragic conventions in the *Apology*, see Alister Cameron, *Plato's Affair with Tragedy*.

account of the wonderful scene his last hours presented, although containing nothing very special, forms an elevating picture, and will be to us a permanent representation of a noble deed. The last dialogue of Plato is popular philosophy, for the immortality of the soul is here first brought forward; yet it brings no consolation, for, as Homer makes Achilles say in the nether world, he would prefer to be a ploughboy on the earth.

(Paolucci and Paolucci *Hegel on Tragedy* 361–62)

Hegel alludes here to the famous interchange between Achilles and Odysseus in the underworld, in which the dead hero rejects the consolation of historical fame:

"O shining Odysseus, never try to console me for dying.
I would rather follow the plow as thrall to another
man, one with no land allotted him and not much to live on,
than be a king over all the perished dead."

(*Odyssey* 11.488–91)

These lines epitomize the generic and sexual paradoxes of Achilles, split in literary history between a superhuman virile militarism on one hand and, on the other, an effeminate withdrawal from his fate. This ambiguity punctuates the legends of Achilles' life and death, from his childhood in women's clothing to his curtained tent outside Troy with Patroclus, to his sullen dismissal of Odysseus' greeting in the underworld. As such, Achilles represents a structural deviation within both epic and tragic traditions of the hero, since he forestalls epic military heroism in his life and refuses tragic fatalism in his death. For Hegel, the stoicism of Socrates, far from reversing the complaints of Achilles, repeats their failings in another key, since the Socratic notion of an afterlife presented in the *Phaedo* remains inadequate to Christian consolation. To align Socrates with the Achilles of generic aberration is to see each as the weak point, the Achilles' heel, of their genres, and of the narratives of generic transformation they define. Not only does the morose figure of Achilles in hell contaminate the integrity of epic and tragedy, but by doing so at their canonical Homeric origin, it disturbs any linear history of generic development. To call

Socrates a second Achilles is to see the "death of tragedy" into
philosophy as already secondary, a nagging repetition of effeminate complaint that faults the dialectical consolations of
philosophy, Christianity, and literature.

For Achilles in the underworld already appears as the philosopher in Plato. Hegel's comparison of Socrates and Achilles
is informed by a pair of contradictory citations of the passage
in *The Republic*. Plato initially rejects the line as an example of
tragedy's encouragement of "moral weakness" (Book 3.140),
but then renovates it in the allegory of the cave, in which
Achilles' complaints in the afterlife become the philosopher's
rejection of the world of phenomenal and artistic illusion:

> There was probably a certain amount of honour and glory to
> be won among the prisoners, and prizes for keen-sightedness
> for those best able to remember the order of sequence among
> the passing shadows and so be best able to divine their future
> appearances. Will our released prisoner hanker after these
> prizes or envy this power or honour? Won't he be more likely
> to feel, as Homer says, that he would far rather be "a serf in
> the house of some landless man," or indeed anything else in the
> world, than hold the opinions and live the life that they do?
>
>   (7:319)

Plato finds the literal meaning of the line unacceptable, but
accepts an allegorical reading of Achilles' unheroic sentiment,
and with it the conventions of figurative reading. As an epic
allusion to the *topos* of the descent to the underworld, moreover,
the passage itself constitutes a descent to the underworld of
dead poets—to the underworld *as* the literary tradition. The
republic of philosophy is pitted by the cave of literature, en-
folding the Homeric line whose double citation in the *Republic*
sows the generic contradiction embodied by Achilles in the
womb-tomb of the philosophical and critical tradition.[4]

Although Nietzsche's *Birth of Tragedy* inherits Hegel's Socrates and the dialectical passage of literature into theory that

4. On Plato's cave as a womb, see Luce Irigaray, "Plato's *Hystera*," in *Speculum of the Other Woman* 243–364.

his death dramatizes, Nietzsche laments the change that Hegel celebrates. Nietzsche echoes the grievance of Achilles:

> Once the complaint has sounded, it is heard again from the short-lived Achilles, mourning the leaf-like change and vicissitudes of the race of men and the decline of the heroic age [*Untergang der Heroenzeit*]. It is not unworthy of the greatest hero to long for a continuation of life, even though he live as a day laborer.
>
> (*Birth* 43; *Werke* 1:31, translation altered)

Nietzsche uses the figure of Achilles to demonstrate the secondary rather than natural state of the Homeric *naïve*, since the life-affirming complaint of Achilles, presented by Nietzsche as a kind of secondary narcissism, comes after and fantasmatically reverses the terrifying insight of Silenus that it is better not to be born.[5] The representation of Achilles figures a work of intertextual mourning in which the *Untergang*, the decline or setting, of literature into philosophy informs both the structure and the thematics of a certain tendency in literary criticism. Achilles in the underworld laments "the *Untergang* of the heroic age," the passing of the epic period he had epitomized; thus the "short-lived Achilles" becomes the melancholic object of his own mourning, a figure of the sentimental within the naïve. Nietzsche's Homeric allusion, "leaf-like change"—a phrase that makes its progress through the underworlds of Virgil, Dante, and Milton—describes and enacts the vicissitudes of culture as a natural history of decay: the fallen "leaves" of literary history

5. Nietzsche continues his argument in the very next paragraph thus: "Here we should note that this harmony which is contemplated with such longing by modern man, in fact, this oneness of man with nature (for which Schiller introduced the technical term 'naive'), is by no means a simple condition that comes into being naturally and as if inevitably.... When we encounter the 'naive' in art, we should recognize the highest effect of Apollinian culture—which must have triumphed over an abysmal and terrifying view of the world and the keenest susceptibility to suffering through recourse to the most forceful and pleasurable illusions." Like the Freudian ego and the Lacanian mirror stage, Apollinian identity is presented as a secondary and fundamentally illusory cultural achievement rather than a natural, original state.

are transmitted as remnants of the temporal mortification to which language is subject.

Moreover, Nietzche's conception of the Homeric career is derived from Longinus, the Hellenistic critic of the sublime who cast the *Odyssey* as the mourning for the *Iliad*. In the *Odyssey*, Longinus suggests, Homer "render[s] to his heroes their meed of lamentation as if it were a debt long due. . . . So in the *Odyssey* one may liken Homer to the setting sun; the grandeur remains without its intensity" (*On the Sublime* 9.12). Longinus's contrast between the epic unity of the *Iliad* and the *Odyssey* as a romance that digressively mourns it rearticulates the distinction between an Aristotelian tragedy of plot and a Euripidean, Baroque, or Romantic *Trauerspiel* of character.[6] Achilles, placed by Nietzsche in Apollinian light, nonetheless slips into the Socratic shadows of Theoretical Man via the recourse to Longinian periodization. In Nietzsche's text and across Homer's *oeuvre*, Achilles speaks for and as the great literature of the past, but only through the critical voice of Longinus, for whom literary sublimity insistently turns into the falling away from the sublime—grandeur without intensity.[7]

Although Achilles does not appear in *Hamlet*, his son does: the "rugged Pyrrhus" of the Player's speech who by taking vengeance for his father's death displays the virtues Hamlet lacks. Like Priam, Hamlet "strik[es] too short at Greeks" (II.ii.465); he is inadequate to the epic ideal. Pyrrhus personifies the epic wrath of Achilles, but Hamlet is not equal to the Pyrrhic example and personifies rather the morose underside of Achilles' heroic legacy, an identification not with the positivity of a generic norm but with the negativity of its internal lapses. If the myth of Oedipus describes the structures of in-

6. Longinus concludes his discussion of Homer's career: "I wanted you to realize how with the decline of their emotional power great writers and poets give way to character-study" (*On The Sublime* 9.14).

7. Neil Hertz compares Longinus and Benjamin: "The comparison suggests that we cannot take either the critics' nostalgia or their structurings of history at face value; each evokes a catastrophe, yet each seems equally concerned with a recurrent phenomenon in literature, the movement of disintegration and figurative reconstitution I have been calling the sublime turn" (*The End of the Line* 14).

heritance for and in literature and theory, the sexual and generic ambiguities of Achilles fault its patrilineal lines. The *Trauerspiel* of *Hamlet*'s intertextual legacy retroactively pins the "Achilles' heel" of classical criticism to the Oedi-pus, the swollen foot, which both names and lames the forward march of literary inheritance. The generic flaw that Achilles represents performs the founding gesture of a post-tragic literary criticism that extends from Longinus to Benjamin. Such criticism, adrift between literature and philosophy, ostends its own self-difference by mourning an ambivalent object—a tragedy turned *Trauerspiel*, like milk turned sour—with which, alas, it has identified.

In *Ecce Homo*, Nietzsche displays and insults his juvenile effort in *The Birth of Tragedy:* "It smells offensively Hegelian, and the cadaverous perfume of Schopenhauer sticks only to a few formulas" (270–71). By reducing the visual paradigm of Hegelian speculation to the residual primitivism of smell, Nietzsche does not simply oppose materialism to idealism but rather locates a materialism *of* the ideal in odor as the vaporization, the rendering into spirits, of matter—a natural history of *Geist* produced not as the transcendence of matter but as the remnant of its decay.[8] Benjamin's *Trauerspiel*, another first book of perverse philology, germinates precisely in the rank space of the "offensively Hegelian" as it links the ghostly machinery of Hegelian aesthetics to the frantic dualism of Nietzsche's early work. If Hegel "smells," it is because something of tragedy— its "cadaverous perfume"—remains undigested in dialectical philosophy; as Hamlet says of the corpse of Polonius, if he can't be found in heaven or hell, "you shall nose him as you go up the stairs into the lobby" (IV.iii.35–36). The Shakespearean pun on "knowing" and "nosing" indicates the birth of epistemological spirit out of the spirits of scatology. The pun suits the body of Polonius, the play's critical know-it-all; theorizing the *Trauerspiel* in his flamboyantly neoclassical label, "tragical-comical-historical-pastoral," Polonius is a figure of Baroque "Bad Taste." Polonius's maladroit conglomeration exemplifies the additive proliferation of generic categories sullying the pas-

---

8. See Jacques Derrida, *Of Spirit: Heidegger and the Question* 99.

sage of tragedy into criticism, in which the very process of division and exfoliation into critical typologies becomes a kind of materialism—a materialism of "kinds" or genres. Moreover, the unburied body of Polonius exemplifies criticism as corpse or *corpus:* as a critico-literary body enzymatically broken down and reassembled by generic classification. Like Polonius, Benjamin founds dramatic criticism on a hybridized non-genre, a genre of genres, whose function, however, is not to further specify the subdivisions of literary kind, but to anatomize the mechanisms, fantasies, and memories of literary historiography.

Whereas for Nietzsche and Hegel tragedy dies with Socrates, for Benjamin, *Trauerspiel* is stillborn from that death, as the material index of tragedy's decay. The intertextual verbarium of Benjamin's book locates postclassical drama in the half-world of the untragic as conceived by philosophy; Benjamin does not contradict the earlier philosophers so much as elaborate and animate their negative examples. The *Trauerspiel*—both the genre and the book—devolves as a kind of shadow play or dumb show, the grotesque image cast on the wall by the sharper forms of literary philosophy. The *Trauerspiel* functions as a play within a play, a parodic miniaturization in and of the history and theory of tragedy: both the philosophical reflection on tragedy and its warped, satiric repetition—a funhouse mirror held up to art.[9]

The title of Benjamin's book, *Ursprung des deutschen Trauerspiels,* signals its baroque relation, at once imitative and metamorphic, to Nietzsche's *Geburt der Tragödie:* not only does Greek tragedy become German *Trauerspiel,* but "birth," *Geburt,* gives way to "origin," *Ursprung:* literally, "primal leap," but also, as Samuel Weber has pointed out, "irremediable split or crack" ("Genealogy of Modernity" 472). In the "Epistemo-Critical Prologue" to the book, Benjamin glosses the word *Ursprung:*

9. On the Baroque convention of the dumb show and the play within a play, see Benjamin, *Ursprung* E 80–84, G 61–67. On the satyr drama as the epilogue to tragedy (and the Socratic dialogue as its heir), see Benjamin, *Ursprung* E 117, G 98.

The term origin is not intended to describe the process by which the existent came into being, but rather to describe that which emerges from the process of becoming and disappearance.... That which is original is never revealed in the naked and manifest existence of the factual; its rhythm is apparent only to a dual insight. On the one hand it needs to be recognized as a process of restoration and re-establishment, but, on the other hand, and precisely because of this, as something imperfect and incomplete.

(E 45, G 28)

If *Geburt* for Benjamin might imply an organic or genetic model, *Ursprung* is necessarily secondary and retroactive: "a process of restoration and re-establishment," a mournful recuperation that is, however, always melancholically short of synthesis, "imperfect and incomplete."[10] One genre springs from the death of another, not through a redemptive dialectic in which physical death is the means to spiritual life, but rather in a natural history in which death leads to the afterlife and half-life of material decay (47).[11] *Ursprung*, following a staggered temporal rhythm, is an originary repetition discerned only in the historicizing gaze of an Orphic criticism that, looking back at what will have been tragedy, repeats its loss and petrifies it as *Trauerspiel*.

Reading Benjamin with Freud, we could say that the *Ursprung* of *Trauerspiel* is coterminous with the dissolution or *Untergang* of tragedy into the philosophical criticism that constructs it as such. "The tragic," imitated and interred in the

10. In Benjamin's substitution of *Ursprung* for *Geburt*, however, he ends up approximating the Nietzschean example he apparently repudiates; cf. Weber, "Genealogy of Modernity" 476.
11. Compare the comments of Siegfried Kracauer on Benjamin, in an unpublished review of Adorno's book on Kierkegaard, itself strongly influenced by Benjamin's work on and in the history and theory of tragedy: " 'The truth-content of a work reveals itself only in its collapse.... The work's claim to totality, its systematic structure, as well as its superficial intentions share the fate of everything transient; but as they pass away with time the work brings characteristics and configurations to the fore that are actually images of truth' " (cited by Robert Hullot-Kentnor in his foreword to Theodor Adorno's *Kierkegaard* xv).

scene of Socrates' death, survives as the lost object of intertextual mourning in the institution of the humanities, guaranteeing the foundational status of a fetishized "Greek culture" as
the vessel and content of Western values. Through the mechanisms of *Trauerspiel*, the dead Socrates returns as the voice of
self-reproach internalized by philosophy and literary criticism—in Freud's mythical narrative, as the "critical agency"
formed by the consumption of the murdered primal father.
Benjamin cites Nietzsche: " '*The dying Socrates* became the new
ideal, never seen before, of noble Greek youths' " (114). In
psychoanalytic terms, through the death of Socrates, or rather
through the over-determined citation of his death, tragedy
comes to represent for postclassical literature and theory both
the *ideal ego*—the lost narcissistic paragon of an endless nostalgia—and the *ego ideal*—the critical position from which ego
and ideal are mercilessly judged.[12] Tragic drama, as both the
object and the mechanism of mourning, divides its criticism in
a "dual insight"; tragedy, by determining the very impulse to
mourn, remains fundamentally unmournable.

To read Benjamin with Freud is not simply to draw theoretical parallels or analogies, but rather to locate both in the
unfolding discourse of tragedy as it moves from and between
the *Oedipus* trilogy, its repetition and abrogation in the *Apology*,
and the post-tragic critical practices that spring up from their
relation. These practices include not only philosophy and
psychoanalysis, but also the event of Shakespearean textuality, as a primal scene in the secondary drama of postclassical
theory.

Hamlet, the *Untergang* of *Trauerspiel*

Benjamin places Socrates at the origin of *Trauerspiel*, and
Hamlet at the efflorescence of the genre in its *Untergang*. In
Benjamin's text, the death scenes of Socrates and Hamlet are

---

12. For the rigorous theorization of this more informal distinction in Freud,
see Lacan, *Seminar I*, chap. 11, and Zizek, *The Sublime Object of Ideology* 105–7.

key narratives of critical awareness, moments that determine *Trauerspiel* from beyond the confines of the German Baroque. Each is an inherited emblem of the postclassical in which paired yet asymmetrical modes of self-division, namely philosophical self-consciousness and the psychoanalytic unconscious, are founded on mourning.[13] The scene of Socrates' death, staged quite literally as the tragedy to end all tragedy, structurally preserves tragic drama as precisely *the unconscious of philosophical self-consciousness,* the eclipsed signifiers of cultural origination whose cancellation underwrites the objects of philosophical reflection. *Hamlet's* Baroque poetics of self-reflection repeat this dialectic. Moreover, as a play not only of the ghostly father but of the too-alive mother, *Hamlet* stumbles on the textual and intertextual materiality, the intransigent stain, adhering to the symbolic bar of relation and repression, of self-conscious and unconscious.

Concluding the first half of his book with an account of the Renaissance mytho-physiology of melancholy, Benjamin ends by replaying the final scene of *Hamlet:*

> This age succeeded (at least once) in conjuring up the human figure who corresponded to this split [*Zwiespalt*] between the neo-antique and the medieval light in which the baroque saw the melancholic. But Germany was not the country which was able to do this. The figure is Hamlet. The secret of his person is contained within the playful, but for that very reason firmly circumscribed, passage through all the stations [*Stationen*] in this complex of intentions, just as the secret of his fate is contained in an action which, according to this, his way of looking at things, is perfectly homogeneous. For the *Trauerspiel* Hamlet alone is a spectator by the grace of God; but he cannot find satisfaction in what he sees enacted, only in his own fate. His life, the exemplary object of his mourning, points, before its extinction, to the Christian providence in whose bosom his mournful images are transformed into a blessed existence. Only in a princely life

13. Rainer Nägele's reading of *Hamlet* in Benjamin also emphasizes the difference between literary melancholia and philosophical self-consciousness (*Theater, Theory, Speculation* 168).

such as this is melancholy redeemed, by being confronted with
itself. The rest is silence.

(E 157–58, G 136–37; translation altered)

In this passage, consistent with Freud's account, melancholia
inhabits a split, a *Zwiespalt,* across a series of textual divides.
The "figure of Hamlet" emerges from the initial cleavage between two postclassical iconographies of melancholia, the neo-
antique and the medieval. The splitting of a specific classical
discourse becomes splitting per se: the self-division between
the mourning subject and the "exemplary object," which is
Hamlet's own life. This split in turn informs the stance of critical spectatorship, at once ironically distanced and narcissistically invested, that marks the strained relations between the
character Hamlet and the play *Hamlet,* between the play and
the genre of *Trauerspiel,* as well as between Benjamin's text and
Shakespearean discourse.

The context of the martyr drama evoked by Benjamin further counterpoints Hamlet and Socrates, who cross precisely
at the Cross.[14] Benjamin describes here a kind of passion play
suffered by *Trauerspiel* as a genre, in which *Hamlet,* incarnating
the form most fully, thereby mortifies it. As Benjamin writes
in the prologue, "A major work will either establish the genre
or abolish it [*hebt sich auf*]; and the perfect work will do both"
(E 44, G 27). Benjamin draws upon an incarnational dialectic
recalled again in the passage on *Hamlet,* in which the play appears as the sublime exemplification, fulfillment, and abrogation of the genre. If Benjamin momentarily adopts the
Hegelian history of spirit, however, he nonetheless derails its
nationalistic teleology, its spatial and temporal unities: when
German *Trauerspiel* finally finds its apogee, "Germany was not
the country which was able to do this." *Hamlet* appears as the
English flower of German drama, which, blossoming before the
fact, cankers all future Germanic production: "It was above all
Shakespeare's drama, with its richness and its freedom, which,

14. On Renaissance martyr drama, see G. K. Hunter, "Tyrant and Martyr,"
and Julia Lupton, "Afterlives of the Saints."

for the romantic writers, overshadowed [*verdunkelnd*] contem-
poraneous German efforts" (E 48, G 31). This displacement of
national history—the "German Tragic Drama" of the book's
title—contorts what is meant by the history of a genre or form
more generally, such that the fragmentation and scattering
implicated in diaspora replace national continuity and influence
as the informing tropes and schemes of Benjamin's aesthetic
historiography.[15] For the same reason, *Hamlet*'s fulfillment of
a particular genre entails not only its shattering, but the shattering of "genre" in its more traditional conceptions, its conception as tradition.

Benjamin's conjunction of sorrowful self-consciousness and
the martyr drama implicitly reads the dialectic of melancholy
through the Christian paradigm (itself inherited from Judaism)
of the over-and inward-turning of the Law.[16] *Hamlet*'s melancholic self-division mirrors Judeo-Christian interiority insofar
as both involve an internal split between subject and object,
ego ideal and ideal ego, conscience and the sinning self. The
fold of self-consciousness, in which the self is dialectically
formed through identification with another, produces and depends upon a more radical division, the bar of repression and
substitution. Thus the fold or hyphen within each representational tradition becomes the allegorical disjunction of figuration per se: the *Zwiespalt* of melancholia echoes the chasm
between "Judeo-" and "Christian," Old and New Dispensations,
letter and spirit. In each case, moreover, an intransigent mark
is left over from the process of interiorization, not simply as
the resistance to dialectical cancellation but as a material scar,
scission, or circumcision left in its wake. As Rainer Nägele has
suggested, the Judaic problematic in Benjamin's work "involves

15. See Nägele's gloss of Benjamin's early statement that "art history does
not exist" (*Benjamin's Ground* 14–18). Nägele also emphasizes Benjamin's ongoing critique of developmental, teleological narratives of history (*Theater, Theory, Speculation* 3, 183, and passim).
16. Freud points out that the conversion of external law into conscience
stems not from the relatively late idea of Christian mercy, but from Mosaic
morality and the rhythm of reforms instituted by the Prophets. See *Moses and
Monotheism* (SE 23:51, 64) and *Future of an Illusion* (SE 21).

not only empirical traces of Jewish thought but perhaps even more the scenarios of a philosophical unconscious" (*Theater Theory Speculation* (124–25)—that is, we would say, not only an unconscious scenario, but the scenario of the unconscious, the residual Judaic rhetoric within the Freudian counternarrative to philosophical self-consciousness and Christian interiority.

Thus Benjamin ends his redemptive gloss of *Hamlet* with an unmarked citation from the play: "Only in a princely life such as this is melancholy redeemed, by being confronted with itself. The rest is silence." Benjamin's assumption of Hamlet's last words mimes the Romantic critic's characterological identification with Hamlet as figure of self-consciousness, but through the citational agency of the letter and at the moment of death. Benjamin's text, that is, identifies with Hamlet and *Hamlet* as dead, as "rest" or residue of generic and dialectical transformation. It is in keeping with this mortified identification that Benjamin chooses to cite Hamlet's last words instead of Horatio's Christian rejoinder to them:

> *Hamlet:* The rest is silence. [*Dies*].
> *Horatio:* Now cracks a noble heart. Good night, sweet prince,
>   And flights of angels sing thee to thy rest.
>   (V.ii.363–65)

Horatio's repetition of the word "rest" imposes a redemptive reading of Hamlet's death: from residue to resurrection, from the silence of the grave to the tranquil music of the spheres. Moreover, the echoing of the word "rest" across the two lines projects the acoustic mirror of the maternal lullaby as the fantasmatic object, both lost and residual, of the play's mourning. Benjamin's selective citation—and our reading of it—serves not to cancel the Messianic turn of Horatio's consolation, but to reassert the obdurate Judaic lining, at once apocalyptic and unredeemed, of the Christian dialectic of salvation.

Unlike the death of Socrates, the scene of Hamlet's death does not produce the self-consciousness of philosophical thought, but is produced by it, as its aftereffect, its accidental detritus. Hamlet's death is neither fated like that of Oedipus nor voluntary like that of Socrates; instead, in Benjamin's description, Hamlet "wants to die by some accident" (*Ursprung* 137). The radical externality of fate, materialized in the stage props that "gather around him," indicates the Baroque contingency rather than classical necessity of *Hamlet*'s plot. Littered with *revenants*, lost and found corpses, misdirected murder, ambiguous suicide, and accidental poisoning, the play stages death not as destiny, but as missed encounter. The aleatory, gratuitous quality of Hamlet's death indicates that, for the traditions that inherit him, *Hamlet isn't quite dead*. Although through Socrates tragedy dies into philosophy, through Hamlet *Trauerspiel* doesn't-quite-die into a not-quite-philosophy—psychoanalysis. Socrates founds the paternal superego of philosophy through resolute self-sacrifice, but Hamlet stages a tragedy of ir-resolution that determines or undetermines a feminine imago for Romanticism and its theoretical heirs.

In the natural historicism of Benjamin's book, the Platonic legend of Socrates, mourning tragedy, constitutes the mythic *Ursprung* of *Trauerspiel*, whereas *Hamlet* marks a second moment of origination, the *Ursprung* of *Trauerspiel* precisely out of its generic abrogation, its *Untergang*. To repeat Benjamin's formulation, "A major work will either establish the genre or abolish it; and the perfect work will do both" (E 44, G 27). The example of *Hamlet* disrupts the line's redemptive logic of aesthetic perfection, since *Trauerspiel* comes to flower as neither the maturity nor the sublation of the genre, but only in and as the genre's decline. This scheme implicates mourning in the procedures of periodization itself, as ways of narrating the past that are themselves "inherited" from the past in acts of mourning. Thus the death of Socrates as a specific plot or *mythos* comes to narrate the relation between periods and modes: the Baroque as the mourning for the Classical, philosophy as the mourning for tragedy. For Romanticism, and *as* Romanticism, as the story of its *Ursprung*, the death of Hamlet enacts the mourning for that mourning, a secondary relation to the secondary. *Hamlet*, as we will argue further in Chapter 4, is melancholically identified—in a relation at once ironic and narcissistic—with the conventions of melancholia: the ghostly machinery of revenge tragedy, the bombast of neo-Senecan drama, the *acedia* of the medieval court, the despair of modern Wittenberg. The Romanticism that such a relation founds is not produced through a dialectical negation of negation (mourning *against* mourning), but rather through a mourning *for* mourning, for the possibility of adequate mourning— hence, through melancholia.

Thus *Ursprung* and *Untergang*, Socrates and Hamlet, are not opposites, but rather two moments of *Trauerspiel*, or even two aspects of the same moment: the simultaneous disappearance and restoration of the tragic *in* philosophy, or, more broadly, of literature *in* theory. Beyond studying literature from a phil- osophical perspective, Benjamin's text traces and enacts the passage of literature into theory, through narratives of expul- sion, vengeance, guilt, and mourning, and through their fail- ure. The mythical *Untergang* of tragedy constitutes the *Ursprung* of *Trauerspiel* as literary object on the one hand and as model of criticism on the other—that is, of literary criticism as post- tragic, since criticism itself springs out of and serves as the narrative of literary origin and dissolution and of literary origin *as* dissolution. *Ursprung* and *Untergang* are confounded in an unclassical plot that informs the passage of tragedy into criti- cism. Origin and dissolution do not function, then, as the be- ginning and end of a closed Aristotelian narrative of a genre's history, but as doubled scenes of temporal and formal rupture that evacuate any "middle" moment of generic purity or ma- turity.[17] Criticism can stage the history of a genre as either a unified tragedy (e.g., Vasari, Hegel, Steiner), in which case it implicitly casts art as its discrete and autonomous object, or criticism can narrate the history of tragedy as a distended *Trauerspiel* (e.g., Longinus, Kierkegaard, Benjamin), in which case literature is implicated *in* theory, thereby conceding the mutual constitution and intrinsic faulting of each. "Literature" itself becomes such only in its guilty internalization by the in-

17. For examples of Aristotelian narratives of generic change, see Giorgio Vasari, *Lives of the Artists,* which narrates the development of art on the model of a human life, and Alastair Fowler, *Kinds of Literature,* which complicates but preserves a similar developmental scheme.

stitutions of criticism; the literary as an autonomous domain
only exists "in theory," as a consequence of its theoretical defense, rationale, or "apology" by philosophy—an apology for,
but, even more important an apology *to* tragedy.[18]

The *Trauerspiel* of Sexuality

For Benjamin, the work of *Trauerspiel* articulates the passing
of Sophoclean tragedy into postclassical theater and theory. In
Freud and the early Lacan, the work of mourning performs
the passing or *Untergang* of the Oedipus complex, a process
that both divides and genders the subject. What would it mean
to say that the relation between tragedy and *Trauerspiel* mirrors,
or indeed is engendered by, the relation of male and female?
This question should be posed not as an essentialist or historicist
alignment of a kind of tragedy with a particular audience, character type, or set of thematic concerns, but rather at the level
of the opposition, or failed opposition, between the two terms.
If *Trauerspiel* is the (mis)translation of tragedy, in what sense
is the girl's relation to the phallus a (mis)translation, in a melancholic key, of the boy's? The intertextual drama played out
between tragedy and *Trauerspiel,* we would argue, parallels the
drama of sexual difference as theorized and narrated—and
theorized as narrative—by Freud.[19]

The breast, we argued in Chapter 1, is (re)constructed as
lost, as the retroactive cause of and compensation for the phallus at the mournful borderline between pre-Oedipal and Oedipal. What, then, is the relation between the engendering of
the parents at the beginning of the Oedipus complex and the
gendering of the subject at its close, a gendering that takes
place in relation to that phallus? For Lacan, the fundamental
contrast between *Hamlet* and *Oedipus Rex* lies in the fact that in

18. On the genre of literary defense or apology, see Margaret Ferguson,
Trials of Desire.
19. On the relation between theory and narrative in psychoanalysis, see
Felman, "Beyond Oedipus."

Shakespeare's play, "the subject *knows*" ("Desire" 43). Lacan frames this distinction in terms of the heroes' different temporal relations to castration: "The play *Hamlet* narrates the way in which something comes to be equated with what was missing—what was missing because of the initial situation insofar as that situation was distinct from Oedipus'—namely, castration" ("Hamlet, par Lacan," in *Ornicar?* 24:17). *Oedipus Rex*, Lacan implies, *ends* with the recognition of castration, whereas Shakespeare's play *begins* with it.

Lacan's implicit reference here, we would argue, is to Freud's attempt in the 1920s to theorize sexual difference. In the first of these essays, "The *Untergang* of the Oedipus Complex," two generically distinct tragedies of castration emerge: "A female child, however, does not understand her lack of a penis as being a sex-character; she explains it by assuming that at some earlier date she had possessed an equally large organ and had then lost it by castration.... The essential difference thus comes about that the girl accepts castration as an accomplished fact, whereas the boy fears the possibility of its occurrence" (*SE* 19:178). Whereas the boy, like Sophocles' Oedipus, recognizes castration at the end of the Oedipus complex, the little girl, like Hamlet, recognizes castration immediately: "She makes her judgement and her decision in a flash. She has seen it and knows that she is without it and wants to have it" (*SE* 19:252). Freud stages her judgment as instantaneous, even precipitous, abbreviating the psychic and dramatic work of anagnorisis; this precocity in turn explains the decidedly anticlassical lack of climax or resolution to the little girl's narrative. In Freud's *mise-en-scène*, the little girl responds by creating a narrative of loss, much like the incessant retelling of loss that characterizes the action, or inaction, of *Hamlet:* "She explains it by assuming that at some earlier date she had possessed an equally large organ and had then lost it by castration" (*SE* 19:178). The phallus ("an equally large organ") exists *only in narrative retrospect:* that is, the penis, never there to be lost, is the imaginary organ retroactively associated with an always-lost bodily integrity.

In his discussion of *Hamlet* in "Seminar VI," Lacan specifically links the Freudian narrative of Oedipal *Untergang* to the work of mourning and the gendering of the subject:

> When does the Oedipus complex, according to Freud, go into its *Untergang*, that decisive event for all of the subject's subsequent development? When the subject feels the threat of castration, and feels it from both directions implied by the Oedipal triangle. . . . As for the boy, he decides he's just not up to it. And as for the girl, she gives up any expectation of gratification in this way—the renunciation is expressed more clearly in her case than in his. All we can say is expressed in a formulation that doesn't come out in Freud's text but whose pertinence is everywhere indicated: the Oedipus complex goes into its decline insofar as the subject must mourn the phallus.
>
> ("Desire" 46)

Lacan recounts the Freudian narratives of sexualization, but implicitly subordinates generic protocols to rhetorical ones by construing each narrative in terms of a relation to the phallic signifier. "Mourning" is the name given to that relation: if both boy and girl "must mourn the phallus," however, the nature of their loss is nonetheless structured differently.

Since the little girl is mourning something that was never there in the first place, we would argue that her relation to the phallus is melancholic rather than mournful.[20] We could say that she *mourns mourning*—that is, that she mourns the lack of any real object that could be mourned, or, more precisely, that she mourns the lack of a lack that could be restored. This melancholia establishes the interminable, unresolved plot of her Oedipal *Trauerspiel:* "The Oedipus complex escapes the fate [*Schicksal*] which it meets with in boys: it may slowly be abandoned or dealt with by repression, or its effects may persist far into woman's normal mental life" (*SE* 19:257). Recall that according to Freud's late essay, "Analysis Terminable and In-

---

20. On melancholia and femininity, see Luce Irigaray, *Speculum of the Other Woman;* Kaja Silverman, *The Acoustic Mirror;* Judith Butler, *Gender Trouble;* and Kenneth Reinhard, "Allegories of Mourning," chap. 4.

terminable," it is the woman's penis envy that prevents analysis from concluding, as the analytic drama fails to reach the closure of Sophoclean tragedy and dwindles into the endless complaints and ostentatious soliloquies of *Trauerspiel*.

The oppositions between male and female, tragedy and *Trauerspiel*, and mourning and melancholia parallel each other, not only in terms of their contents but in terms of the structure and dynamic—the drama—of their oppositions. Melancholia *mourns mourning*—laments, that is, the lack of a genuinely anterior, legitimate, "normative" paradigm. Mourning is "primary" only in the sense that melancholia needs to posit an origin from which to deviate. So, too, the parallel distinction between the male tragedy of castration and its inconclusive feminine translation is subject to a necessary reversal, insofar as the melancholic relation to the phallus is, in the final (Freudian) analysis, the *only* relation to the phallus, which is defined precisely by the inability of *any subject*, male or female, to possess it without being dis-possessed by it. Finally, if *Trauerspiel* presents itself as the mourning for tragedy, its motifs and paradigms can always be located in the "purer," more "classical" plays it appears to translate. The point is not simply that all tragic drama "always already" is *Trauerspiel* (although such a conclusion is fair enough), but that the distinction between tragedy and *Trauerspiel* emerges in an historicism of melancholy that arises as such in defining, imagining, and deforming its categories in retrospect.

In Shakespearean *Trauerspiel*, femininity functions as lost object, divided subject, and alienating Other of *Hamlet*'s generic and discursive practice, as we argue at greater length in the next two chapters. First, as lost object: in *Hamlet*'s repudiation of the mother's flesh in the name of the father's spirit, the violence of maternal loss is both represented and elided by the law of the ghostly father—a phenomenon that explains the dominance of the play's Oedipal interpretation. Second, as divided subject: feminine sexuality manifests a melancholic relation to the phallus, which is activated only in narratives of its loss. Femininity thus describes the lapse of tragic agon into the compromises of *Trauerspiel*, accounting not only for the "weak character" of Prince Hamlet, but also for the interminability of the play's postclassical plot and its plotting of the postclassical. Finally, as alienating Other: following Lacan, we argue in the next chapter that the mother in *Hamlet* functions primarily not as Oedipal object, but as the Other of demand whose excessive enjoyment impedes the classical (masculine) dialectic of desire. This impasse, moreover, extends beyond the staging of desire in the play to the scene of *Hamlet*'s generic and intertextual relations: Senecan drama functions as the Other of demand, which, rather than either complementing or opposing Shakespearean discourse, fundamentally alienates it, locating *Hamlet* in the field of a tradition that is not its own.

Benjamin's excavation of *Trauerspiel* is presented together with a rhetorical project: to retrieve the allegorical underside of Romanticism's aesthetic ideology of the symbol. In its conjunction of the problematics of genre and rhetoric under the rubric of mourning, Benjamin's *Ursprung des deutschen Trauerspiels* allows us to account for the literary dispositions of Freud and Lacan in their distinction and alignment: if for Freud, rhetorical transformations are governed by dramatic and narratival categories (Oedipal tragedy, the primal scene, family romance), for Lacan, Oedipal narrative is always written by the materiality of the signifier in its allegorical determinations by metaphor and metonymy. Moreover, to articulate this imbrication of rhetoric and genre within and between Freud and Lacan is to pose the question of gender as a fundamentally discursive problematic. Gender positions depend on temporal narrations of loss that in turn imply specific structural relationships to a signifier.

Through the semiotic and narratival overdeterminations of gender in psychoanalysis, rhetoric and genre become more than linguistic kin and less than poetic kind. *Genre* here encompasses morphological analysis as it includes and counterpoints Aristotle's conception of *mythos* in tragedy and Benjamin's focus on Aristotelian malformations in *Trauerspiel*. This generic coupling of tragedy with *Trauerspiel* is itself (to speak generically) isomorphic with the gender pair male-female as articulated in the tragic paradigms of psychoanalysis. From the perspective of rhetoric, on the other hand, the morphological transformation of tragedy into *Trauerspiel* is produced by a *tropological* process of metonymic displacement and metaphoric condensation. If *Trauerspiel* materializes as the allegorical (mis)translation of tragedy, which it construes as its lost origin, the phallus as signifier is constituted as the substitute, through mournful allegoresis, for the breast as imaginary object, both "before" the phallus as its prefiguration and "after" it as its fantasmatic compensation. Freud's essays on sexual difference, with their strained narratives of recognition and reversal, are inaugurated by the 1924 "Dissolution [*Untergang*] of the Oedipus Complex," an essay glossed by Lacan in his discussion of *Hamlet* in "Seminar VI." Between these texts, *Hamlet* emerges as the emblematic drama of the object *in* desire, and of literature *in* psychoanalysis.

CHAPTER THREE

Hamlet's Flesh: Lacan and
the Desire of the Mother

The opening line of Hamlet's first soliloquy, the formal vehicle for his famous "interiority," is fractured by a textual crux: "O that this too too *sullied* [or *solid*] flesh would melt, / Thaw, and resolve itself into a dew" (I.ii.129–30).[1] The Quarto reading ("sallied," a variant of "sullied") emphasizes the bad conscience of Hamlet, which bolsters Freud's Oedipal interpretation of the play, in which Hamlet's mourning for his father is tainted by his identification with Claudius. The Folio's "solid," on the other hand, supported by the soliloquy's language of dissolution, materializes the specific gravity of the flesh, its sodden resistance to the flights of fancy that "characterize" Hamlet; in this reading, the solidity of Hamlet's flesh rankly burgeons from the corporeality of Gertrude, whose bestial "increase of appetite" (I.ii.144) leads Hamlet to break into the famous *interruptio*, "Frailty, thy name is woman" (I.ii.146). A psychoanalytic philology might argue that both readings must be valid—not, however, as alternatives available for adjudication or compromise, but as rival readings "sullied" by their coexistence in mutual cancellation. Echoing anxiously through each other, the two words weigh down the symbolic agon of signification (the competing meanings of "sullied" and "solid") with the heaviness of

1. For the textual debate on the reading of Q2 "sallied" versus the Folio "solid," see Harold Jenkins's note to this line in the *Arden Hamlet* (436–38).

the pure signifier (the near-homophony of the words), staging at the linguistic level the structural ambivalence in the soliloquy—as well as in the play and its psychoanalytic criticism—between mourning for the father and disgust with the mother. Although both Freud and Lacan have been associated with readings of *Hamlet* that emphasize the father, in Chapter 1 we excavated the maternal remainders in Freud's coupling of *Hamlet* and *Oedipus Rex*. In this chapter, we unfold the implications of this reading through Lacan's emphasis on *Hamlet's* alienation in the desire of the mother. Whereas in Chapter 2 we traced the deformations of patrilineal transmission in tragic theory as it detours through Benjamin, in this chapter we briefly locate the figure of the mother in Benjamin's account of allegory. Just as psychoanalytic modes of reading inform our tracking of the sexual narratives embedded in Benjamin's rhetoric, Benjamin's text underwrites our approach to psychoanalysis through literature; what mandates the juxtaposition of Benjamin, Freud, and Lacan is their common ground in the history and theory of tragedy as it is configured around *Hamlet,* the primary play of tragic secondarity.[2]

The Mother of All Allegories

Benjamin's *Ursprung des deutschen Trauerspiels* falls into two main segments, the first of which focuses on *Trauerspiel,* the second on allegory.[3] In Benjamin's project, allegory is not only

2. See Juliet Flower MacCannell's suggestive overlay of Benjamin, Freud, and Lacan via allegory: "Lacan characterised his own enterprise as 'commenting' on the texts of Freud, a layering of another text over his. The two form an allegorical relationship in Walter Benjamin's sense of the term" (*Figuring Lacan* xiv).

3. To date, the second half has been more influential, above all through the work of de Man and Derrida. Furthermore, de Man and Derrida, in conjunction with their emphasis on Benjamin's retrieval of allegory, have also championed Abraham and Torok's version of the psychoanalysis of mourning. To restore Benjamin's analysis of *Trauerspiel* to the current discussion of allegory recalls us to the continued imperative of Lacanian and Freudian analysis in their Shakespearean interdependence. For the legacy of Benjamin's theory of allegory, see especially Paul de Man, "The Rhetoric of Temporality," and

a dominant linguistic tendency of *Trauerspiel* as a distinct literary form, but also describes the tropological relation between *Trauerspiel* and tragedy—a relation, that is, of mournful interpretation in which the *Trauerspiel* plays ceaselessly recall their classical paradigms in figures of their difference from them. Near the end of the book, Benjamin, taking up Baroque allegories of evil, derives allegory from mourning through the figurative vehicle of the feminine: mourning, he writes, "is at once the mother of the allegories and their content [*die Mutter der Allegorien und ihr Gehalt*]" (E 230, G 205). Although Benjamin rarely thematizes gender directly, his rhetoric, as Rainer Nägele has recently demonstrated in *Theater, Theory, Speculation*, repeatedly stages scenes of "intersection" between language and sexuality. Here, Benjamin's choice of metaphor manifests through the very act of figuration the role of the "Mother" in the mutual constitution of allegory and mourning. Mourning is the "mother" of allegory in two senses: it derives the structural disjunction of the allegorical sign from originary loss, and it describes the affective condition, the "dominant mood" (*Gemütszustand*), that colors and discolors allegory. Furthermore, in using the mother to figure this double role of mourning, Benjamin's line imagines origin only to hollow it out, since "mother" functions precisely not as the tenor or object of allegorical mourning, but as its vehicle. The origin of allegory can only be presented in an allegory of origin *as allegory*, a paradox embodied and gendered in Benjamin's use of the mother as figure of originary loss.

Most directly, Benjamin's metaphor indicates that mourning is not simply a preferred content of Baroque emblematics, but also describes the structural condition of allegory as the impossible restitution and repetition of the losses attendant upon signification. "Meaning," Benjamin writes earlier in the book, is "the reason for mournfulness" (*Ursprung* 209). Allegoresis is

Derrida, *Memoires*. For other texts that privilege allegory in their reading of the *Trauerspiel* book, see the essays in *Benjamin's Ground*, edited by Rainer Nägele. Nägele's *Theatre, Theory, Spectacle* and Samuel Weber's "Genealogy of Modernity," however, focus on *Trauerspiel*.

a function of the difference between a signifier and its occluded meaning; death, its favorite topic, most clearly marks this difference by revealing the arbitrary, temporary, and constructed quality of the signifying world ("Alas, poor Yorick...").[4] At the same time, allegory also involves the anagogic postulation of a semantic unity immanent in the "amorphous fragments" and "dry rebuses" of disjunctive signification (176). We could say that allegory in its symbolic or disjunctive drift on the one hand and its imaginary or restorative tendency on the other is "in" mourning: constituted in the field of mourning, and in mourning for significance lost.

Like Freud's melancholic women who find pleasure in self-absorbed ostentation, the *Trauerspiel* displays and enjoys its grief: "For these are not so much plays which cause mourning, as plays through which mournfulness finds satisfaction: plays for the mournful. A certain ostentation is characteristic of these people. Their images are displayed in order to be seen" (*Ursprung* 119). If for Benjamin, Baroque mourning describes both the repetition and reparation of loss, it does so not through the symbolic economy of Oedipal tragedy, but as a narcissistic show of feminine lament that exceeds the decorum of catharsis. In Benjamin's figure, mourning is, pointedly, the *mother* of allegory rather than its father, an allegory that stages not a *Trauerarbeit* of tragic dialectics but a *Trauerspiel* of postclassical theatricality whose emblematic gestures of grief, in Benjamin's chiastic phrase, press "convention of expression" into "expression of convention" (175).

Benjamin's reference to the mother, moreover, not only casts her as a metaphor or figure, but implicitly presents the maternal as the ground, origin, or *Ursprung* of figuration as such; as the "mother" of allegory, mourning is not only the structural condition but the affective precondition of rhetoric, its *mater* as well as its *matrix*. Benjamin narrates the Baroque repetition of the mythic fall into language in terms that evoke the symbolization of the infantile somatic processes:

4. See Benjamin, *Ursprung* 166, and Weber's commentary on it, "Genealogy of Modernity" 495.

For the baroque sound is and remains something purely sen-
suous; meaning has its home in written language [*die Bedeutung
ist der Schrift zu Hause*]. And the spoken word is only afflicted
[*heimgesucht*] with meaning, so to speak, as if by an inescapable
disease; it breaks off in the middle of the process of resounding,
and the damming up of the feeling, which was ready to pour
forth, provokes mourning. Here meaning is encountered, and
will continue to be encountered as the reason [*Grund*] for
mournfulness.

(E 209, G 185)

In Benjamin's allegorical narrative, an "anatomy of melancholy" arises through the intrusion of writing onto embodied
voice, an interruption that signifies by cutting short the emotional relief afforded by the proto-symbolic pouring forth of
feeling in sound.[5] In default of the cathartic "cure," which
resolves Aristotelian tragedy, the meaning that "infects" the
allegories of the *Trauerspiel* generates an "inescapable disease"
of pathological, transferential mourning. Benjamin's mythical
account of the cultural birth of language depends on a meta-
phorics of individual psychogenesis subliminally evoked in the
language of an uncanny domesticity. Meaning, writes Benjamin, is "at home," *zu Hause,* in writing; far from establishing
domestic harmony, however, written meaning is the unex-
pected guest who stays on to "afflict" or "haunt" [*heimsuchen*]
speech at its origin. The word *heimsuchen*, literally, to seek or
visit at home, brings with it all the linguistic and sexual ambiguities of *Unheimlichkeit* (the uncanny), which afflict the imagined
unity of the pre-Oedipal home with the shadow of duplicity.
In narrating the Oedipalization of the subject in mourning—
the affective immediacy of maternal speech giving way to the
law of paternal writing—mourning, "the mother of the alle-

5. This distinction is consonant with that made by Julia Kristeva between
the "seemingly very rudimentary representation (pre-sign and pre-language)"
of "mood" in its "semiotic," "deictic" character, and the "symbolic," truly signifying function of language. See "On the Melancholic Imaginary" and *Soleil
Noir.* For Kristeva's further distinction between the "semiotic" and "symbolic"
see her *Revolution in Poetic Language.* On the consonances between Kristeva
and Benjamin, see Nägele, *Theater, Theory, Speculation* 121–25.

gories," has already unsettled the house of being at and as its feminine origination. Thus the narrative of a catastrophic first break is instantly resituated as a scene of repetition that transforms trauma from a single inaugural event into the structural condition of signification: "Meaning is encountered, and *will continue to be encountered* [*wird noch weiterhin begegnen*] as the reason for mournfulness" (emphasis added).

The archetypal "mother of allegories" in Shakespearean drama and its criticism is Gertrude. As Jacqueline Rose has argued, in *"Hamlet*—the 'Mona Lisa' of Literature," Hamlet's mother is the figure of the feminine whose representational inadequacy led T. S. Eliot to formulate the ideal of the objective correlative. Eliot writes:

> The only way of expressing emotion in the form of art is by finding an "objective correlative"; in other words, a set of objects, a situation, a chain of events which shall be the formula of that *particular* emotion; such that when the external facts, which must terminate in sensory experience, are given, the emotion is immediately evoked.... The artistic "inevitability" lies in this complete adequacy of the external to the emotion; and this is precisely what is deficient in *Hamlet*. Hamlet (the man) is dominated by an emotion which is inexpressible, because it is in *excess* of the facts as they appear.... Hamlet is up against the difficulty that his disgust is occasioned by his mother, but that his mother is not an adequate equivalent for it; his disgust envelops and exceeds her.... [I]t is just *because* her character is so negative and insignificant that she arouses in Hamlet the feeling which she is incapable of representing.
>
> (*Sacred Wood* 100–101)

Eliot begins with an Aristotelian semiotics of literary emotion, which judges the appropriateness of a character's affective response in terms of its correlation to his or her dramatic situation, in order to diagnose the problems of Hamlet and *Hamlet*. Hamlet's indecorous disgust with Gertrude "envelops and exceeds her," an image in which the supposedly internal state of the character grotesquely swells outwards, smothering the mother who ought to have been its "external" occasion. Eliot

ends, however, by making the very failure of a maternal objective correlative into the most appropriate condition for Hamlet's particular affect of disgust: "It is just *because* her character
is so negative and insignificant that she arouses in Hamlet the
feeling which she is incapable of representing." It is precisely
the difference between "arousing" a feeling and adequately
"representing" it—a negative quantity rather than a positive
quality—that explains Hamlet's excessive emotion, the emotion
of excess. Rose suggestively links Eliot's criticism of *Hamlet* to
the Oedipal narrative of Eliot's more famous essay, "Tradition
and the Individual Talent": "Eliot's conception of literary
tradition and form could therefore be described as a plea
for appropriate mourning and for the respecting of literary
rites" (130).[6] If Eliot casts the classical literary tradition as itself a classical tragedy of fathers and sons, *Hamlet* emerges as
its melancholic deviation, which, under the sign of maternal
guilt, transforms tragic continuity into the intermissions of
Trauerspiel.

Benjamin's formulation, "Meaning is the reason [*Grund*] for
mournfulness," similarly correlates representation and emotion, meaning and mournfulness. Like the trajectory of Eliot's
analysis of *Hamlet,* moreover, Benjamin's "ground" is fundamentally ungrounded, since the meaning at stake is not the
fullness of a determinant signified but the disjunction of the
sign as such that, "damming up" feeling, provokes mourning.
In this scenario, mourning in turn appears not as an emotion
that precedes language but as a linguistic response to the radical
blocking of pure affect by language. Finally, in both Benjamin
and Eliot, this correlation of two negatives (mourning and
meaning, Hamlet's disgust and the insignificance of Gertrude)
is implicated in the *Abgrund* or abyss of the maternal as the

6. Moreover, Eliot's discussion of "feelings" (which are aligned with representation) and "emotions" (which are aligned with content) in the second
half of "Tradition and the Individual Talent" elaborates Eliot's concern with
the dialectical "correlation" or "fusion" of representation and emotion. On
Eliot and Shakespeare see Gregory Jay, *T. S. Eliot and the Poetics of Literary
History* 114–34.

Grund, the ground, foundation, or reason, of mourning.[7] In Benjamin's text, mourning emerges as both an emotion and a signification, as a "mood" in the affective and the grammatical senses, or rather as the trace and elaboration of the disparity between affect and meaning in language, which for Benjamin is the condition of allegory. The maternal names the site of that disparity, understood not, however, as a person, theme, or signified, but—following Benjamin's rhetoric—as (an) allegory: as the representation of the affect that arises exactly in the loss of immediate or commensurate affect.[8]

The Pound of Flesh

Lacan's discussion of *Hamlet* appears in "Seminar VI," titled "Desire and its Interpretation," a discourse whose title transcribes Freud's *Die Traumdeutung* (*The Intepretation of Dreams*) into a Lacanian register. Lacan's *interprétation* translates Freud's *Deutung,* and the German *Traum,* posited by Freud as the fulfillment of a wish, reappears as the French *désir.*[9] Moreover, just as Freud's *Traumdeutung* couples *Oedipus* and *Hamlet* in an implicit theory of intertextual interpretation through repression and mourning (see Chapter 1 herein), Lacan too takes *Hamlet* as the specimen Shakespearean drama of desire and interpretation. It is here that Lacan reformulates the cliché of

7. On the play of *Grund* and *Abgrund* in Benjamin, see Nägele, "Benjamin's Ground" and *Theatre, Theory, Speculation,* especially chap. 5.

8. On affect, tragedy, and psychoanalysis, see Jahan Ramazani, "Freud and Tragic Affect: The Pleasures of Dramatic Pain."

9. Lacan's remarks on *Hamlet* occur in "Seminar VI"; the sessions on *Hamlet* are printed in the journal *Ornicar?,* a selection of which has been translated into English and published in Felman, ed., *Literature and Psychoanalysis,* as "Desire and the Interpretation of Desire in *Hamlet.*" Ellie Ragland-Sullivan notes the place of "Seminar VI" in the "logical time" of Lacan's thinking: "His remarks offer both a new reading of an old drama and an 'old' reading of Lacan in relation to his own later work" ("*Hamlet,* Logical Time and the Structure of Obsession" 29). For commentary on Lacan's reading of *Hamlet* we have found essays by Bruce Fink, Ellie Ragland-Sullivan, and John Mueller to be especially helpful.

romance, the "object of desire," as the "object *in* desire," not as separate from but constituted by desire. This paradigm, moreover, describes the place of literature "in" psychoanalysis: the status of Shakespeare as a discourse that both informs the rhetorical habits of psychoanalytic thought and is retroactively rewritten by it. Finally, if literature stands in the place of "the object in" the interpretive desire of psychoanalysis, the feminine gendering of that object inflects the critical allegories of desire and its interpretation—an object understood, however, not as the passive, "objectified" recipient of male desire but as the bearer of an alienating enjoyment.

Lacan defines the "object in desire" in the course of explaining the formula for fantasy, $\math$ $◊$ a:

> I express the general structure of the fantasy by $\math$ $◊$ a, where $\math$ is a certain relationship of the subject to the signifier—it is the subject as irreducibly affected by the signifier—and where $◊$ indicates the subject's relationship to an essentially imaginary juncture [*conjoncture*], designated by a, not the object of desire but the object in desire [*l'objet dans le désir*]. . . . This is our starting point: through his relationship to the signifier, the subject is deprived of something of himself, of his very life, which has assumed the value of that which binds him to the signifier. The phallus is our term for the signifier of his alienation in signification. When the subject is deprived of this signifier, a particular object becomes for him an object of desire. This is the meaning of $\math$ $◊$ a.
>
> The object of desire is essentially different from the object of any need [*besoin*]. Something becomes an object in desire when it takes the place of what by its very nature remains concealed from the subject: that self-sacrifice, that pound of flesh which is mortgaged [*engagé*] in his relationship to the signifier.
>
> ("Desire" 28; *Ornicar?* 26–27: 22–23)

The formula of fantasy designates the relation of a subject split and alienated by language to an object that promises to compensate for that fundamental lack. At this point in Lacan's thought, the *a* functions as the imaginary substitute for the real substratum of living being ("something of himself, of his very life") forever blocked by the symbolic accession to language. Here Lacan associates the barring of the subject with the phallus, the castrating mark of linguistic substitution, which guarantees that the object exists only *in* desire, that is, as the opaque "juncture" of real loss and imaginary reparation in the field of symbolic relations mapped by language; later in Lacan's work, as we shall see in Part Two, the affiliation of the *objet a* with the real is increasingly emphasized over its primarily imaginary function in "Seminar VI."

The Shakespearean "pound of flesh," on loan here from *The Merchant of Venice,* emblematizes the bodily *physis* cut off by symbolic castration and imaginarily stitched by the endless string of objects in desire. Lacan alludes to *The Merchant of Venice* when he evokes the phallus through intimations of castration and circumcision, but recall that the flesh demanded by Shylock comes from the breast:

> *Portia:* Therefore lay bare your bosom.
> *Shylock:*   Ay, his breast,
> So says the bond, doth it not, noble judge?
> "Nearest his heart;" those are the very words.
>
> (IV.i.252–55)

Across the text of Shakespeare, Lacan's notion of the phallus is here articulated as the permanent mortgaging of the flesh by language. The "pound of flesh," associated with the corporeality and *jouissance* of the maternal bosom, is canceled and phallicized by its very weighing into pounds, measure for measure: "The subject is deprived of something of himself, of his very life, which has *assumed the value* [*pris valeur*] of that which binds him to the signifier." The subject's corporeal life disappears into its primitive valuation as the phallus, the value of value that underwrites the symbolic economy of linguistic substitution. Through the agency of the phallus, the signifier of the subject's "bond" to and by language, the annulled flesh is remembered as the imaginary object of exchange whose purchase promises to restore the Nature lost in its commodification. The *objet a* is neither referent (the "flesh" of the living being) nor symbol (the "pound" of phallic calculation) but the mask and index of the referent's cancellation by the symbol—in the Hegelian vocabulary of the early Lacan, the *objet a* is the imaginary consolation left over from the murder of the Thing by the Word.[10]

The *objet a*, Lacan says in "Seminar VI," is "at once image and pathos," both imaginary spectacle and remnant of suffering being in the theater of fantasy ("Desire" 15). Lacan's genealogy of the object in desire parallels Benjamin's account of the emergence of allegory from mourning: desire and mourning designate neither the immediacy of an affect nor its cutting off by meaning, but the allegorical mood and mode produced by that scission. In "The Structure of Allegorical Desire," Joel Fineman has argued that allegory is the trope that combines metaphoric condensation and metonymic displacement, the two axes of language theorized by Jakobson, Lacan, and others.[11] The metonymic links of the signifying chain are instituted by a primal metaphor: "the metaphor of the Name-of-the-Father, that is, the metaphor that substitutes this Name in the place first symbolized by the operation of the absence of the mother" (*Écrits* E 200). The father's name—language, the agency of the phallus—replaces not (as one might expect), the body or presence of the mother, but rather, in Lacan's careful formulation, "the absence of the mother," the place of an initial symbolization that marks the loss of corporeal *jouissance* through the entry into language. The "image and pathos" of this doubled metaphor, extended and remembered by metonymic desire, resurfaces in the immobilizing object of fantasy: "The enigmas that desire seems to pose . . . amount to no other derangement of instinct than that of being caught in the rails— eternally stretching forth towards the *desire for something else*— of metonymy. Hence its 'perverse' fixation at the very suspension point of the signifying chain where the screen-memory

---

10. See Lacan, *Language of the Self* 84 and *Seminar I* 173–8, and commentary by Miller ("La Psychose dans le texte de Lacan" 139) and Zizek (*The Sublime Object of Ideology* 131).

11. For a rigorous account of metaphor in Lacan and Jakobson, see Russell Grigg, "Metaphor and Metonymy."

[*souvenir-écran*] is immobilized and the fascinating image of the fetish is petrified [*se statufie*]" (*Écrits* E 167, F 518; translation altered).[12] The object is "in" desire in two senses: both as an interchangeable element produced in the metonymic train of associations that constitutes desire as "the desire for something else," and as the opaque blockage, the fantasmatic girl tied to the tracks, which derails that train with fixed and fixating metaphors of the maternal body in the melodrama of fantasy. As the return of metaphor within metonymy, the object operates both as the lure projected by desire to keep it moving and as the hypnotic "image of the fetish," which stalls and stills the cinematic movement of symbolization in the perverse freeze-frames of fantasy. The metaphoric and metonymic provenance of desire emphasized in Joel Fineman's Lacanian determination of allegory simultaneously evokes the Benjaminian problematic of mourning: "Every metaphor is a little metonymic because in order to have a metaphor there must be a structure, and where there is a structure there is already piety and nostalgia for the lost origin through which the structure is thought" ("The Structure of Allegorical Desire" 44). The object in desire, Lacan writes, is "petrified" or "statufied" [*se statufie*], a tombstone which fetishistically allegorizes "the absence of the mother," imagining her presence by symbolically commemorating her loss.

In "Seminar VI," Lacan derives "the absence of the mother" from the dialectic of need, demand, and desire: "It is insofar as the Mother, site of the demand for love, is initially symbolized in the double register of presence and absence, that she is in a position to initiate the dialectic; she turns what the subject is really deprived of—the breast, for example—into a symbol of her love" ("Hamlet, par Lacan," in *Ornicar?* 26–27:39). The Other of demand, embodied by the mother or primary caregiver, is the locus of the child's first expression of need whose verbalization fundamentally alienates the particularity of bodily

12. See Malcolm Bowie's careful reading of the train imagery in this passage (*Lacan* 132–33). On the construction of the object out of metaphor and metonymy, see Jean Laplanche, *Life and Death in Psychoanalysis*, especially 66–84.

requirements into the universal demand for love. The difference between need and demand, Lacan writes elsewhere, is
desire, "the power of pure loss [that] emerges from the residue
of an obliteration" (*Écrits* E 287). As the demand for absolute
love, demand always exceeds what is expressed; in this difference, the Other emerges as lacking, as unable or unwilling to
fulfill the desire left unexpressed in the demand.[13] Lacan calls
this lack the phallus, the signifier without signified, which marks
both what the Other cannot provide the child and what the
child cannot fulfill in the Other. In this narrative, the "real
privation" of the breast only becomes the initial site of symbolization through the intermediate moment of demand, which
dialecticizes bodily privation into symbolic lack through verbalization. Hence the breast for Lacan is only an example ("le
sein par exemple") rather than an essential origin or source of
symbolization, whereas the phallus, as the signifier of the lack
in the Other, is necessary and unconditional—not because of
its physiological nature or naturalness, but, on the contrary,
because of its arbitrary status by definition as the marker of
the intrinsically nonquantifiable quantity, the x of the mother's
desire.[14] Finally, the *objet a* of fantasy functions as both the
denial and the reminder of this lack in the Other; in Lacan's
algebra, the *Autre* of demand (A), is barred (Ⱥ) by the encounter
with its lack (Φ), a decompletion of the Other as the set of all
signifiers. This lack in the Other is fetishistically crystallized
and compensated through the *objet a* of fantasy ($\$ \lozenge a$); through
this object carved out of the Other, the fantasy both stages the
subject's separation from the Other and re-covers their break.[15]

13. For a clear account of demand in Lacan, see Elizabeth Grosz, *Jacques
Lacan* 61–66.
14. See J.-A. Miller, "To Interpret the Cause": "We do not know what she
wants. And we do not know what and where she enjoys. The meaning of the
phallus, in this sense is, precisely, to give an answer to this X so that . . . the
meaning of the paternal metaphor, of the Freudian Oedipus as inscribed by
Lacan, translates itself as from an unknown *jouissance* to the phallusization of
jouissance, that is, to a significantization of *jouissance*" (46).
15. We are relying here on Bruce Fink's "Lacan's Reading of *Hamlet*," which
emphasizes the relation between *alienation*, the subject's "subjection" to language as the Other, and *separation*, the subject's "subjectification" through de-

As Lacan says, "It is from the phallus that the object gets its function in the fantasy, and from the phallus that desire is constituted with the fantasy as its referent" ("Desire" 15). Whereas in fantasy the phallus is replaced by the *objet a*, the phallus as signifier of lack also maintains the desire which takes fantasy as its "referent" or stopgap: "That is why human desire is adapted not to an object, but rather to a fantasy" ("Seminar VI," 12 November 1958, 15). The formula for fantasy, that is, also describes fantasy as formulaic, as the fixed, conventional, even clichéd narrative—the "formula romance"—which at once stages and delimits the parameters of desire by "adapting" it to a fixed set of relations between the barred subject and its fantasmatic object.[16]

In neurosis, objects of desire partake of the insistent, nagging, fundamentally unspecified, characteristics of demand, becoming impossible objects in obsessional neurosis and unsatisfactory objects in hysteria. In "The Subversion of the Subject and the Dialectic of Desire," the essay that focuses and elaborates the issues of "Seminar VI," Lacan writes, "Indeed, the neurotic, whether hysteric, obsessional, or, more radically, phobic, is he who identifies the lack of the Other with his demand, Φ with D. As a result, the demand of the Other assumes the function of an object in his phantasy, that is to say, his phantasy ... is reduced to the drive ($ \$ \lozenge $ D)" (*Écrits* E 321). In neurosis, the Other of demand gets caught in the place of the object in fantasy, short-circuiting the dialectization of desire with the brute, nonsymbolized, insistence of the drive.[17] At the

---

completing or barring the Other, and carving out of it the *objet a*. See also Fink's "Alienation and Separation."

16. In "Seminar VI," Lacan explains that "fantasy accomplishes a certain accommodation or fixation of the subject onto something which has an elective value" (28 January 1959, 137). Zizek defines fantasy: "What the fantasy stages is not a scene in which our desire is fulfilled, fully satisfied, but on the contrary, a scene that realizes, stages, the desire as such ... it is precisely the role of fantasy to give the coordinates of the subject's desire, to specify its object, to locate the position the subject assumes in it" (*Looking Awry* 6).

17. See Zizek's definition of the drive: "A drive is precisely a demand that is not caught up in the dialectic of desire, that resists dialecticization" (*Looking Awry* 21).

moment of "Seminar VI," this nondialectical quality of the demand is associated primarily with its imaginary function, its configuration of the subject as ideal, specular, and only supposed, as "sujet de la connaissance" ("Seminar VI," 12 November 1958, 23), whereas later this feature will merge, through the affinity of demand to the drive, with the real. In "Seminar VI," the "image" of the *objet a* already glows with the "pathos" of the drive in later Lacan, giving desire its obsessional, repetitive, and regressive character, a situation allegorized for Lacan by the staging of desire and its interpretation in *Hamlet*.

The Object of a *Jouissance*

As Bruce Fink has argued, for Lacan, Hamlet's problem is Gertrude. Rather than identifying Hamlet with Claudius—in the Oedipal narrative established by Freud—Lacan emphasizes Hamlet's subjection to the desire of the mother:

> Our first step . . . was to express the extent to which the play is dominated by the Mother as Other [*Autre*], i.e., the primordial subject of the demand [*la demande*]. . . . This desire, of the mother, is essentially manifested in the fact that, confronted on one hand with an eminent, idealized, exalted object—his father—and on the other with the degraded, despicable object Claudius, the criminal and adulterous brother, Hamlet does not choose.
>
> His mother does not choose because of something present inside her, like an instinctive voracity. The sacrosanct genital object that we recently added to our technical vocabulary appears to her as an object to be enjoyed [*objet d'une jouissance*] in what is truly the direct satisfaction of a need, and nothing else.
>
> ("Desire" 12–13)

Lacan locates the essential vacillation of Hamlet's will in the field of Gertrude's ambiguous desire; in Lacan's reading, we might say, Hamlet is "too much in the mother."[18] Although Hamlet encounters something in Gertrude other than the two of them—the possibility of a third position opened up in the mother/child dyad by the dialectic of demand—this space does not operate as the symbolic lack of an imaginary phallus, but is overfull with the real phallus, the *objet d'une jouissance*, which, in the vocabulary of the Lacan of this moment, provides "the direct satisfaction of a need," rather than the deferral of a desire. Whereas here this object of enjoyment signals an impasse in the drama of castration, later in Lacan's thought it is precisely such a piece of the real that both occasions the barring of the Other and is left over from it. Here, Gertrude's desire has a (real) referent, which exceeds the propriety of symbolization, and an (imaginary) meaning, which puffs up signification with an inflated sense of significance, an answer whose double overfullness stops rather than stimulates the subject's question of desire, "What do you want?" [*Che vuoi?*] In consequence, according to Bruce Fink, Gertrude "converts Hamlet's discourse into demand pure and simple," leaving no place empty for desire (10). Through the dependence of Hamlet's desire on the desire—or rather the enjoyment—of the (m)Other, Hamlet's flesh feels "too too sullied," because his mother's flesh appears "too too solid," insufficiently barred through castration (I.ii.129).

"The phallus," says Lacan, "even the real phallus, is a *ghost* [*ombre*]" ("Desire" 50; *Ornicar?* 25:42). The "reality" of the phallus, that is, designates not its empirical manifestation in an actual penis (itself never more than a poor substitute for the phallus), but rather what Lacan calls a "phallophany," the nauseating emergence of the nonsymbolized phallus from behind

18. As Bruce Fink notes, "While most critics seem to have emphasized the stasis or knots in Hamlet's desire or will, Lacan here shifts ground, pointing to how Hamlet is captivated by his *mother's* desire, that in a certain sense her desire constitutes a space within which his movements are confined" ("Lacan's Reading of *Hamlet*" 3). Compare also Zizek's commentary on Lacan's *Hamlet*: "Hamlet is therefore hindered not by indecision as to his own desire . . . what hinders him is doubt concerning the *desire of the other*, the confrontation of a certain '*Che vuoi?*' which announces the abyss of some terrifying, filthy enjoyment" (*The Sublime Object of Ideology* 120–21).

the veils of signification in the field of the (m)Other's demand
("Desire" 48–49). The phallus, Lacan explains, "is this thing
that is presented by Freud as the key to the *Untergang* of the
Oedipus complex. I say *thing* [*chose*] and not *object*, because it
is a real thing [*chose réelle*], one that has not yet been made a
symbol, but that has the potential of becoming one" ("Desire"
46; *Ornicar?* 26–27:37). This phallic thing is both too real, because it is the object of *jouissance*, and not real enough, because
it fills out and denies the lack in signification. In Lacan's *Hamlet*,
Claudius, the shameless and incestuous usurper, parades the
real phallus enjoyed by Gertrude, an adulterous and adulter-
ating union grotesquely literalized in the enigmatic interchange
between nephew and uncle:

> *Hamlet:* Farewell, dear mother.
> *Claudius:* Thy loving father, Hamlet.
> *Hamlet:* My mother. Father and mother is man and wife, man
> and wife is one flesh; so my
> mother.
>
> (IV.iii.52–55)

In Hamlet's mock syllogism, the "flesh" of Claudius and Gertrude is joined in an antisacrament that corresponds to and
replaces the dialectical union of the Pauline couple, joined in
charity through the mediation of the Divine Third, with the
mutated and contaminated fleshiness of the maternal body ob-
scenely enjoying the real phallus. In *Hamlet,* Lacan says, "the
Oedipal situation . . . appears in the particularly striking form
in the real" ("Desire" 51). Although in the Freudian staging of
desire and its interpretation *Hamlet* offers a repressed, temporally remote version of *Oedipus Rex*, in Lacan's analysis, Oedipus is not so much distanced by repression as too close for
comfort. Claudius real-izes the father of the primal horde in
the boudoir culture of modern Denmark, a mythic Viking too-
too solidly materializing in the study of Shakespeare's sullied
and sullen Kierkegaard-*manqué*.

In Lacan's staging of the play, Ophelia is cast as the "object in
desire" whose death provides Hamlet with some access to castra-

tion, and hence to the articulation of desire, through mourning. In acts 2 and 3, Ophelia, whom Hamlet rejects by equating her with the overbearing corporeality of his mother, comes to embody for Hamlet the flagrant grossness of the real phallus as the *objet d'une jouissance.* Tendentiously glossing her as "*O phallos,*" Lacan comments that Ophelia is "exteriorized and rejected by the subject as a symbol signifying life . . . the bearer of that vital swelling that he curses and wishes dried up forever" ("Desire" 23). In her death, Lacan argues, Ophelia is "reintegrated" as an object in desire: the graveyard scene "is directed towards that furious battle at the bottom of the tomb. . . . Here we see something like a reintegration of the object *a,* won back here at the price of mourning and death" ("Desire" 24).

The object in desire is a dead object, a situation that defines the (masculine) structure of the obsessional neurotic, who can only desire something when it is radically unattainable: "Only insofar as the object of Hamlet's desire has become an impossible object can it become once more the object of his desire. . . . [The obsessional neurotic] sets everything up so that the object of his desire becomes the signifier of this impossibility" ("Desire" 36). This condition of masculine desire, reworked in the poetics of the beautiful dead woman from Petrarch to David Lynch, has the further consequence of not only petrifying the feminine object, but also of deadening the male subject who identifies with loss. In *Seminar XI,* Lacan argues that the first object emerging from the dialectic of demand is the subject's own death: "The first object he proposes for this parental desire whose object is unknown is his own loss—*Can he lose me?* The phantasy of one's death, of one's disappearance, is the first object that the subject has to bring into play in this dialectic" (214). The dialectic of demand and desire also stages the subject's own death in fantasy; whereas the object in desire is constituted in mourning, the subject initially emerges as lost to the Other. This obsessive construction in loss of both subject and object, of subject *as* object, rewrites "To be or not to be" from the stoic's philosophical question about future action into the neurotic's rhetorical question about his present state: am I, as a speaking subject, dead or alive?—since the "I" as living being

is eclipsed precisely in speaking itself.[19] Moreover, we can re-
gloss the obsessive's question as, "Am I (wanted) dead or alive?"
since it is not simply in speaking, but in speaking *to the Other*
as the vehicle of an alienating desire that the subject, in Lacan's
expression, "fades," that is, arises as lost.

The death of Ophelia stages Lacan's question, "What is the
connection between mourning and the constitution of the object in desire?" ("Desire" 36). In order for the object to be "won
back" as an object "in" desire, it must be killed and mourned,
a process Lacan describes as the mobilization of the imaginary
and symbolic orders in relation to a "hole in the real":

> Where is the gap, the hole that results from this loss and that
> calls forth mourning on the part of the subject? It is in the real,
> by means of which the subject enters into a relationship that is
> the inverse of what I have set forth in earlier seminars under
> the name of *Verwerfung*.
>
> Just as what is rejected from the symbolic register reappears
> in the real, in the same way the hole of loss in the real [*le trou
> de la perte dans le réel*] sets the signifier in motion. This hole
> provides the place for the projection of the missing signifier,
> which is essential to the structure of the Other. This is the sig-
> nifier whose absence leaves the Other incapable of responding
> to your question, the signifier that can be purchased only with
> your own flesh and your own blood, the signifier that is essentially
> the veiled phallus.
>
> It is there that this signifier finds its place. Yet at the same
> time it cannot find it, for it can be articulated only at the level
> of the Other. It is at this point that, as in psychosis—this is
> where mourning and psychosis are related—that swarms of im-
> ages, from which the phenomena of mourning arise, assume
> the place of the phallus.
>
> ("Desire" 37–38, translation altered; *Ornicar?* 26–27:30)

19. See *Seminar II*, in which Lacan reads "To be or not to be" as an expression of the connection between the death drive and the insistence of the signifying chain: "This *To be or not to be* is an entirely verbal story. A very funny
comedian tried showing how Shakespeare came upon it, scratching his head—
to be or not . . . and he would start again—*to be or not . . . to be*. If that's funny, it's
because this moment is when the entire dimension of language comes into
focus. The dream and the joke emerge on the same level" (233).

The "hole of loss in the real," evacuated by the occasion of bereavement, Lacan says, reappears in the symbolic order, the field of the Other, which is itself decompleted or barred by that loss; normative mourning arises in turn as the installation of symbolic and imaginary formations that both mark and mask loss, and in the process (re)configure the object of mourning as an object "in" desire.[20] In the symbolic place cleared by real loss, the subject projects "the missing signifier," that is, the phallus that signifies the lack in the Other, S(A). This signifier emerges in the margin of desire left over by demand; in its articulation, verbal or otherwise, demand "purchases" a place in language for the subject at the price of "your own flesh and your own blood," effectively veiling the phallus through and *as* metaphor and metonymy.

In the absence of the phallic signifier, however—and this is the situation in Lacan's *Hamlet*—"the Other [is] incapable of responding to your question," that is, unable to return the subject's demand inverted as the question of desire. In *Hamlet*, the signifier of the lack in the Other does *not* find its place, for the (m)Other does not manifest a symbolic lack: "Yet at the same time it cannot find it, for it can be articulated only at the level of the Other." The subject's access to the object as lost occurs only through a third party: since Gertrude, as Lacan says in "Seminar X," demonstrates an "absence of mourning" (3 July 1963, 397), Hamlet's mourning—and hence his desire—is also dysfunctional. "Swarms of images" bordering on hallucination (the Ghost that his mother cannot see) take the place of symbolic substitutes ("your father lost a father; / That father lost, lost his" [I.ii.89–90]). The death of Ophelia, as well as the murder of Polonius, are, according to Lacan, ritual sacrifices in expiation of the unmourned loss of the father, attempts to institute a lack that can be adequately mourned ("Desire" 39).

20. The very notion of a "hole in the real" is problematic in Lacan's own terms: the real by definition is full, absolutely without lack. In *Seminar VII*, however, Lacan again uses the expression, there equating the "hole in the center of the real" with *das Ding*, the primordial lost Thing; the hole in the real, then, should be understood as the real *as* hole, as the inconsistency in or residue of the symbolic order (146).

The object is constituted in desire through mourning, as a replay and substitute for a loss that always exceeds, precedes, and shadows the object "in question"—in the subject's question to the Other. Lacan links the dialectic of demand and desire to the mournful passage of the Oedipus complex:

> At the moment of the final outcome of his Oedipal demands [*exigences*], the subject, seeing himself castrated in any case, deprived of the thing, prefers, as it were, to abandon a part of himself, which will henceforth forever be forbidden to him.... [T]he subject must explore his relationship to the field of the Other, i.e., the field organized in the symbolic register, in which his demand for love [*exigence d'amour*] has begun to express itself. It is when he emerges from this exploration, having carried it to the end, that the loss of the phallus occurs for him and is felt as such, a radical loss. How does he respond to the necessity [*exigence*] of this mourning? Precisely with the composition [*texture*] of his imaginary register and with nothing else—a phenomenon whose similarity to a psychotic mechanism I have already indicated.
>
> ("Desire" 48; *Ornicar?* 26–27:38)

In acceding to symbolic castration, the subject brings into play the imaginary register as a partial compensation whose delusory, fetishistic dimensions, as Lacan suggestively comments, approach the hallucinatory. In its symbolic assumption and imaginary denial of castration, the dissolution of the Oedipus complex enacts the allegoresis of *Trauerspiel*, itself the passing of Oedipal tragedy. In Benjamin's formulation of allegorical time, "Ultimately in the death-signs of the Baroque the direction of allegorical reflection is reversed; on the second part of its wide arc it returns, to redeem" (*Ursprung* E 232, G 208). Whereas the "death-signs" of Baroque allegory insist on symbolic castration as the (m)ark of the covenant, the rainbow "arc of its return" promises the rehabilitation of significance, but only in the demonic half-light of fantasy. Recall that in Benjamin's rhetorical genealogy, mourning is cast as the "mother of the allegories": allegory springs from an originary loss, which is retroactively both discovered and recovered in the parade of signification. Across the bar that divides the allegorical sign, at once reflecting pool and alienating breach, the real trauma of infantile loss separates into the imaginary *Traum* of the object and the symbolic drama of castration.

If Gertrude holds the place of the *Autre* of demand in Lacan's reading, the lack in the symbolic Other (the something rotten in the state of Denmark), initially filled and filled up by Claudius as the real phallus, is ultimately marked by the death of Ophelia and her reconstitution in mourning as Hamlet's impossible *objet a*.[21] As Bruce Fink has argued in his "Lacan's Reading of *Hamlet*," however, this work of mourning and castration is only partially successful, continually prone to collapse into its foundations in the alienation of demand. Pursuing Lacan's comments in "The Subversion of the Subject" on the infiltration of desire by demand in neurosis, we would emphasize that, although Ophelia appears as the means of Hamlet's separation from his mother through the acquistion of a new object—the "classical" Freudian narrative of Oedipalization—Ophelia is nonetheless continually linked in the play to Gertrude, and to Gertrude not as object of incestuous desire but as maternal Other of demand.

Thus Hamlet's early conflation of Ophelia and Gertrude in the fantasmatic projection of their voracious sexualities is born out in Ophelia's erotic songs, which use the theater of madness to stage the crossing of the Other of demand and the object of desire in the fundamental fantasy of Hamlet and *Hamlet*. In her mad scene, Ophelia insistently demands an audience not with Claudius but with Gertrude: "She is importunate, / Indeed distract," says the Gentleman to the Queen; "Where is the beauteous Majesty of Denmark?" cries Ophelia (IV.v.2–3, 21). Although the two women are separated out for Hamlet in the idealizing aftereffects of Ophelia's death, it is nonetheless Gertrude who narrates Ophelia's drowning, once again merging the two figures in the fluidly specular language of melancholy

---

21. Lacan notes that "the 'something rotten' with which poor Hamlet is confronted is most closely connected with the position of the subject with regard to the phallus" ("Desire" 49).

("There is a willow grows askant the brook / That shows his
hoary leaves in the glassy stream..." [IV.vii.165–6]). At Ophelia's grave, Gertrude's elegiac substitution, "Sweets for the
sweet," weaves the shattered signifiers of Ophelia's scattered
flowers into the formal garlands of elegiac metaphor; and even
as the lines promote the symbolizing work of mourning, their
doubling, quasi-tautological equation also continues to manifest
the intransigent link between Ophelia and Gertrude, object and
Other, in the scene of Hamlet's desire. Finally, the two women
are linked in death; Ophelia's garments, "heavy with their
drink," pull her to her death (IV.vii.180); Gertrude dies by
drinking from the poisoned goblet, as her last words obsessively
reiterate: "No, no, the drink, the drink! O my dear Hamlet! /
The drink, the drink! I am poison'd" (V.ii.315–16). Each dies
"heavy with drink": echoing Hamlet's first soliloquy, we could
say that Gertrude and Ophelia "melt, thaw, and resolve... into
a dew," condensing liquid and solid by virtue of their watery
weightiness.[22]

Motherhood Made Me a Nicer Person

The logic of Lacan's reading is registered in the relation
between the two great Hollywood-style *Hamlet*s, Olivier's (1948)
and Zeffirelli's (1990). On first glance Zeffirelli's version looks
like a weak repetition of Olivier's classically Freudian reading,
with the overdrawn self-consciousness of Britain's knight of
culture replaced by the fast draw of the American action movie
(Mel Gibson) and the easy sleaze of the erotic thriller (Glenn
Close). This "weak repetition," however, through the very ten-
dentiousness of its casting, parallels the shift from a Freudian
to a Lacanian problematic. Olivier's Hamlet tenderly returns

22. Alice Crawford pointed out to us the "drink link" between Ophelia and
Gertrude.

the affections of his mother in a forties-Freudian reading that emphasizes Gertrude as the object of Hamlet's incestuous desire. Zeffirelli's production, on the other hand, places the mother as the Other of demand: at once overanxious and oversexed, Gertrude's hungry kisses and caresses are resisted with barely concealed disgust by her son; ending the first soliloquy prematurely with "Frailty, thy name is woman!" Gibson's Hamlet appears viscerally repulsed by his mother's sexuality. As Lacan writes of Hamlet, "It's not his desire for his mother [*pour sa mère*], but rather his mother's desire [*de sa mère*] that's in question," a distinction that measures out the difference between the "classical" Freudian reading and its postclassical repetition (*Ornicar?* 25:20).

The early sequences of the two films establish their particular inflections of the Oedipal scenario. In Olivier's version, the opening scene on the ramparts is followed by the camera's continuous movement down into the castle, apparently in search of the "something rotten in the state of Denmark" (I.iv.90), which, in Olivier's rearrangement of the text, are the last words spoken by the guards. Slowly probing Elsinore's dark interior, the camera quickens and the music swells when the royal bedchamber distantly comes into view. Zooming in on the marriage bed's triply recessed space (down a hall, within a room, beneath a canopy), the eye of the camera is penetrating and analytic, a tool of discovery in search of psychological depths and their visual symbols, its movement dramatizing the voyeuristic gaze of the infantile sexual researcher who investigates the incestuous sheets of the primal scene.

Zeffirelli's film replaces the continuous shots and patient renderings of Olivier's *Hamlet* with rapid scene changes, shortened speeches, and extended action directed towards the distracted globe and truant disposition of the postmodern audience. Zeffirelli deleted act 1, scene 1, completely and distributed act 2, scene 2, among a series of discrete settings; the first of these, the burial of King Hamlet in the crypt of Elsinore, is also the most confected. Dominated by the figure, face, and voice of the weeping Glenn Close, the scene ends with Gertrude casting herself onto the covered coffin. Beseechingly meeting the gaze of Claudius at the other end of the casket, Gertrude's urgent reach across the tomb rewrites the question of the mother's desire as her demand for satisfaction. The marriage bed, which visually encodes the Oedipal story of Olivier's film, is here replaced by the ancestral tomb; the claustrophobic space of the *Kasten* in Zeffirelli's opening leaves no room for Oedipalization, effectively burying alive the son's desire in the alienating weight of a past that is insufficiently mourned. Zeffirelli's rapid montage of shots and reverse shots, exploited in his staging of overheard conversations, is not so much voyeuristic as the *representation* of voyeurism: whereas in Olivier's *Hamlet*, the camera's gaze implies the fantasmatic mastery of a continuous vision, in Zeffirelli's, voyeurism alienates, fragments, and dislocates.

Zeffirelli's characterization of Gertrude as demanding (m)Other depends upon the cinematic unconscious, the intertextual Other constituted by the relation between the received code of genres and narratives on the one hand and the reflected light of the movie star on the other—the cinematic dialectic, that is, between symbolic culture and imaginary cult. Casting Glenn Close as Gertrude necessarily evokes the history of her previous roles as they both project and are shaped by the publicly imagined persona of the actress. In Adrian Lyne's *Fatal Attraction* (1987), Alex Forest, the character played by Glenn Close, is transposed over the course of the film from object of desire—the one-night stand "discreetly" punctuating the life of the happily married New York attorney (Michael Douglas)— to a very demanding (m)Other, bearing a child, a grudge, and a sharp weapon. In the famous final sequence, a pedantic superimposition of *Psycho*'s shower scene and *Vertigo*'s "death" by drowning, a knife-wielding Glenn Close surprises the newly suburbanized wife in the bathroom. Alex's manic visage, appearing in the mirror where the wife's face should be, uncannily condenses wife and mother in the steamy condensation on the glass: it is not as erotic rival that she threatens the American family, but as terrifying maternal Other who afflicts (*heimsucht*) the Oedipal home, unsettling its foundations from within.[23] Apparently drowned at last by Michael Douglas in the bathtub, she returns screaming from her watery grave only to be killed "for real," this time by the wife. Between the two outbursts of violence (and between two deaths), she half-sinks, half-floats in the tub, suspended in the viscous middle ground of a wavering, translucent, liquefaction. Her white frock "heavy with drink," she is, for that moment, *Ophelia*, the dead object, at once "image and pathos," who both manifests and veils the dreadful lack in the Other.[24] *Fatal Attraction*—the obsessive's attraction to the fatal—describes the neurotic's conflation of demand and desire, in which the object of desire uncannily merges with the maternal figure of demand, insistent, unrelenting, and increasingly *driven*, an embodiment, that is, of pure drive.

With Glenn Close as Gertrude, Zeffirelli's *Hamlet* is fatally attracted to *Fatal Attraction;* the 1990 *Hamlet's* alienation in the demands of the cinematic unconscious indexes its structural and historical differences from the ideal ego represented by

23. See Danielle Bergeron, who writes of the film's conclusion that "This time the Thing is inside, in his own house" ("The Letter against the Phallus" 33), and Lucie Cantin: "The fragility of the system, alluded to throughout the film, is clearly demonstrated in the last scene, where, while looking at her injuries in the mirror, Beth sees the Thing reappear as if it were actually in her" ("The Letter and the 'Thing' in Femininity" 37). These essays appear in a special issue of *The American Journal of Semiotics* devoted to *Fatal Attraction;* Juliet Flower MacCannell, editor of the volume, summarizes the essays: "The anxiety woman can produce has long been regulated to such a degree that 'woman' as she-who-can-not-be-defined has been expelled from the universe of man, cast into what Lacan called 'the Real.' Hence she becomes a repressed 'Thing,' ready to return . . . " ("The Semiotics of *Fatal Attraction*" 6).
24. We owe the connection between *Vertigo's* mock death by drowning and Ophelia's to the conceptual art piece by Victor Burgin, "The Bridge," reproduced in *Between*. (*Vertigo*, incidentally, is based on a French novel, *D'entre les morts.*) Elaine Showalter has explored the iconography of Ophelia's madness. In the denouement of *Fatal Attraction*, Glenn Close, finally shot by the wife, sinks back into the bathtub, staining its waters and her dress with blood; the flowers of Ophelia have here ceded to the flowers of menstruation, echoed as well in her manic cutting of herself earlier in the scene. Christopher Bollas has spoken on the menstrual connections between "cutting" and the "cunt," elaborated in Mary Jane Lupton, *Menstruation and Psychoanalysis*.

Olivier's. As if to repeat and correct this reversion from object in desire to Other of demand traced within and between *Fatal Attraction* and *Hamlet*, a *Ladies' Home Journal* cover story from January 1991 on Glenn Close displayed the reassuring title, "Motherhood made me a nicer person." As a reaction-formation recording and revising the cinematic vicissitudes of the psychoanalytic *Hamlet* in popular culture, the phrase bears the message, "Motherhood made me a *person*," that is, reduced the mother from field of linguistic alterity and alienation (bearer of desire and enjoyment) to a fixed, humanized character (object of desire), effectively reestablishing the more normative Freudian reading of *Hamlet*. Insofar as it is *motherhood* that makes Glenn Close a "nicer person," the headline shifts the object of maternal satisfaction from the dangerous liaison of real incestuous transgression to the symbolic sublimation of the child-as-phallus, the preferred outcome of the Freudian narrative.

These critical, cinematic, and popular transformations of *Hamlet* indicate that Shakespeare's play exists "in" its theoretical and cultural rereadings rather than outside of or prior to them, as their discrete object. In this scenario of desire and its interpretations, critics neither simply read *Hamlet* objectively, diagnosing its problems, nor project their fantasies onto the play in a purely subjectivist model of criticism, but rather take up *positions in fantasy* laid out by the play. In *Hamlet,* the formula for fantasy ($ \$ \lozenge a $) involves an object (Ophelia) whose imaginary outlines are composed and decomposed by their residual origins in the Other of an undialectized demand (Gertrude) whose incestuous enjoyment distorts the symbolic articulation of desire. It is crucial to emphasize the fact of fantasy here, that is, the production of "Gertrude" in and by the play and its criticism: as we will argue in the next chapter, the image of Gertrude's "compulsive ardour" (III.iv.86) is precisely an *image*, a representation of the mother fostered by the language of Hamlet and the Ghost, but not by any lines spoken by "Gertrude herself." The figuration of Gertrude as vulgar drive is founded not in any lack in the character but in a fundamental *lack of characterization:* it is not that Gertrude is not "nice," but that she is not a "person."

Or, to recite Eliot's diagnosis, the problem with *Hamlet* is that Gertrude's character is "negative and insignificant"—a representational as much as a moral criticism. Eliot's "Tradition and the Individual Talent" describes literary influence as an Oedipal subordination of the present to the past, which, rather than simply repeating the past, transforms it; in this drama of patrilineal inheritance, the aesthetic object forms the "objective correlative" adequate to the tragedy played out between the two terms of the essay's title. Although the new poet must, in Eliot's phrase, make a "self-sacrifice"—the pound of flesh of individual being—the result of this "extinction of personality" is not only the fading of the subject but also the decompletion of the "existing order" of tradition (53, 50). The literary object both commemorates and covers this overlapping lack; as a work of cultural mourning, Eliot's literary object is thus itself the objective correlative, which divides, correlates, and reintegrates tradition (the Other) and the individual talent (the subject) in a dialectical symbol of the cultural dialectic.

In Eliot's "Hamlet and His Problems," the perceived inadequacy of the mother's representation signals a certain stalling in the classical dialectic of tradition. Read metacritically, *Hamlet*'s lack of an objective correlative shifts the intersection of tradition and the individual talent from the site of tragic reconciliation through the dialectical symbol, to the scene of their continued allegorical disjunction in the *Trauerspiel* of modern drama and criticism. This problematic is registered in Lacan's emphasis on the mother's role within the classical Oedipal reading, an inflection that affects not only the staging of Oedipus within the play, but also its enactment in and as tradition. Although the three positions of Eliot's classical narrative—tradition, literary object, and individual talent—continue to be operative in the critical scene of *Hamlet* and its interpretations, their scope and interaction suffer a sea change. The basis of the symbolic order of tradition has shifted from the law of the father to the demand of the (m)Other, a reorientation that deflects the symbolic scenario of the classical Oedipus by bringing into focus the enjoyment of the mother—neither as positivity (empirical satisfaction) nor negativity (symbolic castration), but as the lack of an appropriate lack, which leaves inadequate space for the articulation of desire. This is the situation of tradition when it is perceived as complete to the point of excess, tending towards a Baroque *jouissance* in its own signification, whether manifested in bombast, rhetoricity, or punning. In consequence, the literary object produced at the intersection of meaning and being, tradition and the individual talent, does not reconcile their agon but rather insistently flaunts their continued alienation, as their allegory.

This is the relation, as we will see in the next chapter, between *Hamlet* and the Senecan tradition of drama that Shakespeare inherited, a Latinate legacy dominated by Euripidean mothers in the shadow of Sophoclean fathers. Lacan notes *Hamlet*'s metamorphic relation to *Oedipus* in the intertextual dynamics of psychoanalysis: "Freud himself indicated, in a somewhat *fin de siècle* way, that for some reason when we lived out the Oedipal drama, it was destined to be in a warped form, and there's surely an echo of that in *Hamlet*" ("Desire" 44). *Hamlet* neither repeats nor rejects *Oedipus* but "warps" it, re-marking the post-classical swerves from classical tragedy, which are nonetheless internal to it. As an object "in" tradition, *Hamlet* is at once the "image" and "pathos" of classical tragedy in decline. The display of its laments and soliloquies signal the incomplete success of cultural mourning, which, by metamorphically extending tragedy into *Trauerspiel,* ostends and distends it into allegorical criticism.

CHAPTER FOUR

Hamlet's "Ursceneca"

In the *Poetics,* Aristotle sets forth with taxonomic precision the possible relationships between knowledge and action: "The deed may be done by characters acting consciously and in full knowledge of the facts. . . . Or they may do it without realizing the horror of the deed until later, when they discover the truth; this is what Sophocles did with Oedipus. . . . A third alternative is for someone who is about to do a terrible deed in ignorance of the relationship to discover the truth before he does it" (14.1453b 27–36). Here, Aristotle characteristically privileges the plot of *Oedipus Rex,* since it links action with discovery, defined as "a change from ignorance to knowledge" (11.1452a 31). The philosopher goes on, however, to suggest still another possibility, albeit an unsatisfactory one: "The least acceptable of these alternatives is when someone in possession of the facts is on the point of acting but fails to do so, for this merely shocks us, and, since no suffering is involved, it is not tragic" (14.1453b–1454a). Knowledge without action, philosophical cognition without dramatic recognition: it is as if Aristotle had read *Hamlet* and were condemning its lapses from the standards set by *Oedipus Rex.*

Sensing the shape of another dramaturgy, the passage from Aristotle serves as a fitting epigram for reading *Hamlet* "after *Oedipus,*" presented now not in the context of psychoanalytic discourse, but in relation to Renaissance tragic genres and the problem of a postclassical drama. What psychoanalytic criticism (including criticism of psychoanalysis) has not sufficiently addressed in the magisterial pairing of *Hamlet* and *Oedipus* is the question, "Hamlet and *which* Oedipus?" What happens, that is, if we look at the *Oedipus* plays of Seneca, the "Roman Euripides," rather than at the exemplary Greek texts of Sophocles? Such a move would necessarily shift critical attention from character to genre, from the reification of Hamlet as a psyche to analysis of the play in terms of classical models and motifs. The focus on Seneca also changes our sense of the "classical" itself, by insisting on the "secondary" moment of Latin literature as the "primary" object and vehicle of Renaissance classicism. The reception of Seneca's plays provides a specific textual arena for the formulation of an Elizabethan theory and practice of postclassical tragedy, since the Senecan dramatic corpus worked as both the major classical model for Renaissance dramatists and a powerful example of a postclassical (Baroque) poetic.

Senecan tragedy represents a double legacy for Shakespeare, one that enacts the narrative of mourning reconstructed in the previous chapters: the drama of the demanding mother, projected by the play in such figures as Hecuba, Niobe, Fortuna, Dido, and Gertrude; and the drama of the ghostly father, his return from the dead produced by an act of melancholic introjection. Inserting Senecan tragedy into the "classical" Freudian coupling of *Oedipus* and *Hamlet* distends the compass of *Hamlet*'s family romance to include the problematics of pre- and post-Oedipal mourning, structures that come to describe not only *Hamlet*'s narrative and themes, but also its metatheatrical, intertextual, and generic dynamics. In the terms of Chapter 1, we argue that the Senecanism of *Hamlet* is produced through the *introjection* of a *projection*, a procedure not of dialectical self-reflection but of a fundamentally asymmetrical self-deflection. Shakespeare's play internalizes a version of Senecanism that it simultaneously projects as its exterior; in distinguishing itself from "the Senecan," Shakespeare's play melancholically identifies with that very difference. The difference *between* "Shakespeare" and "Seneca" becomes *Hamlet*'s own self-difference, as inscribed by the reflexive, permeable, reversible boundaries of the play's metatheatrical scenes.

After *Oedipus Rex*

The opening of Seneca's *Oedipus* formally announces its departure from Sophoclean tragedy. The character Oedipus begins the play with an image of the sun in mourning:

> Iam nocte Titan dubius expulsa redit
> et nube maestus squalida exoritur iubar,
> lumenque flamma triste luctifera gerens
> prospiciet avida peste solatas domos,
> stragemque quam nox fecit ostendit dies.
>
> (*Oedipus* 1–5)

> Now [already] night is driven away; the hesitant sky returns, and rises, sadly veiling his beams in murky cloud; with woeful flame he brings a light of gloom and will look forth upon our homes stricken with ravening plague, and day will reveal [display] the havoc which night has wrought.
>
> (Trans. Miller)

These lines belong to the prologue, the convention of narrative exposition inherited by Seneca from Euripides and taken as a sign of the postclassical fall, within the Greek canon, from the dramatic perfection of Sophocles. In the same speech, Seneca's Oedipus goes on to explain the prophesies he is trying to escape, and to express in advance his prescient sense of guilt: "Things unspeakable [*infanda*] I fear—that by my hand my father shall be slain" (14–15). His foreknowledge, his position as *pro-logos*, attenuates the interdependent dramatic machinery of tragic irony, recognition, and reversal, an attenuation characteristic not only of Senecan drama, but of Sophocles' own "post-Oedipal" play, *Oedipus at Colonus*. In this passage, the final

verb, "ostendere," to display, well describes this shift from performative revelation to expository narrative, and from dramatic
discovery to theatrical ostentation.

The opening word, "iam," translated in the Loeb edition as
"now" but meaning "already" and "soon" as well, emblematizes
the simultaneously anticipatory and belated status of Oedipus's
knowledge in the play. The character Oedipus can be prologue
to his own tragedy because the Greek play *Oedipus Rex* "already"
(*iam*) exists; the rest of Seneca's play unfolds that "iam" in its
retrospective and prospective valences. Sophocles' play, too,
operates through the "discovery" of a prior event that only
comes into its full meaning in the act of recognition; Seneca's
play does not reject or undo its model in an agonistic struggle,
but rather deflates the Sophoclean machinery of irony and recognition by appropriating and diluting the temporal structure
on which that machinery depends.[1] In Sophocles, the coming-
to-knowledge is fully acted out in and as the plot of *Oedipus
Rex*, whereas in Seneca's play there can be no real progress
because on the one hand, the hero already knows, and on the
other, knowledge is always located elsewhere, in the literary
underworld inhabited by the ghost of Laius and the Latin libraries of Greek literature. Dramatic irony is weakened by our
sense that Oedipus himself as well as the audience is in on the
joke—a derailing of dramatic irony by its *extension* rather than
its *refusal*.

The opening figure of the black sun manifests this technique
of deflationary appropriation by borrowing the Sophoclean distinctions between darkness and light, blindness and insight, in
order to collapse them. The line establishes a homophonic fi-
liation between light—*lux, lumen*—and grief—*luctifica* (causing
grief), *luctus* (grief), *luo* (to atone). The series will later be spa-
tialized by the shady *lucus* or grove, the site of Creon's Descent
to the Underworld in search of Laius's ghost—the play's most
striking and characteristically "Senecan" deviation from the

---

1. On the structure of *Nachträglichkeit* in *Oedipus Rex*, see Cynthia Chase,
"Oedipal Textuality," in *Decomposing Figures* 175–95.

Sophoclean model, as well as its clearest link to *Hamlet*.[2] Like the *iam* and the prologue convention, the melancholy merging of grief and light in the image of the clouded sun effectively "clouds" the temporal and logical division between ignorance and knowledge upon which irony and recognition depend in Sophocles' *Oedipus Rex*. Like Hamlet, Seneca's Oedipus is from the beginning "too much in the sun," already (*iam*) both shadowed and enlightened by the proleptic knowledge of guilt— shadowed *by* his enlightenment, and thus structurally unable to progress from shadow into light.

The plots of Senecan drama, generally Latin imitations of Euripides' revisionary tragedies, typically stage the particular narrative of mourning we reconstructed in Chapter 1, a narrative founded on the elision of projected maternal absence in the act of internalizing her loss in and as the name of the father. In the final act of Seneca's *Phaedra*, two crucial paradigms of Senecan drama cross: the tragedy of maternal lust, violence, and lament (*Medea*, *Trojan Women*) and that of the guilty, punishing, or mournful father ascending from Hell (*Hercules Furens*, *Oedipus*, *Thyestes*). The scene is dominated by Theseus's mournful re-membering of Hippolytus's scattered body, while the last lines of the play resolutely refuse any funeral rites for his wife:

> Patefacite acerbam caede funesta domum;
> Mopsopia claris tota lamentis sonet.
> vos apparate regii flammam rogi;
> at vos per agros corporis partes vagas
> inquirite.
> Istam terra defossam premat,
> gravisque tellus impio capiti incubet!
>
> (*Phaedra* 1274–80)

---

2. Kellie Delaney has pointed out that the syllable *luc-* also echoes in Seneca's name, Lucius Annaeus Seneca, in that of his famous nephew, the poet Lucan (Marcus Annaeus Lucanus), and, looking forward to *Hamlet*, in "Lucianus, nephew to the King," the murderer-avenger in the play within a play.

Open wide my palace, gloomy and foul with slaughter, and let
all Athens with loud laments resound. Do you make ready the
flames of the royal pyre; do you seek through the fields for his
body's parts still missing?
As for her, let her be buried deep in earth, and heavy may
the soil lie on her unholy head!

(Trans. F. J. Miller)

In these lines, Theseus speaks as a "post-Oedipal" hero:
mournful father rather than murderous son, he salvages the
irreparable fragments of the castrated Hippolytus.[3] At the
same time, the play violently expels the sexualized, monstrous
body of Phaedra. In this, it enacts both the pre-Oedipal "abjection" of the mother, which maps the specular difference
between self and other around the experience of loss, and
the post-Oedipal reinscription and effacement of maternal
mourning produced by the introjection of that lack as the
father's no. Formally, the scene extends beyond tragic recognition in a redemptive or recuperative turn—the turn of
Oedipal *Untergang*—a move that in its delusive exclusions
nonetheless works to enforce rather than mitigate the drama's
bleak vision.

Jonathan Crewe has provocatively described Senecan drama
as "post-Oedipal," or even stronger, "anti-Oedipal": "Senecanism is thus excessive with reference to psychoanalysis as well
as deconstruction and is so in refusing to concede any normative or culturally formative authority to the Oedipal sce-
nerio" ("Violence" 115). We would argue, however, that rather
than exceeding the categories of psychoanalysis, Seneca (via
Hamlet) determines those categories *as internally aberrant* exactly
in exceeding them as regulative or normative codes. Here, Benjamin's staging of generic transformation along melancholic
rather than agonistic lines is crucial to our alignment of psychoanalysis with the vicissitudes of dramatic form: through its

3. "Tandemque raptum truncus ambusta sude / medium per inguen stip-
ite erecto tenet" ["A tree, its trunk charred into a stake, stays him with its stock
driven right through the groin and holds him fast"] (1099–1100).

plots and figures of Oedipal dissolution, Senecan tragedy presents itself as *the mourning for classical tragedy,* a mourning whose narcissistic identification is both elegiac and sadistic, commemorative and imperialistic. Seneca's dramas bear many of the formal features that Walter Benjamin attributes to Baroque *Trauerspiel:* the theatrical excess of indecorous onstage violence, the rhetorical excess of interminable offstage narration, and a hypertrophied language of lament and invective.[4] Benjamin presents the drama of the German Baroque, in its heavily rhetorical, stylized, and allegorical deviations from classical aesthetics, as the forgotten analogue and source of a certain current in Romantic and Modern literature—a current that, we would add, also informs key moments of psychoanalytic discourse. Moreover, as the excavation of a specifically German term (*Trauerspiel*) vernacularizing a classical one (*Tragödie*), Benjamin's project suggests translation as a model of the relation between tragedy and *Trauerspiel:* a relation based not on agonistic opposition and overturning but on the slippages of cultural misappropriation through weak misreadings and critical allegoresis.

Benjamin concludes his first section, "Trauerspiel und Tragödie," by associating *Trauerspiel* with a kind of historicism:

> A basic stock of dramaturgical realia, such as is embodied in the political anthropology and typology of the *Trauerspiel,* is what was required in order to escape from the problems of a historicism which deals with its subject as a necessary but inessential transitional manifestation. In the context of these realia one can perceive the special significance of baroque Aristotelianism, which is likely to prove confusing to more superficial consideration. In the guise of this "alien theory" an interpretation won through, on the strength of which the new, in a gesture of submission, secured for itself the most convincing authority, that of antiquity. The baroque was able to see the power of the present in this medium. It therefore regarded its own forms as

---

4. For the first, see Medea's murder of her children; for the second, Theseus's narration of the underworld in *Hercules Furens;* and for the last, see above all the Hecuba of *Trojan Women.*

"natural," not so much the antithesis, as the conquest and ele-
vation of its rival. Ancient tragedy is the fettered slave on the
triumphal car of the baroque.

(*Ursprung* E 100, G 80)

Here, Benjamin characteristically defines the "special significance of baroque Aristotelianism" in terms of its "insignificance," that is, the Baroque use (or abuse) of the *Poetics* to
effect its deviation from them. Benjamin frames this deviation
not in terms of "antithesis" [*Gegensatz*] but of submission or
subjection [*Unterwerfung*] to the authority of the antique. In
psychoanalytic terms, we witness here not the moment of
Oedipal agon, in which son confronts father, but of post-
Oedipal submission to a paternal authority which is subdued
as it is elevated—what Freud calls the *Untergang* of the Oedipus complex.

This submission depends on an act of conquest: the section
ends with the disturbing image of "ancient tragedy [as] the
fettered slave on the triumphal car of the baroque." Benjamin
alludes to a markedly Roman theatrical form, the triumphal
procession, in which the spoils of imperial conquest were displayed in a parade of power. The Roman triumph, tending
toward allegory in both its linear temporal form and its emblematic techniques, acted out the process of translation as a
mode of legitimation—the *translatio imperii* of Roman imperi-
alism. The theatricality of conquest informs the Senecan tradition—see, for example, the display of bodies at the end of
Hamlet and *Lear* or the mournful choral aftermath of conquest
in Seneca's *Trojan Women,* or the Hecuba speech of *Hamlet.*
Moreover, here the conventions of triumph inform the intertextual drama itself: Benjamin describes the Baroque in terms
not only of a *relation to* latinity, but as the *repetition of* Roman
modes of translation, modes in which the elegiac and the imperial are strikingly complicit. Roman *translatio* describes the
mournful appropriation, through allegorical display, of a past
Greek culture, a culture that becomes in the moment of translation an "original language."[5]

5. The mournful retelling of the fall of Troy in book 2 of the *Aeneid* is a

The latinity of *Trauerspiel,* by no means emphasized by Benjamin, indirectly surfaces in this passage through the figure of the triumphal car—surfaces through and, we might say, *as* figure, a rhetorical feature which specifies what Benjamin means here by "historicism." Benjamin's diagnosis of "the problems of a historicism which deals with its subject as a necessary but inessential transitional manifestation" applies not only to the conditional stance of the Baroque towards its own productions, its "history plays," but also to Benjamin's position vis-à-vis the Baroque, whose role is to get him to the matter of his later writing, Romanticism and Modernism. Throughout the book, Benjamin reads the Baroque in terms of Romanticism; when he quotes Shakespeare, he cites the Schlegel-Tieck translation. Benjamin's writing, however, maintains the transitional status of its object: rather than moving forward or backward to the apparently stable symbolic signifieds of Tragedy on the one hand and Romanticism on the other, Benjamin holds in suspension the function of the Baroque as signifier or trope for the periods it translates and anticipates. Only through this act of suspension can Benjamin's book become, in his phrase, itself a "necessary but inessential transitional manifestation": the mirror of rhetoricity which Benjamin holds up to Romanticism. We would call this neither "old historicism" nor "new historicism" but a *historicism in the perfect tense,* which tracks the temporality of signification in its generic, rhetorical, and ideological specificity without reifying "specificity" as an end or content in itself.[6]

T. S. Eliot wrote of the Senecan Shakespeare:

> I propose a Shakespeare under the influence of the Stoicism of Seneca. But I do not believe that Shakespeare was under the

---

paradigmatic example of the Roman complicity between elegy and conquest—or, in psychoanalytic terms, what Melanie Klein sees as the necessary relation between "mourning" and "triumph" (the two phases of manic depression). The mournful narrativization of the fall of Troy is colonized by Seneca's *Troades,* and in turn informs the Player's Speech in *Hamlet.*

6. See Rainer Nägele, "Belatedness: History after Freud and Lacan," in *Reading after Freud.*

influence of Seneca. I propose it largely because I believe that after the Montaigne Shakespeare . . . and the Machiavelli Shakespeare, a stoical or Senecan Shakespeare is almost sure to be produced. I wish merely to disinfect the Senecan Shakespeare before he appears. My ambitions would be realized if I could prevent him, in so doing, from appearing at all.

("Shakespeare and the Stoicism of Seneca," 128–29)

In the apotropaic spirit of Eliot's remarks, we shall not consider Seneca as either a legitimate origin for Shakespeare or a new and better object for literary interpretation. Instead, perversely crossing Eliot and Benjamin, we propose Shakespeare's Seneca not as the positivity of an influence, but as the negativity of an influenza, a Seneca whose critical position "afflicts [*heimgesucht*]" Shakespeare "as if by an inescapable disease" (*Ursprung* E 209, G 185). Put otherwise, we hope to demarcate "the Senecan" as a "transitional manifestation" whose significance is, in Benjamin's phrase, its *insignificance,* its mournful displacement of the classical: both the effects of Senecan secondarity in the literatures that follow and the retroactive appearance of those effects within the classical itself. Crucial for understanding the Senecan tradition, Renaissance literature, and their orientation in Benjamin's project is *the primary status of a secondary literature.* Seneca's plays have been consistently maligned since the hegemony of Greek literature over Latin consolidated in the seventeenth and eighteenth centuries; only now, with the increasing interest in "bad," "belated," and marginal literature, as well as with the not unrelated effort to revive the study of Latin literature, is Seneca beginning to experience something of a renaissance.[7] This return to Seneca describes the dominant trajectory of Elizabethan drama, whose tragic writers knew much Latin but little Greek; for Renaissance tragedians, Seneca

7. As evidence of this revival, see C. J. Herington's defense of Seneca, "Senecan Tragedy"; Frederick Ahl's polemical introduction to his recent translation, *Three Tragedies;* Gorden Braden's study, *Renaissance Tragedy and the Senecan Tradition;* Charles Segal's Lacanian reading of *Phaedra, Language and Desire;* and Jonathan Crewe, "The Violence of Drama." For an earlier psychoanalytic study of *Hamlet* and Seneca, see Wolfgang Rudat, "Ernest Jones' *Hamlet* Interpretation and Nevile's Translation of Seneca's *Oedipus.*"

functioned paradoxically as both the paradigm of classical drama, and as an increasingly problematic exemplar of post-classical taste.[8]

Blood of Fathers, Mothers, Daughters, Sons

Hamlet clearly defines itself in relation to Senecanism, whether that relation is conceived of as continuous, revisionary, or parodic. *Hamlet*'s Senecanism is variously "post-Oedipal": generically, in its melancholic difference from Aristotelian tragedy; thematically and formally, in its language of ostentatious grief and ceremonial, allegorical, and recitative diction; and psychoanalytically, in its dynamics and imagery of maternal and paternal mourning. Gorden Braden writes of Hamlet's occasionally Senecan diction: "It often seems to be somebody else's language" (*Renaissance Tragedy* 217). This alterity of Senecan language within *Hamlet* most clearly characterizes the play's metatheatrical set pieces (the Player's speech, the play within a play), both set off and inset. The Ghost is an almost embarrassing piece of Senecan machinery, which, in its ghostliness, is clearly marked as a creature foreign to the play and its atmosphere of witty skepticism. A similar foreignness infects such moments as Hamlet's speech, " 'Tis now the very witching time of night..." (III.ii.379ff), the "O what a rogue and peasant slave am I" soliloquy, his appearance to Ophelia as a Senecan ghost, "As if he had been loosed out of hell / To speak of horrors" (II.i.82–3), and the bout of competitive mourning in the grave of Ophelia. In such scenes, Hamlet borrows from the surrounding theatrical interchanges a language that does not suit him.

Braden's analysis of the character Hamlet can be extended to the play as a whole, which takes, and *takes in,* Seneca as its

---

8. G. K. Hunter has argued for Seneca's relative lack of influence by emphasizing the importance of Ovid and the gothic, nonclassical quality of Elizabethan classicism. Both these features, we would argue, rather than *opposing* the Senecan tradition, are in fact part of it. Segal (*Language and Desire* 3) and Crewe ("The Violence of Drama 27) both note Seneca's debt to Ovid.

other: as its specular, projected opposite, introjected as its own self-difference. The relation between *Hamlet* and Senecan drama is neither simply parodic, nor straightforwardly emulative, since *Hamlet* identifies with the Senecan precisely as a discourse different from its "own" practice. *Hamlet* emerges, that is, through a process of melancholic identification: it internalizes the Senecan as lost, faulty, and interminable, and consequently subjects itself to the same relentless criticisms.

The Player's speech, characterized by Braden as a "neo-Senecan set piece" (217), is one locus of this construction and absorption of Senecanism. Presented as Aeneas's tale to Dido, it is recitative rather than dramatic in form, and is couched in the rhetorical and representational excess associated with Seneca. Pyrrhus appears

> Roasted in wrath and fire,
> And thus o'ersized with coagulate gore,
> With eyes like carbuncles, the hellish Pyrrhus
> Old grandsire Priam seeks.

> (II.ii.457–60)

Pyrrhus is swelled up, "o'ersized," with the language of violence, the attributes of Hell, and the ponderous formalism of Latinate word order: he is the product and the emblem of a Roman rhetorical exorbitance.

The speech represents Pyrrhus transgressing every family relation: "horridly trick'd / With blood of fathers, mothers, daughters, sons" (II.ii.453–4). For Aristotle, plots of parricide epitomize and guarantee the economic structure of Greek tragedy: "When the sufferings involve those who are near and dear to one another, when for example brother kills brother, son father, mother son, or son mother, or if such a deed is contemplated, or something else of the kind is actually done, then we have a situation of the kind to be aimed at" (14.1453b 19–23). In *Oedipus*, incest and patricide are not simply two themes brought together, but inseparable structural principles: insofar as the son desires his mother, he must displace his father; to

possess the one is, structurally, to kill the other.[9] Tragedy is
thus for Aristotle the genre of the *genus*—both "kind" and
"family"—since its generic operations are perfectly reinforced
by its family plots. The Player's speech, however, both over-
articulates and hopelessly dilutes kinship relations (after all,
these are not *Pyrrhus*'s "fathers, mothers, daughters, sons") so
that they cannot organize the action described. The violation
of kinship, that is, becomes a rhetorical device rather than a
principle of plotting. Yet such a transformation of the classical
functions not as an agonistic revision but as a melancholic
(mis)translation, as in the Baroque German theorist Opitz's
paraphrase of the passage from Aristotle; according to Opitz,
the subject matter proper to tragedy includes "the commands
of kings, killings, despair, infanticide and patricide, conflagra-
tions, incest, war and commotion, lamentation, weeping, sigh-
ing, and suchlike" (cited by Benjamin in *Ursprung* 62). "More
than kin," the figure of Pyrrhus exceeds the limits of tragic
"kind" in its very attempt to remain within it.

An apostrophe to Fortune follows the death of Priam:

Out, out, thou strumpet Fortune! All you gods
In general synod take away her power,
Break all the spokes and fellies from her wheel,
And bowl the round nave down the hill of heaven
As low as to the fiends.

                                    (II.ii.489–93)

The Player's allegorical address aligns Senecan tragedy with
the medieval *de casibus* tradition, which narrates the endless
turns of Fortune's wheel. It is no accident that this figure is
feminine: she is the "*strumpet* Fortune," referred to in the same
scene in all her monstrous bodily specificity.[10] The passage is

---

9. Cf. André Green's Lacanian reading of Aristotle's *Poetics* as a proto-
structuralist theory of tragedy (*The Tragic Effect* 8–9). See also Jean-Pierre
Vernant, "Ambiguity and Reversal," for a structuralist reading of *Oedipus*.

10. See Frederick Kiefer, *Fortune and Elizabethan Tragedy*, on both the *de
casibus* tradition and Elizabethan translations of Seneca. He cites Nevile's translation of Seneca's *Oedipus:* " 'Let Oedipus example bee of this unto you all, /

doubly "projective": as *invocation*, it projects, in the cinemato-
graphic sense, the presence of an absent, mythic being; as *invective*, it expels, throws out, or pro-jects this scapegoated
emblem of historical catastrophe, an allegorical analogue to the
exclusion of Phaedra that ends Seneca's drama.

Seneca, following Euripides, recentered tragic drama
around female protagonists. The Player's speech moves from
the tragic villainy of Pyrrhus to the grief and rage of Hecuba.
The plays of female lamentation by Euripides and Seneca
(*Hecuba, Phoenician Women, Trojan Women*) were paragons of
tragedy in the sixteenth century, not because of their dramatic
action but rather their rhetorical tableaux of heroic feminine
suffering.[11] The Player's Speech presents the "mobled queen"
as a theatrical spectacle: "Who this had seen, with tongue in
venom steep'd, / 'Gainst Fortune's state would treason have
pronounc'd" (II.ii.506–7). The sight of Hecuba divested of
family and station, the Player indicates, should call forth in her
audience the same invective against Fortune that preceded her
representation in the Player's speech. Hecuba is a counterimage
to Fortune: both function as Senecan emblems of the tragic as
feminine, the one in her heroic rageful grief, and the other in
her allegorization of female violence and sexuality.

The Senecan shift to the tragedy of the feminine involves
not only a narratival recentering around women, but also a
more structural alliance of the tragic with the feminine, an
alliance allegorized by the (late classical) Fortuna and the emblematic figure of the mother in mourning. In the Player's
speech, *Hamlet* projects the Senecan as its feminine other, fig-

---

A Mirrour meete, a Paterne playne, of Princes carefull thrall' " (66). See Herington, "Senecan Tragedy" 455–56, on the allegorical aspects of Seneca. On
the femininity of Fortuna, see Hanna Pitkin's *Fortune Is a Woman*.

11. See Martin Mueller, *Children of Oedipus:* "The widowed Hecuba was a
living monument to the 'instability of human affairs' [Erasmus], and it was
through her suffering rather than through any action that for the sixteenth
century Hecuba became the tragic figure par excellence" (21). Crewe notes of
Phaedra, "The Senecan play can be said to repeat and intensify the well-
remarked feminocentric shift in Greek drama for which Euripides stands"
("The Violence of Drama" 107). See also Emrys Jones, *The Origins of Shakespeare*
93–94.

ured in these twinned images of sexual violence and enraged grief. The language of the Player's speech—archaic, elevated, rhetorical—is marked off from the framing play. Like the apostrophe of Fortune, this differentiation at once invokes a version of the Senecan and resolutely casts out and outdates that image as prior to and outside itself.

Ursceneca

If Hecuba and Fortuna are prominent emblems of Senecan theatricality in *Hamlet*, they compete rather strongly with the Ghost, inherited from Seneca's tragedies of paternity, *Oedipus* and *Thyestes*, via such plays as *The Spanish Tragedy*. So too, in metatheatrical and intertextual terms, *Hamlet* can only project the Senecan as its feminine other by identifying with the Senecan, and thereby taking it as its "inside," its internalized ideal; *Hamlet*'s metatheatrical scenes function as an embedded theatrical other simultaneously "interior" and "exterior" to the play as a whole. In the psychoanalytic model of mourning we formulated in Chapter 1, the play within a play is constructed through the *introjection* of a *projection:* the taking in of an imagined other, a discursive infolding that transforms the specular difference between self and mother, text and pretext, into the symbolic difference between subject, object, and law. In the terms of Chapters 2 and 3, Senecan discourse functions at once as the Lacanian (m)Other of demand—the tradition of feminine excess both interrogated by and demanding of *Hamlet*—and the ghostly paternal legacy of a tragedy already (*"iam"*) displaced and remembered by *Trauerspiel*. As a narrative of intertextual relations, this movement elaborates two Senecan legacies: the tragedies of violent or mourning women and those of vengeful, ghostly fathers. The first is generated primarily through acts of negative construction, at once invective and invocation, whereas the second functions in *Hamlet* as a discourse of return that speaks within conscience from beyond the grave. The second, moreover, both founds itself on and reinscribes the first, so that *Hamlet* (mis)represents itself, generically and thematically, as a tragedy more of the father than of the mother.

Senecan *Trauerspiel*, as a "post-Oedipal" genre of mourning, replaces Sophocles' *mythos* of a crime committed in ignorance and gradually discovered, with the *ethos* of a guilty self-knowledge that precedes and conditions dramatic action—the scenario anticipated by Aristotle's disparagement of knowledge without action as inherently untragic.[12] As Lacan writes, "The thing that distinguishes Hamlet from Oedipus is that Hamlet *knows*" ("Desire" 19). This knowledge locates *Hamlet* in the post-Oedipal: dramatically, in the mournful period after tragic recognition, as in *Oedipus at Colonus* or its Senecan analogue, *Phoenician Women;* and psychoanalytically, in the process of Oedipal *Untergang* or dissolution performed by the introjection of the father's name as lack, prohibition, and castration.

In the play within a play, there is no true discovery, since both Claudius and Hamlet already know the crime, and the others apparently infer nothing from the spectacle. If Oedipal tragedy involves the economic discovery of a primal crime or scene, post-Oedipal *Trauerspiel* mournfully repeats and interiorizes a scene it already knows in a theater of conscience, a "distracted globe."[13] The play within a play gives us both the dumb show and the dialogue, doubling Aristotelian discovery into a Baroque mirror game. Reflection, writes Benjamin, "repeats itself infinitely, and reduces to immeasurability the circle which it encloses. Both these aspects of reflection are equally essential: the playful miniaturization of reality and the introduction of a reflective infinity of thought into the finite space of

12. The long dialogue between Oedipus and Antigone that begins the fragmentary *Phoenician Women* elaborates Oedipus's profoundly guilty conscience. C. J. Herington notes the differences between Sophocles' and Seneca's *Oedipus* ("Senecan Tragedy" 455–56). Charles Segal compares Seneca's ghosts to the Ghost in *Hamlet* and notes their congruence with the psychoanalytic account of guilt (*Language and Desire* 26–27). Compare also the intensification of the theme of guilt in Racine's *Phèdre*.

13. On *Hamlet* as theater of distraction, see Timothy Reiss, "Hamlet on Distraction and Fortinbras on Knowledge," in *Tragedy and Truth* 162–82.

a profane fate [*eines profanen Schicksalsraums*]" (*Ursprung* E 83, G 64). Here, *Hamlet* suggests itself as the generative subtext of Benjamin's formulation: "O God, I could be bounded in a nutshell and count myself a king of infinite space—were it not that I have bad dreams" (II.ii.254–6). Although each passage begins as an apparent celebration of the infinite capacities of human reflection, each ends with the abrupt scission of a limit: the "profane fate" of a radically unredeemed, pagan nature in Benjamin, and the "bad dreams," which sicken the ideal of consciousness with the bar of repression, in *Hamlet*.[14]

This limitation of self-consciousness by the unconscious renders radically asymmetrical the vertiginous interplay of inside and outside, introjection and projection, that constitutes the play within a play as *Hamlet's* interior-exterior. The Ghost, the object of Hamlet's obsessive mourning and heightened feelings of guilt, is the (dis)embodiment of this structural interiorization. Braden's judgment that *Hamlet's* Senecanism "seems to be somebody else's language" can be rephrased in Lacanian terms: the unconscious is the discourse of the Other, with *discourse* understood as intertextual and cultural, and *Other* understood now not as the (m)Other of demand or the image of her body but as the name of the dead father enshrined in and as the law. Like *Phaedra's* Theseus, Old Hamlet returns from the dead to assert his marriage rights; this return is intertextual and generic as well as characterological, since the Ghost is so strikingly marked as Senecan. *Hamlet's* "undiscover'd country," as the uncharted maternal region (the "cunt-ry" of "country matters") from which the Senecan ghost returns, revises or effaces—*undiscovers*—Oedipal and Aristotelian discovery.

The Freudian account of guilt stresses the introjection of the father's imago, an act of inclusion that divides the subject, dissolves the Oedipus complex, and institutes what Lacan in

---

14. On the role of "fate" in Benjamin (and in Benjamin's reading of *Hamlet*) as a limitation on the modern (Christian) ideal of self-consciousness, see Nägele, *Theater, Theory, Speculation* 167–206.

"Seminar VI" calls "mourning for the phallus" ("Desire" 46). As we argue in Chapters 1 and 3, however, the installation of the Oedipal narrative rewrites maternal mourning under the governing sign of castration, which definitively orders guilt and mourning in terms of the paternal law and the symbolic order. This rewriting involves a kind of secondary "abjection" of the mother, in Kristeva's expression: recall the final scene of Seneca's *Phaedra,* in which the father's mourning for his dismembered son is complemented by the refusal of funeral rites for the mother. In *Hamlet,* the Senecan is cast out as a discourse of maternal excess ("Out, out, thou strumpet Fortune!"), a specular division between *Hamlet* and its theatrical other, which returns as a figure of paternal anger and filial guilt (the doubled roles of Pyrrhus, the Ghost). In such a dialectic, the primal crime discovered by Aristotelian tragedy can never be fully prior and generative,[15] since, in Nicolas Abraham's phrase, one of the crimes it describes is "le crime de l'introjection," the re-crossing of the preliminary boundary inscribed by projection through the taking in of that difference.[16] In the reflexive play of *Trauerspiel,* the crime cannot be "discovered" because it is both *already known,* and *inherently unknowable;* the fold enabling self-reflection delineates the impossibility of full self-reflection.

Or, to rework the Second Quarto's spelling of the Roman dramatist's name, "Sceneca," *Hamlet* operates not according to an Oedipal *Urszene,* but to a post-Oedipal *Ursceneca.*[17] It is the "sc-" of "science," "conscience," and "scene" that editors take to be a mark of Shakespeare's autograph (*Arden Hamlet* 41). The "Sceneca" here indicates the double status of what is originary in *Hamlet:* both scene and discourse and scene as discourse. The primal *sceneca* of *Hamlet,* we argue, is the plot of maternal projection and repudiation followed by paternal re-

15. Marjorie Garber points to "the paradox of the play as itself a *mise en abyme* without (exactly, precisely, without) the primal scene at which it is constantly hinting, and which we are constantly on the brink of remembering, falsely, fictively" (*Shakespeare's Ghost Writers* 158–59).
16. See Abraham and Torok's essay by that name in *L'écorce et le noyau.*
17. Michael Allen and Kenneth Muir, eds., *Shakespeare's Plays in Quarto:* "*Sceneca* cannot be too heavy, nor *Plautus* too light" (631).

turn, which both tells a story with recognizable characters and themes (an imaginary "scene"), and describes the intertextual drama of *Hamlet*'s engagement with the Latin dramatist (a symbolic "discourse"). The "Ur-" of *Ursceneca* is a compressed signature for the northern or Germanic, a spatial displacement of the "postclassical." This Germanic geography includes the vicissitudes of Baroque *Trauerspiel* and Elizabethan tragedy (with its *Urhamlet* and German cousin, *Der bestrafte Brudermord*) and psychoanalysis (as in part a Germanic reflection on classical culture in the tradition of Winklemann and Goethe).[18]

The primal crime of *Hamlet* is given its first and fullest articulation in the Ghost's retelling of his murder:

> 'Tis given out that, sleeping in my orchard,
> A serpent stung me—so the whole ear of Denmark
> Is by a forged process of my death
> Rankly abus'd—but know, thou noble youth,
> The serpent that did sting thy father's life
> Now wears his crown.
> *Ham:* O my prophetic soul! My uncle!
>
> (I.v.35–41)

The passage renders two accounts of King Hamlet's death, the first of which, although revealed as false by the second, nevertheless offers a fitting emblem for the crime. The initial account of the serpent in the garden is instantly recuperated as an allegory of King Hamlet's death. In the Ghost's next lines, the Eden allusion expands to include Eve: "Ay, that incestuous, that adulterate beast... won to his shameful lust / The will of my most seeming-virtuous queen." The allegory displaces the

18. The play between ancient and modern, southern and northern, is evident in the almost comic intermingling of classical names with Nordic ones: Claudius and Gertrude, Laertes and Hamlet. Jonathan Crewe, in a chapter on the "Germanic" in Surrey's poetry, writes suggestively of *Hamlet:* "The Germanic narrative of Saxo-Grammaticus, which for Shakespeare (or Hamlet) is openly a counter-classical, anti-Virgilian one, seemingly imports an unconquerable death wish/drive into the overlaid, competing, oedipal and homosocial scenarios of the play" (*Trials of Authorship* 108). On Freud and German classicism, see David Damrosch, "The Politics of Ethics: Freud and Rome."

primal crime of the play from the fratricide of Cain and Abel
to the legal transgression of the first parents, Adam and Eve.
Once more, it is as if Oedipal violence between men can only
occur in relation to a woman—not, however, the passive object
of male exchange at the heart of Oedipal and mimetic desire,
but a figure of woman whose demands unnaturally exceed the
domestic parameters of need. According to the Ghost, Gertrude is voraciously sexual even to the point of coprophagy,
desperately filling up the remainder between need and demand
with the rank leftovers of marriage: "So lust, though to a radiant angel link'd, / Will sate itself in a celestial bed / And prey
on garbage" (I.v.55–57). The Ghost's invective against Gertrude threatens to overwhelm the narration of the crime before
it can be recounted, mirroring in its own rhetorical procedures
the ravenous rage of feminine lust.

The Edenic subtext is further reinforced by the lapsarian
logic of the Ghost's prophetically Miltonic exclamation: "O
Hamlet, what a falling off was there, / From me . . ." (I.v.47–
48). The biblical allusion reinforces the moralized mythological
cosmos of the play; at the same time, the alignment of King
Hamlet with Adam complicates the innocence of the Ghost,
suggesting his weakness to rhetorical manipulation, the ethical
vulnerability of his drowsy ear. The positions of tenor and
vehicle are thus subject in the passage to a series of reversals:
what was first given as event, the serpent in the garden, trans-
mutes into a trope of the actual event, the poison in the ear,
which in turn becomes a figure of rhetoric: "so the whole ear
of Denmark / Is by a forged process of my death / Rankly
abus'd" (I.v.36–38). Moreover, the primal status of this *Ursceneca,* like that of the notorious *Urhamlet,* depends on our lack
of access to it. The scene's precise content, location, and veracity
shift among alternate biblical archetypes (Cain and Abel, Adam
and Eve), competing versions of Christianity (the ghosts of
Catholic purgatory versus the Lutheranism of Wittenberg),
and, within psychoanalysis, variants of the Oedipal scenario
(the patricide of Freud and Lacan, the matricide of Kristeva,
the fratricide of Girard).

The passage presents the *Ursceneca* of the play, a generative narrative that consolidates Oedipal crime across the figure of demanding Woman. Woman appears in these lines precisely as *figure:* Gertrude is allegorized under the biblical type of Eve and the demonic substantive "Lust" (capitalized in the First Quarto); decisively included in the biblical allegory, she is nonetheless excluded from the fratricidal scene that the passage strives to narrate, a scene in which only the two men appear as actors. Gertrude is constructed through intertextual allusion and invective without finding a fixed, discernible place in the drama's plot. This imagining of Gertrude is one of the central activities of the play, and of the play's criticism, which, as Jacqueline Rose has argued, "blames" Gertrude for the aesthetic failings of *Hamlet*—among other problems, its failure to live up to Aristotelian (and Oedipal) standards.[19] Hamlet's first and third soliloquies are crucial sites of this maternal imagining.

Niobe All Tears

Formally, *Hamlet* is perhaps most famous for its soliloquies, which are praised for their introspective content, private emotion, and highly subjective form. Yet the soliloquy, like its formal twin, the formal prologue, was associated in the Renaissance with Senecan rhetoric, as witnessed in Nashe's lambast of the so-called *Urhamlet:* "English Seneca read by candlelight yields many good sentences, as *Blood is a beggar* and so forth . . . [the author in question] will afford you whole Hamlets, I should say handfuls of tragical speeches" (cited in the *Arden Hamlet* 83). *Hamlet* is, in part, "a handful of tragical speeches," a phrase that indicates the citational, cut-and-paste character of Hamlet's voicing of and by the Senecan tradition. Like those of *Hamlet*, the soliloquies of Seneca are laced with mythological allusions, tags that simultaneously epitomize the once-maligned

19. Rose writes, "By focusing on the overlap of these two accusations, of the woman and of the play, we might be able to see how the question of aesthetic form and the question of sexuality are implicated in each other" ("Sexuality in the Reading of *Shakespeare,*" 95–96).

rhetoricity of Senecan language and open up—as Charles Segal
argues in *Language and Desire in Seneca's "Phaedra"*—a densely
psychological register operating at a discursive, cultural, and
literary rather than purely individual level. Hamlet's first soliloquy establishes key mythological parallels in a mode one
could term "Ovide senecasé," an allusive vocabulary that aligns
guilt with the two vectors of parental mourning through the
rhetorical use of myth.[20] Hamlet's first soliloquy integrates the
son's grief for his father with his own sense of contamination
and guilt, two affects mediated in the speech by his rage against
Gertrude; it thus exemplifies the play's *Ursceneca*, both the narrative of maternal demand and the specific techniques of mythopoeic projection.

The first soliloquy, recited before any exposure of the crime,
counterpoints mourning and guilt, a kinship even stronger in
the First Quarto, whose soliloquy begins, "O that this too much
griev'd and sallied flesh / Would melt to nothing" (Allen and Muir
Shakespeare's Plays in Quarto 583; emphasis added). The passage's mythological allusions show Hamlet identifying with the
guilty Claudius even as he emblematically distinguishes uncle
and father:

> O that this too too sullied flesh would melt,
> Thaw and resolve itself into a dew,
> Or that the Everlasting had not fix'd
> His canon 'gainst self-slaughter. O God! God!
> How weary, stale, flat, and unprofitable
> Seem to me all the uses of this world!
> Fie on't, ah fie, 'tis an unweeded garden
> That grows to seed; things rank and gross in nature
> Possess it merely. That it should come to this!
> But two months dead—nay, not so much, not two—
> So excellent a king, that was to this
> *Hyperion to a satyr,* so loving to my mother
> That he might not beteem the winds of heaven

---

20. For a nonsubjectivist account of the soliloquy, see David Bevington,
From Mankinde to Marlowe. On Senecan mythopoesis, see Segal, *Language and
Desire* 7 and passim.

Visit her face too roughly. Heaven and earth,
Must I remember? Why she would hang on him
As if increase of appetite had grown
By what it fed on; and yet within a month—
Let me not think on't—Frailty, thy name is woman—
A little month, or ere those shoes were old
With which she follow'd my poor father's body,
Like Niobe, all tears—why, she—
O God, a beast that wants discourse of reason
Would have mourn'd longer—married with my uncle,
My father's brother—*but no more like my father*
Than I to Hercules.

(I.ii.129–53; emphasis added)

Hamlet's chiastic analogies, "Hyperion to a satyr . . . but no more like my father / Than I to Hercules," locate him in the place of the satyr-king, diagnosing through allusion the sullied (and "griev'd") condition of his flesh.[21] We could say that Hamlet knows *that* he knows, but not *what* he knows, since the object of knowledge (the crime of Claudius) also provides the means of knowledge, through guilty identification.[22] It is for precisely this reason that Hamlet falls into the nontragic relation to knowledge sketched by Aristotle: he is "in possession of the facts" but "fails" to act upon his knowledge.

Intervening between these paternal figures, however, is a mythical mother in mourning, "Niobe all tears." This classical exemplum of excessive grief offers at once a counterexample to Gertrude's failings as a widow and an emblem of ostentatious tears, the theatricality of Hamlet's rejected "forms, moods, shapes of grief" (I.ii.82). The "character" of Gertrude, both like and unlike Niobe, is "charactered" or written through and as mythological allusion. Gertrude has very few lines in the

21. Hamlet's refusal of the role of Hercules, the titular character of two plays attributed to Seneca, manipulates mythological tags in Senecan style in order to distinguish himself from the bloody heroics of the earlier dramatist. Cf. Braden, *Renaissance Tragedy* 218.

22. In the line, "O my prophetic soul! My uncle!," the two "my's" connect knower and known through linguistic identification. We thank Lia Hotchkiss and Jacques Duvoisin for this formulation.

play; instead, the play imagines her through descriptions by others (the Ghost, Hamlet) and analogues in myth, literature, and allegory (Hecuba, Dido, Eve, Niobe, Lust).[23] The projective mechanism operative in the construction of Gertrude is epitomized in Hamlet's angry line, rhetorically at once apostrophe and *interruptio*, "Frailty, thy name is woman," in which Hamlet combines invocation and invective, summoning in order to denigrate.

As we suggest in Chapter 3, this task of imagining Gertrude becomes a problem and a vocation for the play's readers. T. S. Eliot, who claimed that the major issue of the play is "the effect of a mother's guilt upon her son" (98), formulated the criterion of the "objective correlative" in reaction to Gertrude's lack of substance in the drama, her imaginary status. Although Eliot can conceive of a play that would expand "the 'guilt of a mother' into a tragedy... intelligible, self-complete, in the sunlight" ("Hamlet and His Problems" 100), Eliot's essay also courts the possibility that this (Euripidean) theme is founded on the impasses of demand, of alienation in "in-significance," and is thus doomed to lapse from aesthetic norms and generic regulation. Shakespeare, Eliot writes, "attempted to represent the inexpressibly horrible," suggesting that the theme, far from being capable of existing "in the sunlight," is already and irrevocably too much in the sun—the clouded sun of Senecan melancholy (102).

Intertextually, the soliloquy's sequence of classical allusions indicates the play's relation to the classical itself: an identification not with the Apollonian or, better, *Horatian* ideals of moderation emblematized by Hyperion, but with the Senecan excess and generic adulteration of the "satyr-play." The play identifies with that comic monstrosity of mixed forms, the "tragical-comical-historical-pastoral," named in Polonius's speech on genres that alludes to "Sceneca":

23. In the closet scene, for example, we learn much more about the sexuality of Hamlet than the guilt of Gertrude; although he presents himself as the doctor of tragic recognition ("You go not till I set you up a glass / Where you may see the inmost part of you" [III.iv.18–19]), he is, figuratively, the one on the couch.

The best actors in the world, either for tragedy, comedy, history,
pastoral, pastoral-comical, historical-pastoral, tragical-historical,
tragical-comical-historical-pastoral, scene individable, or poem
unlimited. Sceneca cannot be too heavy, nor Plautus too light.
For the law of writ and the liberty, these are the only men.

(II.ii.392–98)

The staging of generic criticism here is clearly meant to be
ridiculous; throughout the play, Polonius represents the arch
misreader, and a *weak* misreader at that. The appearance of
questions of genre in general and of Seneca in particular in
the mouth of Polonius exemplifies *Hamlet*'s troubled relation
to (post)classical aesthetics; the play identifies with the classical
precisely in its mediocrity and excess, its "transitional historicism," an identification that, like Hamlet's with Claudius, institutes not a transgressive celebration of an alternate dramatic
tradition, but rather a posture of masochistic self-criticism.

Psychoanalytically, the first soliloquy performs two kinds of
work for the play: it draws the schematic opposition between
the good and the bad father, and it presents Gertrude as failed
widow, hasty in mourning because lustful in bed. The two tasks
are related insofar as the repudiation of the mother provides
the tools of demarcation that enable the subject's formative
splitting by the introjected lack of the father. In *Hamlet*, the
paternal imago itself is split, one half representing the son's
guilty desire, the other the purity and vengefulness of the father as law. The symbolic, we argue in Chapter 1, always retains
its imaginary lining; the opposition between King Hamlet and
Claudius is specular rather than symbolic, as evidenced in the
amount of energy spent maintaining the two brothers on opposite sides of the mythological cosmos.[24] Or, in the terms of
Chapter 3, the (m)Other of demand—"Niobe all tears"—has
been insufficiently dialecticized as Oedipal desire, rendering
unstable the moral opposition between Hyperion and the satyr,
a faultiness of Oedipal "resolution" systemic to the foundation
of paternal law on the effacement of maternal *jouissance*.

24. This point has been argued, for example, by Margaret Ferguson in
"*Hamlet:* Letters and Spirits."

The reference to Niobe signals the pre-Oedipal catastrophe informing *Hamlet*'s post-Oedipal drama of guilty identification—the residual insistence of maternal demand within the rule of desire. Crucial here is the first soliloquy's emphasis on the orality of desire, at once the source of archaic guilt, the precondition of articulated demand, and the mechanism of mournful introjection:

> Why, she would hang on him
> As if increase of appetite had grown
> By what it fed on...

In psychoanalytic terms, this "increase of appetite" can be read in relation to pre-Oedipal fantasies of violence performed by and against the infant (Klein), the introjection of the father as ego ideal, which "dissolves" the Oedipus complex (Freud), and the efflorescence of desire in the difference between demand and need (Lacan). The construction here of Gertrude as voracious mother functions in all three theoretical narratives, facilitates the passage between them, and points to the melancholic remainder of their movement.

The chiasmus, "Hyperion to a satyr . . . I to Hercules" crosses over the figure of the mourning mother, "Niobe all tears": the passage rhetorically stages Oedipal dissolution over the figure of maternal mourning.[25] A similar counterpointing of mythic analogues organizes Seneca's *Oedipus,* in which the traditional story of patricide and incest is continually undercut by allusions to the Euripidean tragedy of Pentheus dismembered by his mother in Bacchic rites. It is as if Senecan drama demands a myth of maternal violence (which, by imagining the rageful mother, inflicts its own rage against her) in order to offset, but also *to set off,* to set into motion, the dominant paternal scene.

25. The oral mechanics of this transition are rearticulated in Hamlet's cynical observation on the economy of mourning: "The funeral bak'd meats / Did coldy furnish forth the marriage tables" (I.ii.180–81). Marjorie Garber connects the oral imagery of the two passages: "For the language of *Erinnerung,* of interiorization, in this play is the language of digestion, of eating" (*Shakespeare's Ghost Writers* 150).

Finally, Niobe, becoming her tears, is a favored Renaissance figure of narcissistic identification with loss; she thus becomes an image of the melancholic petrification to which Hamlet and *Hamlet* are subject. Niobe's metamorphosis materializes the watery fate imagined in the soliloquy's opening line: "O that this too too sullied flesh would melt, / Thaw and resolve itself into a dew." Not only do the lines identify Hamlet and Gertrude in the reflecting pool of Ovidian metamorphosis, but they also melt, thaw, and resolve into the Ghost's words to Hamlet two scenes later: "Adieu, adieu, adieu. Remember me" (I.v.91). Spoken as the rising sun condenses the morning dew, the line "condenses" mourning and morning, "adieu" and "a dew."[26] The play of signifiers manifests Oedipal resolution as Oedipal *dissolution,* a dissolving of identifications and significations into the liquidated letters of maternal mourning.

Identification with and against the mourning mother is played out in Hamlet's third soliloquy. Hamlet begins by reflecting on the Player's identification with the figure of Hecuba and then goes on to imagine the dramatic effectiveness of his own situation:

> What would he do
> Had he the motive and the cue for passion
> That I have? He would drown the stage with tears,
> And cleave the general ear with horrid speech,
> Make mad the guilty and appall the free,
> Confound the ignorant, and amaze indeed
> The very faculties of eyes and ears.
>
> (II.ii.554–60)

Given Hamlet's role, the Player would out-Seneca Seneca, going beyond the tearful distraction of the mourning mother to the powerful bombast, the "horrid speech," of the vengeful son. Working himself up into just such a Senecan rage, Hamlet then

26. The Ghost's "Adieu" is spelled "Adue" in the Quartos and Folio. For the morning dew, see the Ghost's rapid departure in act 1, scene 1, and Horatio's infamously fatuous line heralding his departure: "The morn in russet mantle clad / Walks o'er the *dew* of yon high eastward hill" (I.i.171–72).

sees his rhetorical outburst as itself a cowardly, effeminate, and debased gesture:

> This is most brave,
> That I, the son of a dear father murder'd,
> Prompted to my revenge by heaven and hell,
> Must like a whore unpack my heart with words
> And fall a-cursing like a very drab,
> A scullion!
>
> (II.ii.578–83)

Hamlet can only become the rageful son by mimicking the mother in mourning, and he cannot escape the ostentation of her "fiction and dream of passion," a narcissism inseparable from his "dull and muddy-mettled" melancholy. As Braden writes of the passage, Hamlet's "reflective nature internalizes the aggression to which he is called; declamatory fury becomes relentless self-laceration" (*Renaissance Tragedy* 218). This is the masochistic identification of the melancholic, who, like Niobe, drowns the stage with tears, becoming the lost object.

The rhetorical question "What's Hecuba to him, or he to Hecuba, / That he should weep for her?" becomes the question the play asks itself about its relation to Seneca. As Rose suggests, the figure of the guilty mother not only inhabits the thematics of the play, but infects its form: "It is as if the woman becomes both scapegoat and cause of the dearth or breakdown of (Oedipal) resolution which the play enacts, not only at the level of its theme, but also in the disjunctions and difficulties of its aesthetic form" (*"Hamlet"* 103). Both the theme and form of the scandalous mother of demand in *Hamlet*, we have argued, are Senecan. The third soliloquy uses the topic and dynamics of theatrical identification to reflect on the drama as a whole and its problematic relation to the postclassical. Just as Hamlet passes through Hecuba in order to rise to his rage, so *Hamlet* achieves the "horrid speech" of the Senecan avenger through the flawed discourse of the guilty and mourning mother. Just as the Hamlet of the soliloquies is split by the opaque self-reflexivity of guilt, so *Hamlet* divides around Senecan drama, its interior-exterior that, in marking *Hamlet's* difference from the Senecan, marks the play's difference from itself.

This self-dividing identification of *Hamlet* with Senecan drama helps account for the tonal register of the metatheatrical scenes, which, although clearly not parodic (compare, for example, the play within a play in *A Midsummer Night's Dream*) are also sharply discontinuous with the framing drama. Hamlet's advice to the Players positions itself ambivalently in relation to Senecan conventions: the scene's Horatian precepts of moderation and decorum describe neither the rhetoricity of the Player's speech, nor Hamlet's own erratic, improvisational wit. Seneca's dramas were increasingly associated with recitative bombast, overstepping the modesty of nature, yet remained for the Renaissance the most authoritative body of classical tragedy.[27] This ambiguity is played out in the contrasting subject matter of *Hamlet's* two Senecan set pieces: the epic classicism of Pyrrhus and Hecuba, versus the Italianate modernizing of revenge in *The Murder of Gonzago*.[28] The fracture in the Senecan legacy between classical and nonclassical poetics infects *Hamlet's* alienated yet by no means satiric relationship to the demands of its own classical precepts and of the (non)classical exemplar of Seneca: a posture of ironic ambivalence rather than parodic self-confidence, of melancholic identification rather than agonistic self-mastery.

Seneca's dramas can never be maintained as a solid counterimage to *Hamlet*, since they too powerfully inform the diction, themes, and plotting of Shakespeare's plays. Instead, the Senecan tradition functions as an ironic double of *Hamlet*, the shadow of the object cast both *by* and *on* Shakespeare's play. The "Senecan" revenge plot is critiqued by the play as violent

---

27. Braden characterizes Hamlet as "one of the most influential critics of Senecan furor" (*Renaissance Tragedy* 217). The phrase "out-Heroding Herod" refers above all to the Mystery Plays, but it is no accident that the many Renaissance Herod-dramas (focusing on the tyrant's tragic jealousy over his wife Mariamne) appropriated Senecan dramaturgy to subject matter associated with the Bible. See Braden's *Renaissance Tragedy* 158–71, in which he briefly reads *Othello* in the context of the Senecanized Herod.

28. On Italian Senecanism, see ibid. 99–114.

and self-perpetuating, as theatrically and ethically mechanical, and yet remains a standard of honorable action that speaks from beyond the grave to condemn the play's too much blunted purpose. In this latter sphere, the Senecan model is not introjected by *Hamlet* in an act of self-present agency so much as it impinges upon the Shakespearean text as a generic structure of massive cultural authority and formative power. In *Hamlet*, the Senecan ethics of revenge are not rejected so much as turned inward. Hamlet's notorious inaction, inseparable from the play's nonclassical interminability and its suspenseless delays, stems from the reflexivity of filial guilt, which turns violence in upon the subject and the text in melancholy masochism rather than unfolding outward in the dramatic realization (or discovery) of patricidal motives. The drama's very identification with the ghostly Seneca, with the Senecan as the discourse of paternal return, subverts rather than promotes the execution of Senecan violence by building a metatheater of revenge at the center of the play.

Finally, the place of Woman as a figure of tragedy is both insured and masked by the double generic legacy of Seneca, who offered to the Renaissance both tragedies of mournful or violent women and stories of rageful, grieving fathers who return from the dead. This Senecan reading of *Hamlet* isolates not the role of Gertrude in Hamlet's psychological narrative, let alone the "character" of Gertrude "herself," but rather the specific rhetorical mechanisms of invective, apostrophe, and allusion that imagine the *figure* of Gertrude in the play and its criticism. Through this process of mythopoeic projection and dramatic elision, Senecan discourse acts as both a ghostly father and a mother in mourning, a field of inherited scenes and signifiers in which *Hamlet*'s generic and textual practices are constituted and alienated.

INTER-SECTION

Hamlet's first soliloquy presents a chiastic ratio of mythopoeic equations—"Hyperion to a satyr . . . I to Hercules"—that negatively identifies the son with the dead father by aligning him with the father's evil twin. As we argued in Chapter 4, moreover, Hamlet's doubled paternal identifications intersect across "Niobe all tears," a figure of the mourning mother that indicates the effaced or abjected condition of Oedipalization. In Sophocles' *Antigone*, the condemned heroine also alludes to Niobe, identifying with her as an icon of melancholy:

> Pitiful was the death that stranger died,
> our queen once, Tantalus' daughter. The rock
> it covered her over, like stubborn ivy it grew.
> Still, as she wastes, the rain
> and snow companion her.
> Pouring down from her mourning eyes comes the water that
> soaks the stone.
> My own putting to sleep a god has planned like hers.
>
> (824–831)

In the simile, the symbolic monumentalization of grief that makes Niobe a favorite emblem of funerary art has as its reverse side her immobilization into a thing of stone, the feature linked in the simile to Antigone's burial alive—not the performance

119

but the refusal of the work of mourning. Moreover, the epithet "Tantalus' daughter" both locates Niobe in a tragic genealogy of cannibals and names the mother as daughter; the epithet renders explicit the grounds of mourning in the oral rage of melancholia, whose motifs of scavenging, incorporation, and indigestion serve at once as the archaic precondition of all later interiorizations and as their secreted, literalized aftereffects. *Hamlet's* imbedded allusion to Niobe refracts the play's Oedipal legacy into its Sophoclean components: in the process, *Hamlet,* the Senecan play of bad influences, points towards *King Lear* as the drama of a fundamentally untransmitted classical heritage, figured not in the (m)Other of an alienating tradition but in the sister-daughter walled off by interdicted mourning. At stake in the mapping of Shakespeare onto Sophocles is not the intertextuality of influence, but the *Nachträglichkeit* of canonicity, the order of ancient and modern tragedies that is retroactively configured in literary history and theory. If the lines and lineage of the tragic canon are founded on the model of Oedipus, that order is constitutively confounded by the literalizations, accretions, and repudiations of cultural mourning in *Antigone* and *Lear.*

In this "Inter-Section," we use the *L-Schema,* the earliest of Lacan's quadrilateral diagrams of the subject, to graph Sophocles and Shakespeare onto the axes of imaginary and symbolic identification. Pressing the figure of Niobe in *Hamlet's* soliloquy correlatively unfolds the L-Schema into its Lacanian correction and addendum, the *R-Schema,* which maps the real as the traumatic breach dividing or "inter-sectioning" the fields of imaginary and symbolic representation. The L-Schema demarcates the logic of *Hamlet* in relation to Oedipal narrative; the R-Schema locates the psychoanalytic coordinates of *King Lear* as a drama of the Real. The turning point between the two graphs is marked by the *a* of *Antigone,* whose articulation of the Niobe story represents the intertextual interstices, the hollowed spaces that enable or, in Lacan's sense of the word, "cause" Oedipal narrative and representation. In this mapping of tragic paradigms in psychoanalysis, the *Oedipus* trilogy and its differential repetition and anamorphic distortion by Shakespearean dra-

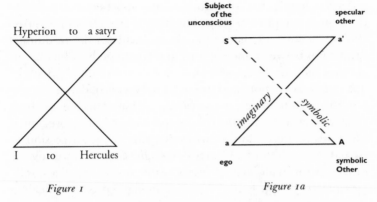

Figure 1   Figure 1a

ma demarcate the basic positions of critical discourse after
Aristotle.

Plotting Parents

The mythological crosscurrents traversing *Hamlet*'s first soliloquy ("O that this too too sullied flesh . . . ") structurally equate
Hamlet with the satyr (Fig. 1). The identification of Hamlet
and Claudius produced by the soliloquy is based not on characterological likeness but on structural analogy—on position
rather than disposition. It is not that Hamlet sees himself as
"like" Claudius, but rather that the massive disparity between
the two brothers parallels that between Hercules and Hamlet
fils, a four-part analogy of differences that inscribes a two-part
mirroring, the relation of rivalry between nephew and uncle.
Lacan's L-Schema, derived from the logical square of Apuleius
and first introduced in *Seminar II*, charts the subject on the
imaginary and symbolic axes, the first describing dual relations
of rivalry and specular identification, the second instituting
ternary relations of symbolic prohibition, repression, and substitution (Fig. 1a). Whereas the axis a–a' represents the ego's
constitutive alienation in the imaginary object (here, the place
held by Claudius), the axis S-A represents the subject as divided
by the discourse of the Other, the dead father of law and
language (the Ghost).

In *Seminar II*, Lacan introduces the L-Schema in order to distinguish the practice of psychoanalysis from that of ego psychology, a contrast that implicitly rearticulates the traditional distinction between ancient and modern tragedy. Thus Lacan chooses the iconography of romance to describe the effects of imaginary alienation and their illusory consolidation in the therapeutic mirror of ego psychology: "One wants him in effect to gather everything which he experienced in the pregenital stage, his scattered limbs, his partial drives, the succession of partial objects—think of Carpaccio's *Saint George* skewering the dragon, with small severed heads, arms, and so on, all around" (*Seminar II:* E 245, F 286). Ego psychology's dream of healing the fragmentation of the psyche by shoring up the ego through identification with the analyst derives from the poetic psychology of a received Romanticism, which putatively gathered the scattered elements of nature and history in the crucible of the lyric imagination. In contrast to this Romantic program of the ego, Lacan here calls the subject to assume its place in the symbolic set of relations into which it was born: "The analysis consists in getting him to become conscious of his relations, not with the ego of the analyst, but with all these Others who are his true interlocutors, whom he hasn't recognized [*réconnu*]... That is where the subject authentically re-integrates his disjointed limbs, and recognises, reaggregrates his experience" (E 246–47, F 288). The early Lacan's staging of recognition as recognition of structure echoes the classical narrative of Oedipal tragedy, which subjects individual *ethos* to the cultural *mythos*—the plot or myth—which has written the hero's story in advance. In *Oedipus Rex*, the exemplary tragedy of Aristotelian poetics, it is not that Oedipus lacks character, but that his character coalesces precisely in and as the act of first fleeing, then unwittingly fulfilling, and finally recognizing the narrative of incest and patricide predicted by the oracles.

In the received narratives of literary historiography, classical tragedy subordinates *ethos* to *mythos*, whereas modern tragedy recontains *mythos* within *ethos*, inventing the bourgeois subject as the proper telos of drama. Classical tragedy insistently locates individual characters in "family plots," in the double sense of

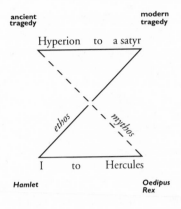

ancient   modern
tragedy   tragedy

Figure 2

Hitchcock's pun; modern tragedy, however, subordinates the tyrannical mechanism of destiny to an individuality whose freedom borders on a monstrous egomania. Its aesthetics of individualism, which reject the affiliated structures of genus and genre, family and narrative, tend to dissolve the parameters of the dramatic as such in the teary gaze of the "sentimental" (Schiller) or the desperate embrace of the "anxious" (Kierkegaard). This dialectical distinction between ancient and modern tragedy describes the mythological sequence of *Hamlet*'s first soliloquy, which, as we suggested in the previous chapter, maps *Hamlet*'s relation to the classical as such (Fig. 2).

The symbolic axis, Hyperion–Hercules, describes the classical order of *mythos*, "Oedipal" in structure as well as content, whereas the imaginary axis, I–Satyr, delineates the modern aesthetics of *ethos*, which characterize *Hamlet*'s deviant relationship to the classical, in which the reign of the ego attempts to consolidate the fragments of classical tragedy in its decline. Rather than effecting a true restoration and organic reordering of classical culture, its only product is a satyr play or *Trauerspiel* of mixed forms, which, like Carpaccio's *St. George*, pieces together the "tragical-comical-historical-pastoral" remnants of classical literature into a thing of shreds and patches.

In *Hamlet*'s first soliloquy, "Niobe all tears" personifies that moment of aesthetic fragmentation and monstrosity which in-

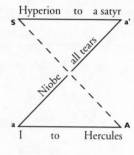

Figure 3

heres in the drama of character's nostalgia for wholeness. The
theatricality of maternal grief projected by the play emblematizes *Trauerspiel* as the dysfunctional, melancholic moment
within the humanist agon between ancients and moderns that
defines the philosophy and historiography of tragedy. Thus
the soliloquy's governing paternal allusions cross at the figure
of Niobe, the emblem of ostentatious grief and ossifying identification with loss (Fig. 3). In this mapping of the soliloquy,
Niobe falls on the imaginary axis, the originary site of maternal
identification and alienation, which Lacan calls in his initial
gloss of the L-Schema "the wall of language": "[True Others]
are on the other side of the wall of language, there where in
principle I never reach them. Fundamentally, it is them I'm
aiming at every time I utter true speech, but I always attain a',
a'', through reflection. I always aim at true subjects, and I have
to be content with shadows. The subject is separated from the
Others, the true ones, by the wall of language [*mur de langage*]"
(*Seminar II* E 244, F 286). This "wall of language" is the screen
of the other's verbiage, first encountered by the subject as complete, seamless, and impenetrable. In his fifth and sixth seminars Lacan reformulates this function as the Other of demand
whose reflective mirror-play (the demand for love) deflects the
question of desire addressed to the "true Others" of the symbolic order. The mother holds the place of the Other as the
battery of signifiers, imaginary in its wall-like, reflective totality,
and symbolic in its instantiation of a protolinguistic order. De-

mand both leads to desire as the difference between need and its expression and continues to erect an imaginary screen of love that prevents the enunciation of desire.

The story of Niobe allegorizes the mortifying alienation of the subject in the field of the mother's overweening love (Niobe's prideful praise of her children) as well as the petrification of desire in the specularity of melancholia (Niobe's endless tears at their death). In *Hamlet*'s soliloquy, the interminable grief of Niobe is the inverse of the over-hasty mourning of Gertrude, whose obscene pleasure, her lack of lack, is projected by the play as further blocking the way to Hamlet's desire. In our graph of the soliloquy, "Niobe all tears" abuts against the "Satyr" of incestuous, unprohibited enjoyment, the "real phallus" incarnated by Claudius (see Chapter 3). In such a scheme, the work of the play would be to shift Hamlet's imaginary demand onto the axis of symbolic desire—in literary-historical terms, to bring *Hamlet* to Colonus, as the scene of the dialectical subjectivization of the Oedipal *mythos*.[1] Insofar as *Hamlet*'s allusion to Niobe, however, represents the stilling of desire in the very demand that should occasion it, the figure comes to embody the cryptic walls that seal Antigone within the valences of the same simile—totalizing "walls of language" lacking the chinks through which desire might slip, like the whispers of Pyramus and Thisbe.

Twisted Sisters

As we saw in Chapters 3 and 4, Gertrude's various allegorical projections mark a critical impasse in the classical narrative of symbolic expropriation. By arguing in "Seminar VI" that *Hamlet*'s dialectic of desire is impeded by Gertrude's enjoyment of a "real phallus," Lacan points the way to his introduction in *Seminar VII* of *das Ding*, the Thing as real: the archaic maternal

---

1. See in "Beyond Oedipus" 133 and passim, Felman's reading of *Oedipus at Colonus* as staging the subject's dying into his history.

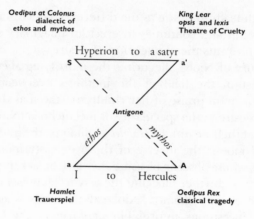

Figure 4

pre-object, at once resistent kernel, hole, and residue of rep-resentation.[2] In his later work, Lacan describes the production of the subject as the cancellation or crossing out of primal *jouissance* (associated with the maternal flesh and *das Ding*) by the symbolic order, the Other instantiated in the name of the father. Incursive rather than discursive, this "real thing" is alle-gorized for Lacan in *Seminar VII* by the remaining play of the Oedipus trilogy, *Antigone*, which we can now map in relation to the axes of Sophoclean and Shakespearean tragedy in psy-choanalysis (Fig. 4).

We take the figures of Niobe and Antigone—and of *Hamlet* and *Lear*—to allegorize two affiliated faces of the feminine in a narrative of subject formation as elaborated by the whole of Lacan's work, moments whose inflection at different points in the career manifests the shifting rhythm of that work's un-folding. In this narrative, the traumatic encounter with *das Ding* of maternal *jouissance* inhabits and disturbs originary need, whose consequent cancellation by demand leaves its traces in the *objet a* of fantasy, the "cause" of desire. Whereas the paternal

2. Lacan comments, "Thus the phallus is this thing that is presented by Freud as the key to the *Untergang* of the Oedipus complex. I say 'thing' and not 'object,' because it is a real thing, one that has not yet been made a symbol, but that has the potential of becoming one" ("Desire" 46).

mythographics of the soliloquy cross *over* "Niobe all tears," rearticulating the subject's alienation in the mother, stressed by Lacan in "Seminar VI," the soliloquy's graphic extrapolation here into the field of ancient and modern tragedy crosses *out* the drama of *Antigone*, materializing the *objet a* as the real excess of the dialectic between imaginary demand and symbolic desire introduced in *Seminar VII*.

In this diagram, Sophocle's Oedipus trilogy lays out three apexes of the Oedipal triangle in its correlation of the discourses of psychoanalysis and classical tragedy. *Oedipus Rex* epitomizes the *mythos* retroactively discovered as the structure of narrative, the discourse of the Other, which returns in later literature as the patrilineal plot of cultural transmission. *Oedipus at Colonus*, inventing the subject of ethics at the cusp of tragedy and philosophy, represents the dialectical sublation of *mythos* and *ethos* that pushes the tragedy of Thebes toward the philosophy of Athens at its outskirts in Colonus. In this scheme, *Antigone* is the sublime object rather than the structural model of philosophical reflection, the play whose dynamics of live burial belie the cultural work of mourning that its heroine so uncompromisingly demands. For the humanist tradition, the vector of modern tragedy, conventionally exemplified by Shakespeare, brings to fruition the bourgeois subject anticipated in Greek drama and its passage into philosophy. The trajectory of this vector, however, is warped by the assonant interferences that accompany its double Shakespearean legacy: whereas *Hamlet* signals the narcissistic disturbance of the governing dialectic between *ethos* and *mythos*, *King Lear*, as the drama of the radically refused object, collects the material dregs of the remaining Aristotelian categories, above all the *lexis, melopoeia,* and *opsis* paraded by the Fool.

Hamlet is generically specified by *Trauerspiel*, but *King Lear* points to the possibility—or rather, the constitutive impossibility—of the "Theater of Cruelty" of Antonin Artaud, which follows the history and theory of tragedy as its denial and remainder. *Trauerspiel* stages the failed mourning for tragedy—its allegory and its reflection, its Ovidian metamorphosis and its theoretical elongation. The Theater of Cruelty, on the other hand, repudiates rather than mourns the classical tragedy of representation by positing a theater of the real in its place. Artaud's goal is to separate out the materiality of props (lighting, gestures, music, voice) from their superadded signifying properties: "Here too intervenes (besides the auditory language of sounds) the visual language of objects, movements, attitudes, and gestures. . . . We must speak now about the uniquely material side of this language—that is, about all the ways and means it has of acting upon the sensibility. . . . Abandoning Occidental usages of speech, it turns words into incantations. It extends the voice" (*The Theater and Its Double* 90–91). In Artaud's theatrical hieroglyphics, "voice" and "visual language" function not as the privileged vehicles of a metaphysics of self-presence and meaning, but as thing-like props with the deictic corporeality of gesture; in this, they border on the Lacanian account of the voice and the gaze as residual objects left over by representation. In Aristotelian terms, Artaud's theater gathers up the spectacular remnants of the *ethos/mythos* dialectic, reclaiming them as the originary ground and refuse of Western drama. In the "First Manifesto," Artaud includes *Lear* in his example of stage sets—"*manikins ten feet high representing the beard of King Lear in the storm*" (97–98)—and returns to Shakespeare in his program of projects: "*Works from the Elizabethan theatre stripped of their text and retaining only the accouterments of period, situations, characters, and action*" (100). In "stripping" Elizabethan theater to the physical "accouterments" of the stage, Artaud repeats the exposure of "the thing itself, unaccommodated man" dramatized in *Lear*'s storm scene—not, however, as a humanist essence or *ens* beneath costume, but as the properties of costume itself, the pure surface without depth presented in Lear's grotesquely nonmimetic beard. In Artaud's *Lear*, the "thing itself" is an unaccommodated manikin.

The polarization of the L-Schema's imaginary axis by *Trauerspiel* in the place of the ego and the Theater of Cruelty in the place of the object necessarily presses the L-Schema into its Lacanian expansion and addendum, the R-Schema, which maps the partition of the imaginary and symbolic fields of representation by the incursion of the real (Fig. 5). In the move-

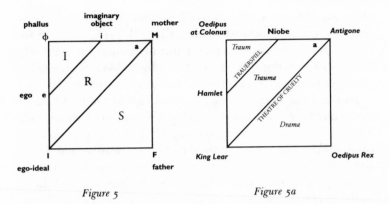

Figure 5   Figure 5a

ment from the L-Schema to the R-Schema, the rending of the
imaginary axis by the introduction of the real bifurcates the
positions of both the object and the ego. The imaginary ego
(*e*) is here distinguished from the symbolic ego ideal (*I*). So
too, the object divides into its imaginary embodiment (*i*) and its
real kernel. The latter is designated by the *M* of the maternal
Thing ("the signifier of the primordial object" [*Écrits* 197]) and
its avatar, the *objet a,* which bears the remainder of *das Ding* in
its symbolic cancellation. In our graph of ancient and modern
tragedy, we have glossed the resulting bands of imaginary, real,
and symbolic as the fields of *Traum,* trauma, and drama (Fig.
5a). Lacan associates the real with trauma, an event, that is,
whose affective quantity both occasions and breaks through the
capacities of mental representation.[3] Around this pure incursion collect the representational modes of the imaginary and
the symbolic, the first characterized by the *Traum* or dream of
wholeness masking the scandal of the real, the second introducing the Oedipal drama, which attempts to symbolize rather
than cover trauma by organizing its void into differential sig-

---

3. "Is it not remarkable," Lacan asks in *Seminar XI,* "that, at the origin of
the analytic experience, the real should have presented itself in the form of
that which is *unassimilable* in it—in the form of the trauma, determining all
that follows, and imposing on it an apparently accidental origin?" (55).

nification.[4] Whereas the symbolic presents itself as the dialectical drama of *Traum* and trauma, the real, precipitated in the intransigent *objet a* of fantasy ("the phoneme, the gaze, the voice—the nothing" [*Écrits* 315]), continues to riddle the order of representation with enclaves of obdurate, "cruel" materiality. In this final graph, *Trauerspiel* and the Theater of Cruelty are dramatic modes that border on the real, once again indicating *Hamlet*'s alienation in the (m)Other of demand and *Lear*'s catastrophic encounter with the Thing, represented by its strained relation—parasitical rather than parricidal, an invasive encroachment more than a family resemblance—with *Antigone* in the tragic discourse of psychoanalysis. Hamlet's first line to Claudius, "A little more than kin, and less than kind," summarizes the textual and intertextual relations between *Trauerspiel* and tragedy in the family romance of psychoanalytic discourse; Hamlet's line to Gertrude, "I must be cruel only to be kind," points to the rupture of tragic kind by its own cruelty staged in *King Lear*. "Cruelty" here indicates not so much the representation of violence as violence done to representation, that is, the drive to reduce mimesis to the visceral stuff of its media, signifying nothing. As such, the eruption of cruelty is fitful and momentary rather than sustained and systematic, not a practical possibility for modern theater but a necessary impossibility that conditions the Western drama of representation as its effaced ground. In Jacques Derrida's analysis of Artaud, "the 'grammar' of the theatre of cruelty, of which he said that it is 'to be found,' will always remain the inaccessible limit of a representation which is not repetition, of a *re*-presentation which is full presence, which does not carry its double within itself as its death" (*Writing and Difference* 248). So, too, *Lear* cannot rightly be said to incarnate a Theater of Cruelty, but rather to indicate its ongoing force as the foreclosed condition of Western drama. Derrida describes the effects of the theater

4. The drama of Sophocles, according to Aristotle, introduced the third actor into the Aeschylean theatre of two (*Poetics* 4. 1449a 19); Sophoclean drama is "Oedipal" not only in content but in the triangular structure of its exemplary family plot.

of cruelty within classical representation: "A certain stage has maintained with the 'forgotten,' but, in truth, violently erased, stage a secret communication, a certain relationship of *betrayal.* ... This explains why classical theatre, in Artaud's eyes, is not simply the absence, negation, or forgetting of theatre, is not a nontheatre: it is a mark of cancellation that lets what it covers be read" (236). Moreover, this theater of the real will have emerged only within the Oedipal drama of tradition: "The murder of the father which opens the history of representation and the space of tragedy, the murder of the father that Artaud, in sum, wants to repeat at the greatest proximity to its origin but *only a single time*—this murder is endless and is repeated indefinitely" (249). In Derrida's account, Artaud's attempt to destroy the narrative of the dead father—to replace Oedipal tragedy with the Theater of Cruelty—is no more than to kill the dead father once again, repeating the Oedipal narrative as the *mythos* of tradition.

In a late gloss of the R-Schema, Lacan writes that the parallelogram of the real "isolates a Moebius strip" (*Écrits* 223) in which the pair of points at each end would be joined with their diagonal opposites, twisting the field they define into a continuous looped surface. As a result, the planar logic of the two-dimensional graph is wrenched into a new topology. In our modification of the R-Schema, *Hamlet* would curl back onto *Antigone*, and *Lear* onto Niobe. This torsion of the plane describes the warping of the opposition between *Hamlet* and *Lear* in psychoanalysis: whereas the obsessive object in *Hamlet* condenses both image and pathos, imaginary and real, the sublime object of *King Lear* shifts between christological redemption and its existential negation. By extension, the traditions or countertraditions of *Trauerspiel* and the Theater of Cruelty converge and separate in their crossed poetics of the real, as the *momento mori* of Baroque emblematics changes places with the living hieroglyphs of Artaud's modernism. The passage of tragedy into psychoanalysis bends the linear history of literature into a Moebius strip that twists the parallel strands of modern drama within the classical tradition of Oedipus.

Hanging Caskets

Percy Bysshe Shelley wrote in 1821 to John Gisborne, " 'You are right about Antigone—how sublime a picture of woman! ...Some of us have in a prior existence been in love with an Antigone, and that makes us find no content in any mortal tie" (cited in George Steiner *Antigones* 4). As Shelley's lines testify, the image of Antigone exerts a critical fascination whose hypnotic luminescence exceeds the dialectical scene in which Hegel frames her. In our graphs of ancient and modern tragedy in psychoanalysis, *Antigone* holds the place of the feminine Thing which sublimely persists in the intertextual and canonical dynamics of Western literature and theory. Chapters 3 and 4 take Eliot's "Tradition and the Individual Talent" as a theory of Oedipal transmission whose *mythos* is blocked by the aesthetic deficiency of Gertrude diagnosed in "Hamlet and his Problems." Here we read Kierkegaard's "The Ancient Tragical Motif as Reflected in the Modern" from *Either/Or* as enunciating an account of tradition that precipitates around the insistence of the refused daughter in *Antigone*.[5] Not a countertheory but an "undertheory" buried within the governing Oedipal dialectic, the intertextual modes theorized and manifested in Kierkegaard's essay mark the vicissitudes of *Antigone* in the canon whose lines the play both follows and disturbs. *Antigone* and *Lear* represent "De-Terminators" of the canon; that is, they manifest the symbolic *determination* of literary order by the constitutive *deterrences* and punctual *terminations* of its own structure.

Just before introducing and restaging *Antigone* in "The Ancient Tragical Motif as Reflected in the Modern," Kierkegaard suggests the "posthumous" nature of tradition:

Let us, then, designate our intention as a venture in fragmentary endeavor or the art of writing posthumous [*efterladt*, left behind]

5. Although we cite passages from the Howard and Edna V. Hong translation (1987) of Kierkegaard's *Either/Or*, we have retained the more readerly translations of the title and subtitle from the David and Lillian Swenson translation (1959).

papers. A completely finished work is disproportionate to the poetizing personality; because of the disjointed and desultory character of unfinished papers, one feels a need to poetize the personality along with them. Unfinished papers are like a ruin, and what place of resort could be more natural for the buried? The art, then, is to produce skillfully the same effect, the same carelessness and fortuitousness, the same anacoluthic [*anakoluth-isk*] thought process; the art is to evoke an enjoyment that is never present tense but always has an element of the past and thus is present in the past. This is already expressed in the expression "left behind." Indeed, in a certain sense everything a poet has produced is something left behind, but it would never occur to anyone to call a completely finished work a work left behind, even if it had the accidental feature of not having been published in his lifetime. I also assume it to be a feature of all authentic human production in its truth, as we have interpreted it, that it is property left behind, since it is not granted to human beings to live with an eternal view like the gods'. Consequently, I shall call what is being produced among us property left behind [*Efterladenskab*], that is, artistic property left behind; negligence [*Efterladenhed*], indolence, we shall call the genius that we prize; the *vis inertiae* [force of inertia] we shall call the natural law that we worship.

(Either/Or Part 1, 152–53)

At first glance the passage appears strikingly close to Eliot's account of literary transmission in "Tradition and the Individual Talent"—in both accounts, literature only becomes itself by dying into a heritage. The basic lines, emphases, and literary models informing Eliot's and Kierkegaard's senses of the past, however, are fundamentally different. Eliot, reasserting the classical ideal of *mythos*, advocates the "self-sacrifice" and "extinction of the personality" of the individual talent in relation to tradition, whereas Kierkegaard, operating within the Romantic ethics of *ethos*, lingers on the "need to poetize the personality." Eliot's text legislates a program of symbolic introjection, assimilation, and reordering against any historicist understanding of "the past as a lump, an indiscriminate bolus" (51). Yet it is exactly the past as bolus that Kierkegaard exhumes and cherishes, a heritage or *Efterladenskab* that is incorporated rather than introjected, an undigested fragment that does not fit into the "simultaneous order" posed by Eliot (49). As the translation indicates, Kierkegaard plays on the prefix *Efter-* (after), indicating in contrast to Eliot's sublationary vocabulary a predilection for the residual and accidental. Eliot's emphasis on the discipline of the poetic work is countered in Kierkegaard's text by an aesthetics of negligence, *Efterladenhed*, which, like the German *Nachlässigkeit*, combines the senses of the lax or careless (*nachlässig*) and of heritage (*Nachlaß*), of remission and transmission. For Kierkegaard, a heritage is not so much what is passed on as what is left over—posthumous or *efterladt*, left behind.

The subtitle of Kierkegaard's chapter, "An Essay in the Fragmentary Read before a Meeting of the *Symparanekromenoi*," alludes to a fanciful fraternity—in Steiner's translation and gloss, "fellow moribunds, companions in live burial, brethren in decease and mortuary readiness" (*Antigones* 53). Eliot's implicit model of tradition derives from *Oedipus Rex;* but the motif of live burial in Kierkegaard clearly identifies *Either/Or* with *Antigone*, the play that suffuses and distracts his essay on tragedy. *Antigone* functions more as an embedded *object* than as a structural *model* for Kierkegaard: not, however, the passive object of philosophical reflection, but a fascinating fragment that has been "buried alive"—that is, taken up as a symbol of the unsymbolized. If the conjunction of *Oedipus Rex* and *Hamlet* exemplifies literature *in* theory—its organizing *mythos* or ego ideal—the disjunction of *Antigone* and *King Lear* allegorizes literature as "cause" of theory: an irruptive, radiant piece of traumatic pleasure, "an enjoyment that is never present tense," retroactively lodged in critical discourse as the irritant rather than the object of its desire. Tradition for Eliot represents the symbolic Other, itself divided between the paternal law of the classical tradition and the maternal demands of its romantic postponements. For Kierkegaard, tradition crystallizes as the object "left behind" in the cavernous "ruins" of the symbolic order, its fissures and discontinuities.

It is not that Kierkegaard is nondialectical or antidialectical in his definition of tradition, since the most pronounced subtext of his essay is in fact Hegel's *Aesthetics;* so, too, Kierkegaard does not abandon the Oedipal scenario but rather inflects it towards the daughter. The imaginary umbra of *ethos* extends from the personality of the author to the mesmerizing image of his or her characters—like Shelley, Kierkegaard presents himself as more than half in love with Antigone's sublime picture of woman:

> So, my dear *Symparanekromenoi,* come closer to me, form a circle around me as I send my tragic heroine out into the world, as I give the daughter of sorrow a dowry of pain as her outfit. She is my work, but still her outline is so indistinct, her form so nebulous, that each and every one of you can *forliebe sig* [fall in love] with her and be able to love her in your own way. She is my creation, her thoughts are my thoughts, and yet it is as if in a night of love I had rested with her, as if she in my embrace had confided a deep secret to me, had breathed it out together with her soul, as if she had then instantly changed before me, had disappeared, so that the only trace of her actuality was the mood that remained behind, instead of the reverse situation that she is brought forth by my mood to ever greater actuality.
>
> (153)

Whereas Eliot's structural reading of tradition implicitly identifies the critic with Oedipus as the patricidal son of Laius, Kierkegaard's narrator is positioned as the incestuous father of Antigone. Put otherwise, the passage rewrites *Oedipus Rex* as *King Lear,* anticipating the character of Cordelia in "The Seducer's Diary," which ends the first part of *Either/Or.* Endowing the classical "daughter of sorrow" with a modern "dowry of pain" in a scene of negative inheritance like that which opens *King Lear,* Kierkegaard also shifts the object of Oedipal incest from the mother to the daughter, with whom the narrator imagines he has rested "in a night of love." Kierkegaard uses the incestuous condensation of daughter and lover to figure the condition of the literary object in tradition as not the passive effect, but the active cause of its own creation. Whereas on the one hand, Kierkegaard casts himself as the (Oedipal) author and father of a modern Antigone, on the

other, Antigone is encountered as the sole possessor and source
of (Oedipal) truth, "as if she in my embrace had confided a
deep secret to me, had breathed it out together with her soul."
In Kierkegaard's revision of the story, Antigone knows the
incest that Oedipus himself never recognizes; the truth that
paradoxically passes from creation to creator is transformed
from the *oracle* of classical drama to the *secret* of the modern.
Whereas the classical oracle lays down a narrative structure of
inheritance, the secret operates as an encrypted object traumatically cut off from all narratival paths of transmission: in
structurally identifying with Oedipus as the father of Antigone,
Kierkegaard's persona identifies with Oedipus *as written* by *Antigone,* the earliest play of the cycle. In the process, the Oedipal
mythos is cast as an iterative structure produced by an intract-
able, thing-like content. In the process, incest, the matter of
Antigone's secret, shifts from the order of structure—the Aristotelian link between genus and genre, family and narrative—
to the condition of a fantasy object, ultimately the primal fantasy of becoming one's own cause. If in Kierkegaard's analysis
the secret of incest is an object as well as a structure, it is not,
however, reducible to a positive message or theme; hence the
"mood" that is its precipitate is the index not of Antigone but
of her disappearance, her "actuality" as the absent cause of
Oedipal narrative.

In Kierkegaard's rewriting of the classical play into its modern reflection, Antigone goes to the grave with her secret knowledge undisclosed and undiscovered, "in her heart like an arrow
that life has continually plunged deeper and deeper, without
depriving her of her life, for as long as it is in her heart she
can live, but the instant it is taken out, she must die" (164).
Here, the motif of live burial is repeated or "secreted" within
Antigone herself; in Kierkegaard's involuting revision, the *mythos* of *Oedipus Rex,* far from functioning as a model of order,
itself is reduced to a thing-like, invasive arrow that enters and
sustains the "heart" of tradition in the act of traumatically vi-
olating it. This foreign body constituted by secret knowledge
is the heart that keeps it and is pierced by it, the "arrow" becoming a metonymy lodged in the governing synecdoche, both

repeating and perforating its life-sustaining emblematics. The incisive secret of Kierkegaard's Antigone describes the traumatic encounter with language distilled into pure signifier, "real" in its efficacy, that both punctures and sutures the order of tradition.

If the narrator of Kierkegaard's essay encounters the Antigone of his creation as a literary object fundamentally not-his-own, this condition derives from her transmission as an icon of aborted transmission. In the play, Antigone represents (in the legal sense) the symbolic imperative to mourn, which, under Creon's prohibition, turns into the melancholic identification with grief; "My life," she says, "died long ago" (559). In Sophocles' *Antigone*, Tiresias describes the disastrous effects attendant on the refusal to bury the dead:

> All of the altars of the town are choked
> With leavings of the dogs and birds; their feast
> was on that fated, fallen Polyneices.
> So the gods will have no offering from us,
> not prayer, nor flame of sacrifice. The birds
> will not cry out a sound I can distinguish,
> gorged with the greasy blood of that dead man.
> . . . .
> Yield to the dead. Why goad him where he lies?
> What use to kill the dead a second time?
>
> (1016–30)

Here, Tiresias enunciates the "second death" as the refusal to allocate the dead a proper place in the symbolic order of history, an act of radical exclusion whose severity borders on foreclosure. As we will see in Chapter 8, Lacan locates *Antigone*, *Oedipus at Colonus*, and their Shakespearean repetition, *King Lear*, in the uncanny space "dans l'entre-deux-morts," between biological death and its symbolization in mourning. The "between-two-deaths" is, in Zizek's gloss, "a place of sublime beauty as well as terrifying monsters, . . . the site of *das Ding*, of the real-traumatic kernel in the midst of symbolic order" (*The Sublime Object of Ideology* 135). In the passage from *Antigone*, the distension of this space through the refusal to mourn results in cultural indigestion. The unburied flesh of Polyneices, refused assimilation into the remembrance of things past, returns in the "leavings" of the birds and dogs to clog the lines of communication that establish the oracular structure of tragedy.

The scavenging bird of Tiresias's speech finds its lyric antistrophe earlier in the play in the famous image of Antigone as a bird grieving the loss of her young. The guard describes Antigone engaged for the second time in the forbidden work of mourning:

> We saw the girl. She cried the sharp and shrill
> cry of a bitter bird which sees the nest
> bare where the young birds lay.

$$(423-25)$$

As in her self-comparison to Niobe later in the play (824–30), the bereaved sister is conflated with the mourning mother; metaphor verging here on metamorphosis, Antigone, like Niobe "all tears," momentarily becomes a living emblem of her grief. In his discussion of *Antigone* in *Seminar VII*, Lacan points out the power of this image in later poetry and drama, from Ovid into Shakespeare (307–8). The figure does not compare Antigone to a bird so much as her laments to its cry, reducing language to voice, to the pure affect of the signifier's keening edge.

Sophocles' simile, Homeric in form as well as content, finds its precedent in the scene of reunion between Telemachus and Odysseus in book 16 of the *Odyssey* (Müller *Sophokles Antigone* 118–19):

> . . . but now Telemachus
> folded his great father in his arms and lamented,
> shedding tears, and desire for mourning rose in both of them;
> and they cried shrill in a pulsing voice, even more than the outcry
> of birds, ospreys or vultures with hooked claws, whose children
> were stolen away by the men of the fields, before their wings
> grew strong; such was their pitiful cry and the tears their eyes wept.
>
> (*Odyssey* 16: 213–19)

In Homer, the climactic scene of recognition and reunion between father and son is sublimely couched or "folded" in the
simile's counterscene of maternal loss; the birds named, moreover, are scavengers (the vulture) and birds of prey (the osprey),
carnivorous resonances that, like the Niobe story, implicate
melancholic cannibalism in the simile's dominant theme of
mourning. The epic simile traditionally functions as the pastoral pocketing of one scene within another in order to gloss
or counterbalance it. Thus this lyric parenthesis of an empty
nest in Homer is itself gathered, nestled, or "empty-nested"
into *Antigone,* and its motifs of mourning, cannibalism, and
metamorphosis are dispersed throughout the drama. "The
birds," complains Tiresias, "will not cry out a sound I can distinguish, / gorged with the greasy blood of that dead man."
This cry is repeated in the inarticulate wail of Haemon at Antigone's grave, stitching together the lament of Antigone and
the shrieks of the glutted birds; as Rebecca Bushnell comments,
Haemon's "cry is said to be *asēma,* 'inscrutable' or 'unintelligible'
(1209). Like Tiresias . . . Creon finds himself striving to interpret a sign or *sēma* which is *asēmon,* as were the cries of the
birds that haunted the prophet" (*Prophesying Tragedy* 62). In
Antigone, the piercing cry of grief merges with the garbled
sound of the birds whose prophetic song is reduced to the
insignificant gurgles of indigestion. In this textual transference,
the symbolic introjection of epic by tragedy is structurally de-
pendent on the archaic cannibalism of incorporation, an encounter with the thing-of-loss imperfectly transformed into the
lost object of cultural mourning. At the same time, the thing
emerges not as the ground but as the residue of symbolization,
its necrophagic "leavings" choking the altars of augury with
the disgusting secretions of the oracular itself. In the alluvium
of allusion, Oedipal reconciliation and pre-Oedipal loss are
nested in each other through the mechanism, at once oracular and oral, introjective and incorporative, of forbidden
mourning.

The space of the Greek theater, divided between the open
stage depicting the public, masculine domain of the *polis,* and
the always hidden inner stage devoted to the domain of women,

is variously crossed and rearticulated throughout Greek tragedy, as Fromma Zeitlin has demonstrated. Although in both
Oedipus Rex and *Antigone* the inner stage is construed as the
realm of women, the differing composition of those spaces
shifts the contours of the feminine between incest and encasement, castration and *Kasten*. In *Oedipus Rex,* the inner stage is
imaginatively dominated by the incestuous *thalamos,* the marriage bed in which the paths of father and son have met; in
that imagined room offstage, Oedipus blinds himself with the
brooch from his mother's gown, an act that not only symbolizes
castration but symbolizes castration *as symbolic,* linking blindness
to insight, repression to knowledge. In *Antigone,* the inner stage
also represents the domestic domain of the palace, but a palace
now occupied by the mourning of Creon's wife Eurydice for
their son Haemon; as the Messenger glosses the topography
of the stage, "But we can hope / that she has gone to mourn
her son within / with her own women, not before the town"
(1247–50). This interior localization of feminine lament confirms the play's climactic construction of the inner stage as the
cave of live burial, the hole in the symbolic produced by the
"second death" of refused mourning around which the drama's
catastrophes collect. Antigone apostrophizes the place of her
burial: "O tomb, O marriage-chamber, hollowed out / house
that will watch forever, where I go" (891–92). Here the two
functions of tomb and marriage bed are not integrated in a
continuum, but rather interfolded as heterogeneous spaces.

This disarticulation of catacomb and wedding chamber is
registered, as we argue in Chapter 3, in the contrast between
the opening sequences of Olivier's and Zeffirelli's *Hamlet*s, the
first centered on the curtained space of the marriage bed and
the second staged in the family vaults of Elsinore. Although
the interior division of the Sophoclean kingdom finds its Shakespearean counterpart in the psychoanalytic relation of *Hamlet*
and *Lear,* what is at stake in such an analysis is not a typology
of essential distinctions, but a topology of encasement deployed
in and between Sophocles and Shakespeare in their foundational passage into culture and theory. In the Oedipus trilogy,
the heteromorphic spaces of *Antigone* and *Oedipus Rex* are linked

by the hanging of both mother and daughter, Jocasta in the bedroom of the symbolic and Antigone in the cavern of the real. Moreover, recall that Cordelia, too, dies offstage by hanging, an act that uncannily locates her in the inner house of Labdacus. The shared *Verhängnis* or destiny of the women suspends the opposition of the plays in the literal suspension of hanging. As such, the hanging of the women executes a corporeal emblematization of the "between-two-deaths" as a liminal state not of symbolic mediation but of radical exclusion, not an "in-between" but an "out-between"—in Lacan's coinage, an "extimacy," at once intimate and exterior.

The death of Cordelia hangs *Lear* between the cave of *Antigone* and the marriage bed of *Oedipus Rex*, an act that does not reconcile the topographies of the two plays in the dialectical *Aufhebung* of *Oedipus at Colonus*, but rather, like the Moebius strip, twists and distorts symbolic space in the process of graphing the plays' interimplication. The mapping of *Hamlet* and *Lear* onto the Oedipus trilogy performed in this chapter occurs not so much in the register of the intertextuality of influence—the genealogical interweaving of allusive passages—but in the intertextuality of the canon, the symbolic cross-referencing and real interpenetration of works by virtue of their ordering in the history and theory of tragedy. Composed first, yet diegetically last, *Antigone* "causes" *Oedipus Rex*, catalyzing the symbolic structures of the Oedipal *mythos* that provide a framework and prehistory for its trauma. If *Oedipus Rex* comes to function as the symbolic reference point for *Hamlet* through the affiliated structuralisms of Aristotle and Freud, *Antigone* marks the scandalous contingency of the real, which sets into play the necessity of Oedipal narrative and its material sedimentations in the internested *Kästen* of *King Lear*.

PART TWO

THE *LEAR* REAL

CHAPTER FIVE

The Motif of the
Three Caskets

The *Lear* Real

In the first scene of *King Lear,* the king of France responds
to Lear's disavowal of Cordelia:

> This is most strange,
> That she, whom even but now was *your best object,*
> The argument of your praise, balm of your age,
> The best, the dearest, should in this trice of time
> Commit *a thing so monstrous,* to dismantle
> So many folds of favour. Sure, her offence
> Must be of such unnatural degree
> That monsters it, or your fore-vouch'd affection
> Fall into taint.
>
> (I.i.212–20; emphasis added)

The passage's language of indication falls from "best object"
to "thing so monstrous." Whereas "object" functions in an economy of representation and value ("the argument of your
praise," "the best, the dearest"), the word "thing," egregiously
placing itself beyond appraisal, operates at the limits of the
representable as such: "monstrous," "of such unnatural degree
/ That monsters it." Cordelia's unspeakable act can only be
named, or unnamed, as "thing," the butt of bastardizing dis-
inheritance, or, in Shakespeare's coinage here, of "fore-vouch'd

affection": both a love earlier avowed ("fore-" as "before"), and one now retracted or disavowed—the "for-" of "forfeiting," "forbidding," or "foreclosure."

This decline from "object" to "thing" is repeated in the final scene of the play. Albany, caught up in the business of reestablishing order, answers Kent's query about Lear's absence:

> Great thing of us forgot!
> Speak, Edmund, where's the King? and where's Cordelia?
> [*The bodies of Goneril and Regan are brought in.*]
> Seest thou this object, Kent?
>
> (V.iii.236–38)

The "object" presented in the corpses of Goneril and Regan functions as the object of vision, disclosure, and exemplary representation—an "object lesson" in the rhetoric of display. The word "thing," on the other hand, is consistently placed beyond figuration in the play, either as the guarantor of representation or as its negative excess. The word can evoke a humanist essence or presence, culminating in Lear's stormy tribute to the naked Edgar as "the thing itself: unaccommodated man." At the same time, the "thing" is that which is absent, offstage, intrinsically "forgot," echoing the "for-" of "fore-vouch'd." The redemptive hope summoned by Albany's recollection of forgetting ("Great thing of us forgot!") fails to secure its promised end; even when brought into view Cordelia is "gone for ever," "dead as earth" (V.iii.258, 260). In the first scene and the last, the shift between "object" and "thing" signals a negativity within both appearance ("object") and essence ("the thing itself"), an elemental absence that disturbs their opposition by unfolding the "thing" as the "nothing" upon which the distinction between appearance and essence depends.

Freud's 1913 essay, "The Theme of the Three Caskets," reads *King Lear* by way of the casket motif in *The Merchant of Venice.*[1] Freud's three-part fable of the feminine as womb, wife,

---

1. On "The Theme of the Three Caskets" and Renaissance textuality, see Timothy Murray, "Translating Montaigne's Crypts."

and tomb supplements the Oedipal construction of woman as object of desire with the pre-Oedipal figure of woman as mother and her uncanny post-Oedipal complement, woman as death. In the Shakespearean textuality of psychoanalysis, Freud's three caskets pass into and are retroactively allegorized as Lacan's three fundamental orders: if the first casket (womb) pictures the Imaginary and the second (wife) represents the Symbolic, the third casket, death, indicates the Real. Freud's *Kasten*, like Lacan's *Chose*, is a "hole Thing," an enclosed hollowness whose contents are its emptiness. The language of "thing," "object," and "nothing" marks the intersection of *King Lear* and psychoanalysis insofar as each discourse describes and is marred by a textual (and sexual) hole at the core of representation and exchange. In the *lingua franca* of Shakespeare's English, Lacan's "Real" is an anagram of Freud's "Lear": boxed up in Lacan's *Seminar VII* lies "The Theme of the Three Caskets," which in turn encloses its Shakespearean subtext, *King Lear*. The unstable opposition between inside and outside articulated by *Kasten* and *Chose*, however, elicits an impossible topology in which *Lear* functions as both the hidden thing inhabiting the discourses nestled around it, and the outer limit that conditions and situates their modes of disclosure.

This intertextual modality, we argue, is repeated in *King Lear*'s disfigurative invasion by the Book of Job. In legislating a redemptive paradigm of Judeo-Christian tragedy for Shakespeare's play, Job also leaves over an abandoned husk of "extimate" textuality figured in the motif of skin disease transmitted between the two works. The narrative of patience in Job is the Biblical cocoon in which the pagan tragedy of *Lear* is christologically transformed; the empty chrysalis left over from that metamorphosis is constituted by the two works' lyric excesses of invective and complaint, the sloughed skin of dramatic and historical innovation. If, in our reading, *King Lear* holds the place of the third casket—the feminine origin and boundary of representation in the Shakespeare of Freud and Lacan—the play's generic and allusive mechanisms also refuse to fix the third casket as a specific position, space, or type. Instead, the allegory of the *Kasten* requires a morphology of

continuous surface without depth, a "superficial" representational skin stretched, folded, and perforated into pockets of
intertextual occlusion. At once intimately interior and inva-
sively exterior, *Lear* functions not as the "best object" of psychoanalysis, but as its "thing so monstrous," dismantling the
folds of representation into an anamorphic topology of the real.

Hidden Motifs

In the opening scene of *King Lear,* Regan and Goneril each
vie to offer their father a rhetorical mirror that claims to banish
all others from a perfect union of two. They each promise incest
without castration, an exclusive love undistracted by a third.
Cordelia interrupts this series of bids for undivided attention
by stressing the necessity of division:

> Why have my sisters husbands, if they say
> They love you all? Happily, when I shall wed,
> That lord whose hand must take my plight shall carry
> Half my love with him, half my care and duty:
> Sure I shall never marry like my sisters,
> To love my father all.
>
> (I.i.98–103)

Cordelia insists on the ordered expenditures that govern political and familial patriarchy. Rather than a specular relation
of two, her language of halving and separation functions in a
symbolic structure of three; Cordelia's "bond" binds her to
husband as well as father in defining her as object of exchange
in the reproduction of the Oedipal family, and the Oedipal
state. Like Antigone, Cordelia enters the play as the spokes-
person of cultural renunciation and substitution; both heroines,
moreover, uphold the law of the symbolic in opposition to the
father figures who should hold that place. And whereas Antigone demands the right to mourn, Cordelia enunciates the
compromises of marriage in her insistence that, rather than
gaining a son, Lear must lose his daughter.

In the opening scene of *Lear*, what appear initially as alternate erotic economies are in fact interdependent: Cordelia's "nothing" expresses at once the necessity of renunciation in exchange and the inherent quality, "the thing itself," which, in placing her beyond exchange, guarantees her market value. Thus Cordelia, "herself a dowry" (I.i.240), can be both the "unpriz'd precious maid" who transcends the debased currencies of uncourtly love (I.i.258), and the play's primary advocate of the tragic social necessity of substitution. So, too, Goneril and Regan duplicate each other in duplicating Lear; yet these specular relationships, far from settling into a dual unity secured by reciprocal love, threaten from the beginning of the play to collapse into mutual aggression. The play's narcissistic economy of competitive praise functions not as the opposite but as the support of triangular desire: Cordelia's symbolic value is underwritten by the contention of France and Burgundy, "great rivals in our youngest daughter's love" (I.i.45). In psychoanalytic terms, the play only imagines the regressive pleasures of pre-Oedipal unity from within the frame of gendered desire; in *Lear*, infantilization is always disclosed as Oedipal fantasy.

In France's speech, the shift between "object" of exchange and "thing" outside of value both supports and further complicates this simultaneous differentiation and collusion of the Bad sisters and the Good. France's reference to the "thing so monstrous" transvalues the inexpressibility topos motivating the speeches of all three daughters; here, that which cannot be figured in language appears as the site of vacuous horror rather than the overfullness of idealization. Thus Cordelia's "Nothing" invokes not only the mesh of essence and appearance assumed by every system of exchange, but also contains the particle of negation, "No-" or "Not-," the thing of loss that cannot be adequately measured by representation or accommodated by subjectivity. The diacritical *difference*, that is, between "object" and "thing itself," and between use and exchange values, itself requires the disavowal of a *negativity*, a void marked by the thing as "monstrous" and "unnatural," a radical absence that both gives rise to and threatens to collapse differential systems of representation. At stake here is the distinction between *lack*—the gap or spacing repeated, displaced, and regulated by signification—and *loss:* the sheer quantity of a *jouissance* indifferently in excess or deficit of symbolic quantification.[2] Again the analogy with *Antigone* is compelling, since both heroines in voicing the requirements of symbolic lack come to embody the trauma of real loss.

In Freud's essay "The Theme of the Three Caskets" ("Das Motiv der Kästchenwahl"), the psychoanalytic and Shakespearean discourses of the Thing are knotted together around the "not" of maternal negativity, the *Kasten*. Rather than a theoretical concept, or even the metaphor of a concept, the *Kasten*, in Freud's word, is a "motif" [*Motiv*]: a literary topos "motivated" not by psychological intention but by intertextual repetition. "Motif," we might say, indicates motive without motivation, an intentional structure that nonetheless expresses no particular intention; in Aristotle's terms, "motif" would imply a formal cause disconnected from a final one, or in Heidegger's terms, a "thing" rather than a "tool." The organizing motif of Freud's essay, the feminine hollowness or void of the *Kasten*, casts the motif *as* a *Kasten* or occlusion—not a "hidden motive" but a motif of the hidden. As such, the *Kasten*-motif corresponds to Lacan's account of "cause" as the critical failure or non-functioning—the hole, gap, or *thing*—which occasions the retroactive plotting of a cause-effect relation.[3]

In terms of literary history, a later text "causes" an earlier text through the repetition and formalization of a motif, thereby constituting a tradition of which it is the telos.[4] This

---

2. In comments presented at Lacan's seminar on 15 March, 1967, André Green distinguishes "the category of loss insofar as it is related to *objet a*" and "the category of lack insofar as it is related to the big Other" ("Seminar XIV" 198).

3. In both English and German the use of the French word "motif" indicates its literary difference from psychological "motive." In *Seminar XI* Lacan writes, "Cause is to be distinguished from that which is determinate in a chain, in other words the *law*. . . . Whenever we speak of cause . . . there is always something anti-conceptual, something indefinite. . . . In short, there is only cause in something that doesn't work" (E 22; F 25).

4. The fictional, retroactive dependence of cause on effect has been most

nachträgliche construction of a cause, however, is itself the effect (or "special effect") of a radical failure of historical and linguistic connection and influence. In psychoanalysis, a trauma is that which, only gaining symbolic meaning retroactively, nonetheless always exceeds that signification, as its Real cause. This is the distinction and relation between an "historicism in the perfect tense," which studies the retroaction of meaning, and the permanently past tense of a "was," which, irrevocably and always already past, is at once unavailable to and the paradigm of historicity. Such a dynamic describes the function of the *Kasten* motif not only in the literature Freud analyzes but in the unfolding of Freud's own work and its critical reception. The essay represents Freud's most explicit refiguration of the *Kasten* memory, the scene of maternal loss that framed his remarks to Fliess on *Hamlet* and *Oedipus;* as such, the 1913 essay retroactively splits the 1897 letter into two Shakespearean legacies, the Oedipal *Hamlet* and the *Lear* of "The Three Caskets." Moreover, *Lear,* in its negative (non)relation to Oedipal law, functions not as the retroactive fantasy or primal scene of psychoanalysis (the part played by *Hamlet* and *Oedipus*), but rather as that scene's residual "motif" or "cause." In psychoanalysis, the *Kasten* that allegorizes *King Lear* repeats the live burial of historical nonconnection in *Antigone*, emblematizing the irruptive trauma of maternal loss and feminine *jouissance* whose cancellation motivates Oedipal fantasy and interpretation.

Beginning with the scene of the three caskets in *The Merchant of Venice* and then passing via the oneric algebra of myth and folklore to the three daughters of *King Lear*, Freud's essay maps the vicissitudes of the feminine object in male desire. The emblematic conclusion, at once allegory and epitaph, summarizes and extends Freud's reading of the three caskets motif:

> The regressive revision which [Shakespeare] has thus applied to the myth, distorted as it was by wishful transformation, allows us enough glimpses of its original meaning to enable us perhaps

_____

famously theorized by Hume and Nietzsche (cf. Hayden White, *Metahistory* 35–36).

to reach as well a superficial allegorical interpretation of the three female figures in the theme. We might argue that what is represented here are the three inevitable relations that a man has with a woman—the woman who bears him, the woman who is his mate and the woman who destroys him; or that they are the three forms taken by the figure of the mother in the course of a man's life—the mother herself, the beloved one who is chosen after her pattern, and lastly the Mother Earth who receives him once more. But it is in vain that an old man yearns for the love of woman as he had it first from his mother; the third of the Fates alone, the silent Goddess of Death, will take him into her arms.

(SE 12:301)

The passage revises the Sphinx's riddle by narrating man's life not according to the steps of his physical progression, but rather in terms of the declension of the feminine object. The dominant course of the passage describes the linear unfolding of woman as womb, wife, and tomb; informing and countering this temporal sequence, however, is a regressive movement, attributed both to the intertextual process (Shakespeare's "regressive revision" of the myth as well as Freud's own recourse to folklore and fairy tale), and to the itinerary of the hero's desire. The latter shapes Lear's "darker purpose" to "unburthen'd crawl toward death" (I.i.35, 40), a desire that draws the linear sequence of the Sphinx's riddle (from four legs to two to three) into a circle: the old man ends up on all fours again. Throughout the play, Lear's regressive fantasy turns, and returns, on the necessity of death. Lear is doubly "unburthened": in returning to the idylls of infancy, he is unbirthed, disencumbered of the burden of life, as the first casket lapses into the third.

Freud's essay lays out the basic directions taken by later psychoanalytic criticism of the play: Oedipal readings, which stress Lear's incestuous desire for Cordelia, take place in the symbolic space of the middle casket, whereas pre-Oedipal ones, which emphasize the play's dream of maternal unity, are projected onto the fantasmatic screen of the first.[5] Maternal ne-

---

5. For the latter, see especially Coppélia Kahn, "The Absent Mother in *King Lear*."

gativity, which may support as much as undermine paternal authority, has not been easily accommodated by feminist criticism.[6] Yet "The Theme of the Three Caskets" represents a momentary mutation of the phallic economy in Freud's writing, an aberration that, in its necessary appropriation and misappropriation, continues to regulate his account of sexual difference.

In Freud's essay, the three modalities of the object—womb, wife, and tomb—are keyed to three modalities of absence, absences that anticipate the three Lacanian orders, the *imaginary*, the *symbolic*, and the *real*. If the first casket imagines "the thing itself," the idealized yet alienating maternal other, and the second represents the object of Oedipal substitution, the third points to the "thing so monstrous," the radical negativity that faults the imagined unity guaranteeing the symbolic exchange of women. The *Kasten* is a thing rather than a person, a figure of hollowness that evokes both the foundational fantasy of subjective interiority and the limits of subjectivity in the fine and private place of the grave. The motif of the casket represents "what is essential in woman" (*SE* 12:292) as neither the presence of a hypostatized femininity nor the absence inscribed by castration, but rather as an enclosed void, a structure of occlusion whose contents are its dis-contents.

The three moments are interfolded, or, to use the coinage of Freud's *Kasten* memory, *eingekastelt*, boxed up in each other, forming a sort of Klein bottle that interimplicates rather than demarcates inside and outside, one casket and another.[7] The image of the nurturing mother figured in the first casket represents at once a fantasy of original oneness and, contaminated by the specter of mother-as-death, signals the constitutive fracture of the pre-Oedipal by loss, aggression, and *jouissance*. This contamination in turn disturbs the exchangeability of the pas-

6. A notable exception is Jacqueline Rose's lecture, "Controversial Discussions: Negativity in the Work of Melanie Klein," on Melanie Klein and maternal negativity.

7. On Lacan's use of the Klein bottle, a space whose interior and exterior are continuous, see Jeanne Granon-Lafont, *La topologie ordinaire de Jacques Lacan* 93–106.

sive Oedipal object (the second casket), while also triggering the object's original (over)valuation. This relationship between the destablization of value and the construction of value as such is enacted in France's slippage from "best object" to "thing most monstrous," a shift that, in France's word, "unfolds" the ideal of intrinsic worth as the fantasy necessitated by the monstrosity of the maternal Thing, objectified and attenuated under the law of Oedipus.

Fetish/Object/Thing

The movement between the first and the second caskets describes the construction of the Oedipal object. The movement between the third and the first caskets describes the threatened (re)emergence of the Thing. The movement between the second and the third caskets locates the Freudian concept of the fetish, both mapping and masking the nonrelation of Thing and object. The *Kasten* and the fetish are linked in Freud's writings insofar as they are physical objects that verge on thingness in their anxious attempt to contain or veil the overabundant negativity of the maternal body. According to Freud, the fetish veils not a presence but an absence: the default of the maternal phallus. Moreover, this default is of a peculiar kind, since, as feminist critics have insisted, the maternal phallus never existed as such.[8] Freud's fetish, then, marks the absence of an absence, absences which, like the three caskets, are organized incommensurately. The fetish, that is, figures the *lack* of "something" that was always already *lost*—it indicates not a lost thing, but *the Thing as loss.* Thus the fetishist does not so much assert the existence as deny the nonexistence of the maternal phallus, a vertiginous negativity rather than an insistent and consistent negation, in excess of the "having/not having" distinction that is designed to control it.

8. Barbara Spackman, for example, has analyzed the fetish as "a *catachrestic* synecdoche that puts 'something' in the place of 'nothing' " (*Decadent Genealogies* 1989).

By oscillating between an imaginary plenitude and a symbolic deficit, the fetish effaces, and in the process allows us to articulate, the gap between object and thing. Rather than a transitional *object* (in D. W. Winnicott's sense of something bridging inside and outside), the *Kasten* in its fetishistic aspect is what we might call a transitional *thing*. As such, it designates not a point of exchange but of noncommutability, not a relation but a nonrelation between the modalities of the object represented in Freud's three caskets.[9] The traces of this "transitional thing" are visible in the language of melancholia at work in Freud's essay, "Fetishism": the maternal phallus, Freud writes, "should normally have been given up, but the fetish is precisely designed to preserve it from extinction" (*SE* 21:152). "The horror of castration," he writes further on, "has set up a memorial to itself in the creation of this substitute" (154). The fetishist "reveres his fetish" (157)—suggesting mournful idealization—but also finds it "uncanny," indicating the kinship between femininity and the death drive.[10] These lines are situated in a dense network of motifs in Freud's writing that tie the scandal of maternal flesh to the invention of castration and the disavowal of death, motifs emblematized above all by the Freudian motif of motifs, the *Kasten*. In the homophonics of Freud's vocabulary, the *Kasten* of maternal loss and mortification becomes—and in turn is both effaced and made visible by—the *Kastration* of Oedipal lack.[11]

The paired logics of the *Kasten* and the fetish work not to

9. See D. W. Winnicott, "Transitional Objects and Transitional Phenomena." See Lacan in "Direction of the Treatment and the Principles of Its Power": "I showed the value of a conception in which child observation is nourished by the most accurate reconsideration of the function of mothering in the genesis of the object: I mean the notion of the transitional object, introduced by D. W. Winnicott, which is a key point for the explanation of the genesis of fetichism [*sic*]" (*Écrits* 250). See also Lacan's letter to Winnicott (*Television* 77), and "Le fétichisme et la question de l'objet," in *Traits de perversion dans les structures cliniques*, ed. Dominique Miller and Guy Trobas, 307.

10. Following a similar logic of disavowal, the Medusa's head "offers *consolation* to the spectator: he is still in possession of a penis, and the stiffening reassures him of the fact" (*SE* 8:273; emphasis added).

11. On this homophony, see Stephen Bröser, "Kästchen, Kasten, Kastration."

discover the concealed truth of loss behind or before lack, but
rather to locate the incommensurability between loss and lack
disavowed in the Oedipal production of the diacritical equivalents that govern representation and exchange. In Jacques
Lacan and Wladimir Granoff's gloss of Freud, the perversions
are "the residue of development toward the Oedipus complex"
("Fetishism" 272), a phrase that indicates the fetish's position
at once subordinate to and in excess of the law of castration.
In its temporal precocity ("*toward* the Oedipus complex") and
its *nachträglich* constitution by it (as the "*residue*" of the Oedipus
complex), the fetish circulates in the interstices of the three
caskets. The fetish, as well as the theory of the fetish, remains
as the perverse sign, surplus, and disavowal of the unmappable
transition between *Kasten* and *Kastration*, thing and object.

Freud's 1909 remarks on fetishism to the Vienna Psychoanalytic Society implicate fetishism and theory through an account
of representation whose three-part division corresponds to the
orders allegorized by the three caskets: "Some parallels to [the
patient's] interest in clothes occur in other of his characteristics.
The patient became a speculative philosopher, and names play
for him an especially great role. In this patient something similar to what took place in the erotic domain occurred in the
intellectual domain: he turned his interest away from things
onto words, which are, so to speak, the clothes of ideas; this
accounts for his interest in philosophy" (154). Freud's (and the
fetishist's) distinction of the "word" not only from the "thing"
but also from the "idea" defines theory as the separation of the
signifier from both signified and referent. In the process, the
pure signifier, the word as "name" unattached to any concept
or object, functions not only as the symbolic other of the thing,
but in turn becomes itself a kind of thing—the material remnant of signification, or again in Lacan's phrase, "the residue
of development toward the Oedipus complex." This constellation and circulation of "thing," "word," and "idea" inscribes
the structure of fetishism within the Lacanian triad of the real,
the symbolic, and the imaginary, where the encounter with real
loss is retranscribed as symbolic lack supported by the imaginary appearance of meaning. Insofar as the fetishized "word"

is absolutely denuded of "idea," it retains its connection with the real in the materiality of the signifier; thus the fetish, like the *Kasten*, and like each of Freud's three caskets, is defined by the momentary, failed articulation of a hole and a difference, of a thing and an object.

The *Kasten*, we might say, is a "motif" of the signifier in its thing-like aspect. First and most simply, it is a figure of the signifier as shaped material, a *Kasten* "cast" or "thrown" around a void. By extension, it is a motif in the sense of a motive or cause, in Lacan's formulation of cause as "something that doesn't work," as a breakdown in interpretation, the failure of signification. Finally, "motive" indicates both origin and end, the ground or source of an act on the one hand, and its telos or trajectory on the other; by boxing womb and tomb up in each other, the *Kasten* figures both the uncanny origin and the deathly residue of signification.

In "The Theme of the Three Caskets," death, the specter of feminine negativity, appears not only as the casket's hidden content, *das Verborgene*, but is also aligned with *das Sichverbergen*, the act of hiding or concealing oneself; thus death metonymically shifts in the two passages from revealed message to act of concealment, from contained to container, and, more specifically, to the container of an emptiness, a signifier without a signified. In *Lear*, the king of France wonders that Cordelia could "commit a thing so monstrous, to dismantle / So many folds of favour"; here the thing is that which dismantles and unfolds, disclosing, however, not an object but its disappearance. France's association of "thing," "monster," and the topology of unfolding reappears in Albany's castigation of Goneril: "Thou changed and self-cover'd thing, for shame, / Be-monster not thy feature" (IV.ii.62–63).[12] Like Freud's *Sichverbergen* (self-hiding) used to describe the self-occlusion of the third casket, Shakespeare's "self-cover'd thing" figures subjectivity as a structure of concealment that, rather than sheltering

12. Missing from the Folio, the Quarto's "self-covered" has been recovered through such editorial emendations as "self-converted," "false-cover'd," "self-discover'd," and "sex-cover'd" (*Arden Lear* 148).

the self as a hidden interiority, constitutes the self *as* a cover
or tegument that hides precisely nothing. The "self-covered
thing" rewrites the "thing itself" of subjective autonomy as "itself a thing," an internal-external reference point that displaces
subjectivity in the act of causing it. Together, these passages
cast representation as a continuous and sinuous surface
creased, punctured, and pitted not by signifieds but by their
loss.

Of Testaments and Teguments

In *Lear*, this "extimate" topology finds its extreme expression
in Lear's horrendous image of the daughter as skin disease, "a
boil, / A plague-sore, or embossed carbuncle" in Lear's "corrupted blood" (II.iv.221–3). Moreover, the passage's allusion
to Job specifies the generic coordinates of the play not in terms
of the ancient-modern dialectic of the humanistic canon emphasized in Chapter 5, but in terms of the intertextual dialectic
of "Old" and "New" Testaments as it is played out by the legacy
of Job in Shakespeare's play. The typological dynamic of biblical allegoresis describes the movement of Freud's "Theme of
the Three Caskets" from *The Merchant of Venice* to *King Lear*, a
division that counterpoints two dramas of the bond: in the first,
the father represents the letter of the old Law, whereas in the
second, the father is caught in an imaginary love ungrounded
by the bonds of cultural order. In the allusive ligatures binding
King Lear to the Book of Job, the incommensurability of the
Old and New Testaments is allegorized by the casting of representation as ruptured tegument or abandoned casing, as surface marred in its failed separation and translation of "Old"
and "New." A similar problematic is registered, although not
theorized, by Freud's juxtaposition of *The Merchant of Venice*
and *King Lear*, which implicates the testamentary thematics of
the first play in the biblical intertextuality of the second.

In act 2, Lear, confronting Goneril at the castle of Gloucester, implores her,

I prithee, daughter, do not make me mad:
I will not trouble thee, my child; farewell.
We'll no more meet, no more see one another;
But yet thou art my flesh, my blood, my daughter;
Or rather a disease that's in my flesh,
Which I must needs call mine: thou art a boil,
A plague-sore, or embossed carbuncle,
In my corrupted blood. But I'll not chide thee;
Let shame come when it will, I do not call it;
I do not bid the thunder-bearer shoot,
Nor tell tales of thee to high-judging Jove.
Mend when thou canst; be better at thy leisure;
I can be patient; I can stay with Regan,
I and my hundred knights.

(II.iv.216–229)

In the image of the "plague-sore" and "embossed carbuncle," Goneril is figured not as Lear's offspring but as his "inspring": like a disease, the bad daughter is presented as flesh that has mutinied from within. She is both one with the subject ("And yet thou art my flesh, my blood, my daughter") and an invasive foreign body ("Or rather a disease that's in my flesh"). Like "the thing so monstrous, dismantling so many folds of favour," the daughter-as-disease carries the incursive topology of the Thing, pocking and puckering the skin of representation imagined to separate inside and outside into the "embossed," raised, welts of an inflamed rim. This imagery of pierced, creased, or broken skin is distributed throughout the visual emblematics of the play, from the cruel punctuality of Gloucester's blinding to Edgar's theatrical embodiment of the Bedlam beggars who "Strike in their numb'd and mortified bare arms / Pins, wooden pricks, nails, sprigs of rosemary; / And with this horrible object, ... Enforce their charity" (II.iii.15–20).[13] The phrase "horrible object" activates the etymology of "horrible" in *horridus,* "rough, shaggy, bristly" in conjunction with the sense of "object" as spectacle. Edgar's "horrible object" presents a Medusan fetish-

_____

13. See also Lear's earlier curse against Goneril: "Let it stamp wrinkles in her brow of youth, / With cadent tears fret channels in her cheeks" (I.iv.282–3).

object of multiple pricking and self-mutilation, visually materializing Lear's "plague-sore" as the abraded surface, the suffered and suffering *opsis* of a theater of cruelty.

Lear's railing against Goneril concludes with a quavering attempt at equanimity, "I can be patient," a line that connects the play's imagery of folded, pierced, or imploded skin to one of *King Lear*'s tragic subtexts, the Book of Job.[14] The reference to patience effectively appropriates the metaphor of skin disease from the last test of Job, his affliction "with sore boils from the sole of his foot unto his crown" (Job 2:7), which finally drives him from patience to complaint. In this intertextual transaction, *King Lear* takes up Job's skin disease not simply as figure (daughters = plague sores), but, more important, as the *literalization of figure* whose radical superficiality points to the failure of interiorizing symbolization. Thus the passage shifts from the language of affiliation and communion in the incarnational symbolics of "flesh" and "blood" to their grotesque realization as the visceral, unaccommodated stuff of the invaded body. As the "horrible object" that *Lear* must call its own, not simply the thematics but the textuality of Job becomes the disease suffered or endured by Shakespeare's play.

Lear suffers, that is, Job in its partition: in the Book of Job, the violation of bodily integrity inflicted by the "sore boils" also articulates the generic break in the text, which is divided between a frame narrative of virtue rewarded, written in prose and derived from oral folklore, and the lengthy central sections, probably composed later, whose experimental lyrics situate an ethics beyond the consolations of retribution.[15] This generic division marks—or rather "pock-marks"—the encounter between the Book of Job and *Lear:* whereas the biblical prose tale enters Shakespeare's play through the *mythos* or narrative of patience, the lyric mode enters through the operation of *lexis,* that is, through metaphors which painfully disfigure the textual and intertextual surface with the verbal excess of complaint

14. On *Lear* and Job, see, for example, G. Wilson Knight, *The Wheel of Fire* 209.

15. On the textual history of Job, see Lawrence Besserman, *The Legend of Job in the Middle Ages.*

and invective. Moreover, the passage's splicing of the prose Job
of consolation literature ("I can be patient") with the lyric Job
of unmitigated complaint ("Thou art a boil, a plague sore")
recapitulates the broader intertextual dialectic between Old and
New Testaments. The prose narrative of Job operates for *Lear*
as a prefiguration of Christ's suffering that serves to reinforce
the christological current of the play, culminating in such New
Testament allusions as Cordelia's "O dear father! / It is thy
business that I go about" (IV.iv.23–24; cf. Luke 2:49). The
prose narrative, that is, slips easily into the dialectic of conversion that maps the Old Testament as the prophetic anticipation
of the New. Transformed and transcended through its Christian reworkings in the Griselda story of Boccaccio, Petrarch,
and Chaucer, the narrative of patience feeds into the strained
mythos of redemption in *King Lear*. The lyric Job, on the other
hand, functions in *Lear* to signal precisely the failure of conversion, insofar as the figure of the plague sore literalizes the
incarnational metaphors of flesh and blood into their diseased,
putrifying residue. The text of *King Lear*, we could say, has the
lyric Job "under its skin": invasive, foreign, and obdurately
unconverted rather than transformed and transformative.

What is left over from the allegorical transumption of the
Old Testament into the New is the Jew after the advent of
Christianity: the antihero, that is, of the play Freud pairs with
King Lear, The Merchant of Venice. Although Freud clearly does
not have *Lear*'s biblical textuality in mind, his unlikely juxtaposition of the two plays suggests a further reading of the *Kasten*
as a figure of failed transmission—namely, non-conversion.
Here, the scene of legacy concerns neither the riddling dowry
left by Portia's father nor the division of Lear's kingdom, but
the dialectic between Old and New Testaments and their fallout
in the historiographical embarrassment and "embossment"—
the tumid protuberance of the real that swells and distorts the
texture of the symbolic order—represented by the unconverted
Jew. Slavoj Zizek analyzes the Jew as a species of the real in
the cultural psychosis of anti-Semitism: the Jew functions as
"an external element, a foreign body introducing corruption
into the sound social fabric. . . . In other words, what is excluded

from the Symbolic (from the frame of the corporatist socio-symbolic order) returns in the Real as a paranoid construction of the 'Jew' " (*The Sublime Object of Ideology* 126, 127). A phrase from and about the New Testament, "New wine in old skins" (Matthew 10:17)—a line to which we will return in the next chapter—sums up the logic of this testamentary textuality. Whereas Christ's parable argues the need to renovate the forms of the old religion to fit the new message (new skins for new wine), the carbuncled skins of Job and Lear, grafted onto the trials of Shylock through the structural movement of Freud's essay, literalize the "old skins," punctured and patched, left over by the divine distillery that constitutes "my father's business."

Generically, the "old skins" of the Old Testament left over by epochal conversion point to the lexical and optical literalizations that abrade the christological *ethos* and classical *mythos* of *King Lear*. The effect of such a reading is to accommodate the traditional christological interpretations of the play without capitulating to them, by locating the play's Christian current as a compelling yet fundamentally imaginary impulse that must be coordinated with the real and symbolic fields of the play's generic and intertextual functioning. This point reinforces our earlier structural and historical mapping of a psychoanalytic criticism that neither embraces nor disavows character analysis, but rather accounts for it as a necessary error in reading that must be theoretically situated in the registers of imaginary, symbolic, and real.[16] Finally, this reading of *Lear,* Job, and "The Theme of the Three Caskets" construes the *Kasten* motif as a feminine topology of infolded surfaces, each spun within and around the others. At stake in this mode of generic analysis is not a taxonomy of cultural and literary forms but a "taxidermy" of intertextual teguments that project the stretching, stuffing, and puncturing of representation by the pressure of the real.

16. On prosopopoeia, which includes the attribution of reality to a character, as the fundamentally ethical problematic of reading, see J. Hillis Miller, *The Ethics of Reading* and *Versions of Pygmalion*.

CHAPTER SIX

The Lacanian Thing

"Miel, j'essaie de vous apporter mon miel—le miel de ma re-
flexion" [I am trying to bring you my honey—the honey of my
reflection]. So Lacan begins "Introduction de la Chose" (*Seminar
VII* 27). The question of Lacan's "honey," the essence of his
teaching distilled over time, leads Lacan immediately to the
problem of containers, of how to present and represent the
substance of a discourse that, like honey, is always either too
hard (resistant, gnomic, dense) or too fluid (rapid, associative,
and rather messy): "Hence the problem of jars. The honey jar
recalls the mustard jar which I once used as an example" (27).
Lacan rewrites the figure once again a few pages later in order
to describe the relevance of Aristotelian categories—another
kind of container—to psychoanalysis: "These schemas can be
recomposed and transposed in such a way that we will not be
putting our new honey in the same old skins" (32). Lacan is
moving figuratively between figures of figurality: the image
begins as an intratextual link—from the mustard jar of an
earlier paper to the honey pot of this seminar—and then becomes, through scriptural allusion, both a figure and an example of intertextuality per se. Christ's allegory of allegory
(Matthew 9:17) presents a model of dialectical transformation:
the textual container (pot, skins, Old Testament, philosophy,
Freud) holds new meanings (honey, wine, New Testament, psychoanalysis, Lacan), meanings that in turn transform the con-

tours of the original container or figure itself, thus putting new wine in renewed skins.

Inhabiting Lacan's apparent appropriation of the Christian dialectic, however, is an act and model of nondialectical non-transformation: old wine in new bottles, the same old thing presented in newfangled forms. Yet for Lacan the same old "thing" implies not the rehashing of a tired truism (repetition without transformation), but rather a Thing that emerges as such only through the displacements of its repeated figurations. The Thing is represented in the relation between "wine" and "skin"; that is, it appears in and as the structurality of containment that logically precedes both container and contained.

In Lacan's *Seminar VII* on the ethics of psychoanalysis, the Thing emerges in and as an act of refinding. In designating an object always only refound as lost, the Thing [*das Ding*] is also theorized as such in an inter- and intratextual sequence of returns. Our phrase, "the Lacanian Thing," alludes to Lacan's 1955 essay "La chose freudienne" in order to reread that essay's initial enunciation of the Thing in terms of the symbolic order from the position of Lacan's later elaboration, in *Seminar VII*, of *das Ding* as real. Furthermore, the expression "the Lacanian Thing" writes "Lacan" for "Freud," an intertextual reinscription of the Thing's intratextual path within Lacan's oeuvre. Thus, both in its theoretical formulation and in its discursive dynamics, the Thing names that which is necessarily articulated after the fact as the irreducible cause, *causa*, or *chose* of symbolic ordering and interpretation. Freud's essay "The Theme of the Three Caskets" operates as the covert model, object, and pivot of this dynamic: in taking a Shakespearean thing, the casket, to allegorize the declension of the object as feminine, Freud's essay is itself taken (or boxed) up in Lacan's seventh seminar as a textual residue, a thingly motif.

To trace the textual vicissitudes of the Thing by attending to the specific temporality of Lacan's work as it unfolds around a notion of the real is not to "reify" Lacan's thought into a developmental chronology. Although Lacan's teaching is constellated by a shift in emphasis from the symbolic order of Oedipal law and lack to the real trauma of radical loss and *jouissance,* that trauma will have been there—theoretically and textually—as the cause of symbolic and imaginary representation. The retroactive causality of "the Lacanian Thing" both diachronically distinguishes and synchronically cross-references Freud and Lacan, the earlier years of the *Seminar* and the later, as well as their Shakespearean emblems, *Hamlet* and *Lear.*

Refindings

Within Lacan's ongoing retheorization of the object, the notion of the Thing coalesces as the negative intersection of psychoanalysis, philosophy, and literature by collecting *topoi* and tendencies from Freud and Heidegger around the Shakespearean motif of the casket.[1] In *Seminar VII,* Lacan introduces *das Ding* as "cette realité muette," this mute reality:

> *Das Ding* is originally what I will call the outside-of-the-signified [*le hors-signifié*]. It is in terms of this *hors-signifié* and of a relation to it characterized by pathos, that the subject maintains its distance, and constitutes itself in a mode of relation, or primal affect, prior to all repression...something comes to be organized at that same place which is at once its opposite, its flipside [*l'envers*], and yet identical to it, and which, in the end, substitutes for this mute reality which is *das Ding*—namely, the reality which commands and orders.
>
> (67–68)

As the *hors-signifié* or "outside-of-the-signified"—both outside or beyond signification and the first outside to be signified—*das Ding* is the "mute reality" of the real, which is replaced by the speaking reality of the symbolic. Lacan's phrase "this mute reality"—associated soon after with Harpo, the silent Marx

1. On the Lacanian theory of the Thing, see Zizek, *The Sublime Object of Ideology;* Nathalie Charraud, "Topologie de *das Ding*": and Mark Taylor, "The Reel Thing," in *Altarity* 83–96. On the confluence of Heidegger and tragedy, see Jahan Ramazani, "Heidegger and the Theory of Tragedy."

Brother (69)—evokes the laconic third sister in the *Lear* of
Freud's three caskets, an affinity reiterated in Lacan's discussion of *Antigone* and *Lear* later in the same seminar.

Following Freud, Lacan defines the Thing as "l'objet *wied-
ergefundene*, retrouvé," the object constituted as lost in the act
of refinding it: "Such is for Freud the fundamental definition
of the object in its directive function, whose paradoxical nature
I have already indicated, because we are never told that this
object has been really lost. The object is by its very nature a
refound object. Its having been lost is a consequence of this—
but after the fact [*aprés coup*]. And thus, it is refound without
our knowing in any other way than through its refindings that
it had been lost" (143). The object in its "directive function"—
the object, that is, as cause—is a lost object, but not, Lacan
insists, "really" lost; rather, it is constituted, and constituted-
as-lost, in the narrative of refinding that underlies every motivated gesture, every act of desire.

Although the most explicit account of *das Ding* occurs in
Seminar VII, throughout Lacan's work the problematic of a
primitive object, a feminine Other at the margins of the phallic
economy, appears—or rather *reappears as disappearance* in the
backward glance of the critic. In *Seminar II* Lacan rereads the
specimen dream of psychoanalysis, Freud's dream of Irma's
injection, through the categories of the imaginary, symbolic,
and real. For Lacan, symbolic reading, more than a method
external to the dream text, also constitutes its message and
its desire: "What gives this dream its veritable unconscious
value, whatever its primordial and infantile echoes, is the quest
for the word [*la recherche du mot*] . . . there is no other word of
the dream than the very nature of the symbolic" (*Seminar II* E
159–60, F 191). Yet the "primordial and infantile echoes" min-
imized by this accentuation of the symbolic nonetheless rever-
berate in Lacan's interpretation of Freud's dream—a textual
echo chamber set into play by "The Theme of the Three
Caskets":

> The first time around, accompanying Irma's *ego* we've found
> three feminine characters. Freud remarks that there is such a

profusion of intercalations at this point that in the end things are knotted together [*les choses se nouent*] and one ends up confronted with some unknown mystery [*on ne sait quel mystère*].

When we analyse this text, we must take into account the text in its entirety, including the notes. This is when Freud indicates that point in the associations where the dream is connected up to the unknown [*l'inconnu*], which he calls its navel.

We've arrived at whatever it is that lies behind the mystic trio. I say *mystic* because we now know its meaning. The three women, the three sisters, the three caskets, Freud has since shown us its meaning. The last term is death, as simple as that.

(*Seminar II* E 157, F 188–89)

According to Lacan, the meaning of dreams, which is revealed in Freud's specimen dream, is precisely that dreams mean symbolically—that is, through and as a process of concealment in which what is hidden is always another signifier.[2] Just as dreams signify through wishful substitution, so the relation between *The Interpretation of Dreams* and "The Theme of the Three Caskets" is in Lacan's analysis itself a system of symbolic equations: "The three women, the three sisters, the three caskets, Freud has since shown us its meaning." Paradoxically, however, the meaning of the third casket (death) is precisely the excess of meaning, the dream's "navel," the knot where symbolic saturation points to the limits of interpretation in the real, the "unknown" which hermeneutics necessarily leaves over.[3]

Thus, whereas here Lacan appears to present death as the meaning of the third woman and the third casket ("The last term is death, as simple as that"), further on in *Seminar II* Lacan casts both death and femininity as the limit of meaning, at once

2. Cf. Samuel Weber on Freud's insistence that the meaning of dreams is the *dream work*, rather than the dream's latent thought (*The Legend of Freud* 65–67).

3. In *Seminar XI*, Lacan defines interpretation and its limits in terms of a primal signifier: "Interpretation is a signification that is not just any signification. . . . What is essential is that [the subject] should see, beyond this signification, to what signifier—to what irreducible, traumatic, non-meaning—he is, as a subject, subjected" (E 250–51, F 226). On the interpretive implications of the dream's navel, see Weber, *The Legend of Freud* 75–82.

(primal) cause and (side) effect of the series of symbolic equivalents:

> The first [part of the dream] leads to the apparition of the terrifying anxiety-provoking image, to this real Medusa's head, to the revelation of this something [*ce quelque chose*] which properly speaking is unnameable, the back of this throat, the complex, unlocatable form, which also makes it into the primitive object *par excellence*, the abyss of the feminine organ from which all life emerges, this gulf of the mouth, in which everything is swallowed up, and no less the image of death in which everything comes to its end. . . . Hence there's an anxiety-provoking apparition of an image which summarises what we can call the revelation of that which is least penetrable in the real, of the real lacking any possible mediation, of the ultimate real, of the essential object which isn't an object any longer, but this something faced with which all words cease and all categories fail, the object of anxiety *par excellence* [*l'objet essentiel qui n'est plus un objet, mais ce quelque chose devant quoi tous les mots s'arrêtent et toutes les catégories échouent, l'objet d'angoisse par excellence*].
>
> (E 164, F 196)

In the horrific vision of Irma's throat, the oral and genital cavities—embodiments of the first and second caskets—converge and decompose in death, the third casket, "the abyss of the feminine organ from which all life emerges, this gulf of the mouth, in which everything is swallowed up, and no less the image of death in which everything comes to its end." In the very process of producing meaning through combining or condensing a series of meanings, the throat becomes the site of meaning's collapse. As a gorge rather than an organ, the throat indicates the "unnameable," the "unlocatable," "the real lacking any possible mediation." Lacan identifies this site with "the primitive object *par excellence*," the "essential object which isn't an object any longer, but this something [*ce quelque chose*] faced with which all words cease." As symbolic nexus—the overdetermination of meanings—Irma's throat is the object of interpretation; as the collapse of the symbolic, Irma's throat functions as the "something" or *Thing* in excess of interpretation, meaning's termination.

In this passage, Lacan aligns "ce quelque chose" with the Medusa's head and the "object of phobia," references that theoretically and allusively situate the specter of Irma's throat in the same (dis)continuum between object and thing as the Freudian fetish. In an essay written with Wladimir Granoff around the same time as the second seminar, "Fetishism: The Symbolic, the Imaginary, and the Real," Lacan positions fetishism between imaginary anxiety and symbolic guilt:

> Anxiety, as we know, is always connected with a loss—i.e., a transformation of the ego—with a two-sided relation on the point of fading away to be superseded by something else, something which the patient cannot face without vertigo. This is the realm and the nature of anxiety.
>
> As soon as a third person is introduced into the narcissistic relationship, there emerges the possibility of real mediation, through the intermediary, of the transcendent personage, that is to say, of someone through whom one's desire and its accomplishment can be symbolically realized. At this moment, another register appears, that of law—in other words, of guilt.
>
> (273)

As in *Seminar II*, Lacan's emphasis at this point is on the ethical and theoretical transumption of the imaginary by the symbolic; also as in *Seminar II*, however, this symbolic imperative is already pierced by the simultaneous yet necessarily subordinated claim of the real as it is manifested in the imaginary. Indicative of this moment in Lacan's thought, the real is not implied in the references to "real mediation" and the "symbolically realized," since the real is precisely that which "lack[s] any possible mediation" (*Seminar II* E 164, F 196). Instead, the real, appearing as the vanishing point in the ego's imaginary hall of mirrors, begins to emerge as a theory in anxiety's connection with loss and with the "something" that cannot be faced without vertigo.

Lacan's account of symbolic mediation and its difference from loss resembles Freud's reading of *Hamlet* in his 1927 essay "Dostoevsky and Parricide," written in the same year as his article "Fetishism." In *Hamlet*, Freud writes, "We see the hero's

Oedipus complex, as it were, in a reflected light, by learning the effect upon him of the other's crime. . . . We know that it is his sense of guilt that is paralysing him. . . . There are signs that the hero feels this guilt as a superindividual one. He despises others no less than himself: 'Use every man after his desert, and who should 'scape whipping?' " (*SE* 21:188–89; *SA* 10:281–82). In the two passages, both Freud and Lacan emphasize the mediation of a third party in the enactment of guilty desire—Lacan's formulation "someone through whom one's desire and its accomplishment can be symbolically realized" confirms Freud's figure, "We see the Oedipus complex, as it were, in a reflected light." In both cases, the triangulation of guilt leads to its transcendentalization: Lacan's "transcendent personage" onto whom guilt is displaced echoes Freud's "guilt [felt] as a superindividual one." Finally, in each passage, this dialectical transumption masks the nondialectical remainder of one kind of negativity (pre-Oedipal loss) within another that appropriates it (castration). In Lacan, the nonidentity of the "something which the patient cannot face without vertigo" and the "third person introduced into the narcissistic relationship" registers the disparity between *loss,* the imaginary experience of the real, and *lack,* the symbolic recuperation of that loss. In Freud, "paralysis" afflicts the Oedipal Hamlet much as the Medusa's head arrests its viewer, melancholically petrifying and confounding subject and object in the very moment of their dialectical differentiation.

If the psychoanalytic *Hamlet* unfolds on the reflected stage of symbolization, *Lear* looks into the abyss of anxiety unregulated by symbolic mediation, the abyss that connects the vertigo of Dover cliffs to the horrific gorge of Irma's throat via Lacan's allusion in *Seminar II* to "The Theme of the Three Caskets"— a motif which, apposed to Lacan and Granoff's essay on fetishism, *realizes* the real already nascent within it. The term that affiliates the two plays across the defile formed by anxiety and guilt is *mourning;* thus in 1927 Freud re-cites his earlier citation in "Mourning and Melancholia" of *Hamlet*'s misanthropic line ("Use every man after his desert, and who should 'scape whipping?"). On the one hand, mourning is associated with loss at

the borders of the imaginary and the real ("Anxiety . . . is always
connected with a loss"), and on the other hand, with the imperfect symbolization of loss as guilt. As such, mourning marks
the passage of maternal negativity through fetishistic disavowal
into the father's law. The work of mourning, we could say, is
always fetishistic insofar as it signals the faulty masking of the
thing by the object.[4]

In *Seminar II*, Lacan links the three caskets to Freud's image
of the dream's "navel," a figure that describes the knotting of
meaning in and around a transitional thing, not a part object
but a *post partum* object, a "parting object," which remembers
loss as maternal. In *Seminar XI: The Four Fundamental Concepts
of Psychoanalysis,* Lacan returns to the figure of the navel, aligning it with "the gap so characteristic of cause" (E 22–23, F 25–
26). In the sudden rupture in speech or understanding constituted by parapraxis, the unconscious is momentarily discovered or rather *re*-discovered as the encounter with the real:[5]

> Now, as soon as it is presented, this finding [*trouvaille*] becomes
> a refinding [*retrouvaille*] and, furthermore, it is always ready to
> steal away again, thus establishing the dimension of loss.
>
> To resort to a metaphor, drawn from mythology, we have,
> in Eurydice twice lost, the most potent image we can find of the
> relation between Orpheus the analyst and the unconscious.
>
> (E 25, F 27; translation altered)

In Lacan's association of cause with loss, the unconscious is cast
as feminine and (twice) dead in a tragic narrative of male
mourning that rediscovers loss retroactively. More than a lost

4. The sequence thing-fetish-object is paralleled by the negative operations of *Verwerfung* (foreclosure), *Verleugnung* (disavowal), and *Verdrängung*
(repression). On the connections between mourning, anxiety, and pre-Oedipal
loss, see Freud, *Inhibitions, Symptoms, Anxiety*, section 8 and addendum C, *SE*
20; and Lacan, "Seminar X," 3 July 1963, 2:389–400.

5. Lacan further associates cause with *tuché* (chance), which he translates
as the encounter with the real, and distinguishes both from the dominance by
the pleasure principle and from repetition, which characterizes the unconscious: "The real is beyond the *automaton*, the return, the coming back, the
insistence of the signs, by which we see ourselves governed by the pleasure
principle" (*Seminar XI* E 53–54, F 53–54).

object, Eurydice represents here "the dimension of loss" per se: as Lacan goes on to argue, loss does not occur "against the background of a totality" but rather designates the first "one," the "*un*" ("one") of French as it is echoed and negated by the Anglo-German "*un-*" ("non-"): "the *Un* of the *Unbewußte* [unconscious]" (E 25–26; F 28). The loss in question, that is, involves not the loss of something but loss as some Thing. Loss, logically prior both to the experience of objects as positive totalities and to acts of symbolic substitution, is chronologically secondary, since it can be signified as such only in the double movement of "Eurydice twice lost."

The double loss of Eurydice allegorizes the shifting articulation of the object in Lacan's work: whereas she initially appears as an imaginary object of desire in the symbolic economy of male *poesis*, Eurydice "twice-lost" figures the *objet a* as real, Lacan's definition of the object as cause of desire in *Seminar XI*. In the backward glance of Orpheus, Eurydice comes to represent the materialization of speculative vision as thing-like *gaze*, the opaque residuum that smears the theoretical dream of visual mastery and possession from within. Lacan's allusion to Eurydice allegorizes the psychic and theoretical emergence of the *objet a* in the logic of refinding: initially defined as imaginary, the object can only be conceived as real from the vantage point of a secondary moment of theorization. This rhythm of refinding characterizes not only Lacan's account of analytic experience and its implications in and for the constitution of the subject, but also the temporal structure of his own *oeuvre*, in which the fragment of the real—*ce quelque chose* (*Seminar II*), *la Chose* (*Seminar VII*), or *causa* (*Seminar XI*)—is always found later, psychically, theoretically, and intertextually.

From *La Chose Freudienne* to *das Ding—Encore*

The most telling case of this refinding occurs in the passage between Lacan's essay "La chose freudienne," first delivered in 1955, the conceptualization of *das Ding* as maternal in *Seminar VII* four years later, and the transvaluation of the Thing as

feminine in *Seminar XX*. In "La chose freudienne," Lacan no-
toriously stages an allegory in which Truth speaks; in Lacan's
studied locution, "ça parle" (it speaks) (*Écrits* E 125, F 413). In
Lacan's prosopopoeia, the truth that speaks is not the voice of
imaginary meaning, as content or *énoncé*, but rather the word
as signifier, as the fact and agency of symbolic utterance, or
énonciation. *La chose freudienne*, associated with the unconscious,
the *ça*, at this point falls under the rule of the symbolic. In "La
chose freudienne," the "it" that speaks is not the "real" Thing
as cause of signification, but is rather, in Lacan's phrase, "de-
pendent on the signifier, namely on the word" (E 132, F 421).
In *Seminar VII*, however, Lacan reconceives the Thing as a
fragment of the real, the first exterior that, by instantiating the
kernel of the subject, persists as the residue of the subject's
relation to reality:

> The *Ding* as *Fremde*, foreign and even hostile on occasion, in any
> case as the first outside, is that around which all the movement
> of the subject is oriented.... By nature the object is lost as such.
> It will never be refound [*retrouvé*]. Something is there until some-
> thing better, or something worse comes along, but is there only
> in awaiting.... [I]t's this object, *das Ding*, as the absolute Other
> of the subject, that it is a question of refinding. One refinds it
> at best as regret.
>
> (65)

At once beyond the pleasure principle and prior to signification, the Thing of *Seminar VII* is the "excluded interior" of the
subject, a bit of the real whose internalization does not digest
its alterity. Rather than an object of or in desire, the Thing
anticipates the object as cause of desire, which, in Heidegger's
German, *be-ding-t*—conditions or "things"—the subject in the
terminal melancholia of "regret."

The textual phenomenology of *das Ding* across Lacan's discourse resists the binarisms of both "early versus late" and
"word versus thing." In *Seminar VII*, *das Ding* indicates not the
"real thing" in any simple opposition to the symbolic word, but
rather the materiality of the signifier at the painful intersection

of the symbolic and the real: the Thing is "ce qui, du réel primordial . . . pâtit du signifiant" ["that part of the primordial real which suffers the signifier"] (142). This formulation in turn both derives from and rewrites the scene of enunciation in "La chose freudienne," in which Lacan declares that "it speaks [*ça parle*], and, no doubt, where it is least expected, namely, where it endures [*là où ça souffre*]" (E 125, F 413; translation altered). From the vantage of *Seminar VII*, the "ça parle" of Lacan's earlier essay—frequently taken as the most distilled Lacanian apothegm defining the unconscious as a symbolic formation— is already shot through with the irreducible affect of the real.

Moreover, both formulations repeat with a twist Lacan's still earlier Hegelian statement in the "Rome Discourse" from 1953: "The symbol manifests itself first of all as the murder of the thing" (*Écrits* E 104, F 319).[6] In moving from *symbol* to *signifier* and from the thing *murdered* by language to the Thing that *suffers* language, Lacan shifts emphasis from the symbolic register to the conjunction of the symbolic and the real. "Suffering" rather than "murdered," the Thing now survives the signifier as its remnant and material body, as that part of the real which "bears" the signifier and supports the symbolic order.[7] Although the shift from murdered thing to suffering Thing appears to mark a certain progress from symbol to signifier, Lacan's return to *la chose* in *Seminar XX* brings with it a renovated notion of the signifier turned into a "sign": "You can understand this 'sign' however you like, even in the sense of 'thing' in English, *la chose*. The signifier is a sign of a subject" (130). By "sign" Lacan means the signifier reduced to a thing by its isolation from the network of signifiers; falling out of the symbolic order of meaning, the "sign-thing" is the talismanic

6. On this statement and its permutations in Lacan, see Jacques-Alain Miller, "La psychose dans le texte de Lacan" 139, and Zizek, *The Sublime Object of Ideology* 131.

7. The shift from the murdered thing to the suffering Thing implicitly genders it as well: if the paradigmatic murder in psychoanalysis is of the primal father, the suffering Thing—both she who suffers, is patient, bears, and she who causes suffering, is unbearable and overbearing—is the mother.

relic of the real that precipitates the subject around the residue of signification.

Three distinct moments trace a loop of return in Lacan's thinking about the sign. For the Hegelian Lacan, symbol and thing are set against each other in the dramatic scenario of murder. This approach is in turn rejected by the structuralist Lacan, who emphasizes the production of objects in language under the rule of the signifier. Finally, in *Encore* Lacan returns again to the "primitiveness" of the pre-Saussurian conception of the sign as magical name in order to real-ize the density of the signifier bound up in it. Just as *das Ding*, "lost as such," is only ever refound by the subject, so, in the temporality of Lacan's work, the concept of the Thing must not only be distinguished from the symbolic "chose freudienne," but in turn refound within it, in a movement of return, *encore*, that constitutes the object in Lacan's work in and as a series of textual displacements and theoretical reversions.[8]

Running through the Lacanian discourse of the Thing is the association of femininity and death emblematized by the Freudian *Kasten* motif. In "La chose freudienne," the myth of Diana and Acteon, like the narrative of Orpheus and Eurydice, casts Freud in the role of the transgressive voyeur in search of truth. The analytic chase "leads him on so far that he cannot stop until he reaches the grottoes in which the chthonian Diana in the damp shade, which makes them appear as the emblematic seat of truth, offers to his thirst, with the smooth surface of death, the quasi-mystical limit of the most rational discourse in the world, so that we might recognize the place in which the symbol is substituted for death in order to take possession of the first swelling of life" (*Écrits* E 124, F 412).

8. In a 1966 footnote to his 1958 essay, "Remarque sur la rapport de Daniel Lagache," Lacan suggests that his use of the term "la Chose" there antedates his later concept of *das Ding*, "which wasn't brought out until my seminar in 1959–1960" (*Écrits* F 656). By extension, Lacan would imply here that *la chose freudienne* (1955–56) differs from *das Ding*. In *Seminar VII*, however, Lacan insists on the continuity between *la chose freudienne* and *das Ding* (157–58).

Like Eurydice, Diana appears here as a feminine allegory of the unconscious as punctual truth, an allegory distributed, we could say, among the registers of the three caskets: the "symbol" of the Oedipal middle casket is substituted for "death," the chthonian truth of the third casket, in order to possess through representation and exchange "the first swelling of life," the "grotto" of the maternal first casket. Diana, a figure of "la chose freudienne" as the symbolic truth that arises through the disjunction of utterance and statement, becomes, in her affiliation with the three caskets, a prefiguration of *das Ding* in its alliance with the real.

The gendered personification of *das Ding* in "La chose freudienne" shifts in *Seminar VII* from a rhetorical figure of the feminine to an account of the maternal object. Whereas the exchange of feminine objects is the business of the symbolic order, the feminine Thing points to the impossible pleasure which renders satisfaction unsatisfactory and gives exchange its monotonous tone. Lacan, aligning *das Ding* with the Kleinian mother under the rubric of "la chose maternelle" (82), defines the maternal thing as the impossible goal and residue of the Oedipal order:

> That which we find in the law of incest is situated as such at the level of the unconscious relation with *das Ding*, the Thing. Desire for the mother can never be satisfied because it is the end, the termination, the abolition of the entire world of demand, which is what structures man's unconscious most profoundly. It is precisely insofar as the function of the pleasure principle is to make man continually seek for [*cherche*] what he must refind [*retrouver*], but can never attain, that we encounter what is essential, the mainspring, the relation known as the law of incest prohibition.
>
> (*Seminar VII* 83)

Lacan does not oppose "la chose maternelle" to the Oedipal object, but rather presents it as its painful core: the constitutive loss that defines desire as impossible, and leads to the inherently prohibited status of the feminine object at the center of moral law. Hence Lacan writes that man seeks (*cherche*) what he should refind (*retrouver*), but which he will not attain, since what is sought—the mother as object of desire—is not the same as what he always refinds, refinds as lost, in that search, the mother as *Ding,* her sullied flesh "as dead as earth."[9]

In *Seminar XX: Encore,* Lacan defines femininity not only in relation to *das Ding* as primordial loss, but also in terms of "an Other *jouissance*" which exceeds that of the phallus. Toward the end of *Encore,* Lacan returns to woman as the juncture of "la chose freudienne," the allegory of symbolic truth, and *das Ding,* the indicator of the real: "If you re-read somewhere this thing I wrote called 'The Freudian Thing,' take note of this: there is only one way of writing Woman [la *femme*] without having to cross the word out [*barrer le* la], and that is at the level where woman is truth. That is why one can only half-speak [*mi-dire*] about woman" (94). Lacan refers here to "La chose freudienne" as the essay in which the truth of the unconscious, manifested in parapraxis, had been given a feminine voice. The truth that the unconscious half-speaks is both structurally allegorical—speaking an other, displaced meaning—and allegorized as feminine.[10] Here, however, the feminine prosopopoeia of the unconscious in "La chose freudienne" is rewritten in terms of *Encore*'s account of Woman as *pas-tout*—not wholly under the law of phallic *jouissance.* Whereas in the earlier essay, truth was represented as feminine in the symbolic necessity of half-speaking, in *Encore,* woman is represented as truth, but now in relation to the real as a logical impossibility that can only be written. Here Lacan suggests that the one way to write "the woman" without placing the definite article under erasure is to reread the earlier essay, in which the truth of *La*

9. This is one of Lacan's many reworkings of Picasso's version of the biblical phrase ("Seek and ye shall find"): "I do not seek, I find." Lacan uses the dictum to emphasize the role of refinding, *retrouver,* in the temporality of understanding. Cf. *Seminar XI: "You would not seek me if you had not already found me.* The *already found* is already behind, but stricken by something [*quelque chose*] like oblivion" (E 7, F 12).

10. Joel Fineman has shown that Lacan's definition of the unconscious as "the discourse of the Other" is a "direct translation of the etymology of allegory" (literally, "to speak other") ("The Structure of Allegorical Desire" 46). For the concept of truth in Lacan, see especially his essay "La science et la vérité" in *Écrits,* translated by Bruce Fink.

chose was allegorized as feminine, through *Seminar VII*, in which
the feminine was bound up with the traumatic real of *la Chose*.
The difference between the thing as Feminine and the feminine
as Thing hinges on the difference between the truth of the
slippages of speech ("on ne peut qu'en mi-dire") and a truth
that inheres in the resistant materiality of writing ("pouvoir
écrire *la* femme"). The first is aligned with the symbolization
of the imaginary, the analytic imperative of the earlier Lacan;
the second is aligned with the real-ization of the symbolic, Lacan's redirection of analytic treatment around the *objet a*.[11] For
das Ding in its later incarnation as *objet a* indicates the matter
of the signifier, the writing that does not reflect but *supports* the
"mute reality" of the real.

Thus the passage urges that we reread Lacan's earliest voicing of the Thing *as writing*, a textualization of the Thing that
radically inflects its femininity as Real. As such, the passage manifests the titular movement of *Encore* as a text of return, above
all the return to and of *Seminar VII*, where *das Ding* is articulated
as the point of (no) return. Both intertextually and theoretically, *das Ding* represents not the symbolic scene of the return
of the repressed, but the resistant obstacle of the real, at once
wall and kernel, around and against which the repetitions of
the signifying chain circulate.[12]

From Hegel to Heidegger in Lacan

In the major Freudian pre-texts for the Lacanian Thing,
"The Project for a Scientific Psychology" (1895) and "Negation"

11. Thus whereas the earlier Lacan places the *Autre* between the analyst
and analysand as the goal of their discourse, the later Lacan situates the analyst
in the place of the *objet a*, the place the subject should in turn assume in what
Lacan calls in his late seminars "traversing the fantasy."

12. *Encore* (*Seminar XX*) begins with Lacan's statement that he is returning
to *The Ethics of Psychoanalysis* (*Seminar VII*): "As it turned out, I never published
The Ethics of Psychoanalysis.... That is no doubt why after all this I am still
[*encore*] here, and you are here as well. I can *still* [*encore*] never get over it"
(*Seminar XX* 9; emphasis Lacan's). See also *Seminar XX* 91, where Lacan associates "la chose freudienne" with *das Ding* of *Seminar VII*.

(1925), Freud locates *das Ding* at the genesis of a rudimentary grammar. In the "Project" Freud writes, "The perceptual complex, if it is compared with other perceptual complexes, can be dissected into a component portion, neurone *a*, which on the whole remains the same, and a second component portion, neurone *b*, which for the most part varies. . . . [Language] will call neurone *a* the *thing* and neurone *b* its activity or attribute" (*SE* 1:328). The passage describes a pre-rhetorical, purely grammatical apposition of noun (the thing) and verb (its attributes), which are differentiated by the relation of stasis and change. At the same time, the difference between thing and attribute establishes the circulation of rhetoric—the attribution or signification of the thing—around the pure grammar of the noun qua deictic pronoun, a shifter without specific content.

In "Negation" Freud returns to this scene of elementary grammar in his discussion of the nascent ego's first judgments of attribution: "The attribute to be decided about may originally have been good or bad, useful or harmful. Expressed in the language of the oldest—the oral—instinctual impulses, the judgement is: 'I should like to eat this', or 'I should like to spit this out'; and, put more generally: 'I should like to take this into myself and to keep that out [*Das will ich in mich einführen und das aus mir ausschließen*]" (*SE* 19:236–37; *SA* 3:374). Freud's account of judgments of attribution once again displays the originary constitution of rhetoric and grammar in relation to the unrepresentable trauma of *das Ding*. On the one hand, the binary oppositions of good/bad and useful/harmful establish the diacritical play of signifiers that appear to qualify the object, but in fact only substitute for each other in the displacements of the signifying chain. On the other hand, Freud's reduction of attribution to the pure pronominal form of "this" and "that" (*das* and *das*) suggests the grammatical precondition of this rhetorical exfoliation, in which the Thing is pointed at rather than troped. In Lacan's gloss of Freud's essay, "There are no good and bad objects, there is only good and bad, and besides that, there is the Thing. Good and bad already enter into the order of *Vorstellung* [representation] as indices of that which orients the position of the subject" (*Seminar VII* 78). Lacan emphasizes not "good and bad *objects*" (the order of signifieds), but rather the diacritical difference between "good" and "bad," a distinction between signifiers, which "already enter into the order of representation." Moreover, he distinguishes this binary order of signification from the Thing, whose absolute alterity is kept at bay precisely by the network of rhetorical displacements. The Thing is indexically registered rather than rhetorically troped by the signifiers whose movement it constellates; hence good and bad are "indices" of "that which orients the position of the subject," namely the Thing.

After Freud—but also, as we shall see, after Hegel and Heidegger—the Lacanian Thing, situated at the limits of tropology, is the cause of both grammar and rhetoric. The Thing deictically *designates* rather than rhetorically *signifies* the real, and is itself indicated rather than troped in the network of language that preserves the Thing at a distance. The rhetorical dimension of language produces figures that displace each other in the production of representations. Deixis, indicational rather than representational, is the grammatical function by which language points to rather than substitutes for other signifiers or objects through pronouns such as "I" and "you" and adverbs such as "now" and "then," "here" and "there," *fort* and *da*. The word "thing," kernel of the indefinite pronouns "anything," "something," and "everything" as well as the noun "nothing," is often used as a deictic. Since the shifter has no content in itself, but merely indicates itself as shifter, any specificity of reference depends on its context.

In *The Phenomenology of Spirit*, Hegel argues that the apparent particularity of every act of deictic pointing is both supported and negated by the universalizing structure of language. Thus Hegel writes, "When I say: 'a single thing', I am really saying what it is from a wholly universal point of view, for everything is a single thing; and likewise 'this thing' is anything you like" (66).[13] In his reading of this section of the *Phenomenology*, Paul

13. Hegel writes, "The pointing-out shows itself to be not an immediate knowing [of a point], but a movement from the Here that is *meant* through

de Man shows how consciousness and language are united for
Hegel in the functioning of deixis: consciousness "determines
by showing ... or pointing ... that is to say in a manner that
implies the generality of the phenomenon as cognition (which
makes the pointing possible) in the loss of the immediacy and
the particularity of sensory perception (which makes the pointing necessary): consciousness is linguistic because it is deictic"
(*The Resistance to Theory* 42). According to Hegel, the specificity
of perception is drained off in the universality of language,
which enables cognition. Hegel locates the mutual exclusivity
of perception and consciousness in the disjunction of statement
and utterance: "Of course, we do not *envisage* the universal
This or Being in general, but we *utter* the universal; in other
words, we do not strictly say what in this sense-certainty we
mean to say" (60). Although deictic pointing is meant to isolate
a specific thing, the utterance of the "this," by implicitly negating all other *this*'s, loses the thing in the universality of
Things.

In Lacan's essay "La chose freudienne," the symbolic structure of the unconscious, undergirded by the differential Saus-
surian sign, implicitly depends on this Hegelian dialectic of
specific and universal reference.[14] In discussing the role of the
signified in the production of meaning, Lacan writes, "The
dominant factor here is the unity of signification, which proves
never to be resolved into a pure indication of the real, but
always refers back to another signification. That is to say, the
signification is realized only on the basis of a grasp of things
[*des choses*] in their totality ... it always proves to be in excess
over the things that it leaves floating within it" (*Écrits* E 126, F
414). Lacan's "unity" of signification, of "things in their total-

many Heres into the universal Here" (64 and passim). See also de Man's discussion of deixis and subjectivity in Hegel's *Encyclopedia* (in "Sign and Symbol"
768–70); Cynthia Chase, *Decomposing Figures* 5–8 and passim; and Andrzej
Warminski, *Reading in Interpretation* 163–79.

14. Lacan's discussion of indication in "La chose Freudienne" is directly
followed by comments on Hegel's critique of the "Belle âme," suggesting the
Hegelian context for his thought here.

ity," implies Hegel's universality of cognition and its transumption of specific instances of deixis. Thus, following Hegel, Lacan writes that there is no "pure indication" of the real—no simple fact of pointing to an object of perception—but rather an act of signification that operates through its connection to all other signifiers. At this moment in Lacan's thinking, the deictic "it" of the "ça parle" indicates the dialectic of universal and specific signification that subordinates the objects of sense-certainty to the structure of language, and by extension, the images of consciousness to the symbolic formations of the unconscious.[15] Although Hegel and Lacan both emphasize language as what divides consciousness from perception, Hegel equates language and consciousness, whereas Lacan identifies the alienating function of language with the unconscious. Lacan's understanding of the unconscious at this point in his thinking, moreover, is precisely in terms of the gap between statement and utterance that according to Hegel was produced in the dialectic of sense-certainty and that will be formalized by Emile Benveniste as a function of the shifter.[16] The deictic Thing that speaks in Lacan's essay passes through the Hegelian dialectic and rearticulates it as the grammar of the unconscious that symbolically subsumes and mediates all references to the real.

In *Seminar VII*, Lacan's philosophical reference point for *la Chose* is Heidegger rather than Hegel, an inflection that brings with it a modified notion of deixis—a shift in the function of the shifter. Whereas Hegel emphasizes the assumption of the particular into the universal, Heidegger insists on the phenomenology of pointing in our relation to things *qua* things. In Heidegger's lectures of 1935–36, published as *What Is a Thing?*, the thing's "being-*this*-one" (15, emphasis added), our relation to it as *pointed* to, is how we encounter and frame it. Heidegger explicitly engages the Hegelian dialectic of sense-certainty, revising and extending it: "The 'this' is a general characteristic of the thing and belongs to its thingness. But the generality of

---

15. Cf. Kaja Silverman, *The Subject of Semiotics* 163–64.
16. See especially Emile Benveniste, "The Nature of Pronouns" and "Subjectivity in Language," in *Problem in General Linguistics*.

the 'this' demands generally always to be determined as particular" (30). Far from designating the *Ding an sich* of the Kantian noumena, which implicitly takes the Thing as a substantive or concept, deixis is the pronomial indicator of both the thingness of the thing and our human being in the world. Such thingness, however, rather than being firmly located in empirical reality, as the object of sense perception, is marked by an infinite recession or withdrawal, since thingness is precisely what is lost in attempting to describe "objectively" its characteristics and conditions. In his 1954 volume of lectures, *What Is Called Thinking?*, Heidegger posits a withdrawing real, and defines human being as that which points at its withdrawal:

> The event of withdrawal could be what is most present in all our present, and so infinitely exceed the actuality of everything actual.... As we are drawing toward what withdraws, we ourselves are pointers pointing toward it.... Something which in itself, by its essential nature, is pointing, we call a sign. As he draws toward what withdraws, man is a sign. But since this sign points toward what draws *away*, it points, not so much at what draws away as into the withdrawal. The sign stays without interpretation.
>
> (9–10)

Heidegger's pointer, at once man and sign, indicates loss itself rather than a lost object. As such, it unfolds the ontological implications of Hegel's epistemological category by presenting the faulty trajectory of reference as a constitutive dilemma of Dasein. Whereas for Hegel, the object of sense-certainty, in being pointed at, is subsumed into the alienating structure of language, Heidegger precipitates pointing from out of the significatory dialectic of subject and object. In this sense, "The sign stays without interpretation," since it is "in itself, by its essential nature" pointing, and pointing not at an object in a symbolic economy, but at the withdrawal of and as the real.

In his 1950 essay "Das Ding," Heidegger, taking the jug as the paradigmatic thing, writes that "the vessel's thingness does not lie at all in the material of which it consists, but in the void that holds" (*Poetry, Language, Thought* 169). Rather than spring-

ing forth from either a void or the clay, the jug exists as the
very articulation of inside and outside, something and nothing.
In Heidegger's expression, "das Ding bedingt": the thing
"things" or "conditions." The thing exists not as an entity or
ens, but rather in and as its primal act of division, gathering
and separating "earth and sky, divinities and mortals" (178).[17]
What connects "thinging" and "thinking" in Heidegger's
thought is the orientation of each around or toward a void or
withdrawal that sets into play representational thought while
remaining radically other to it.

Whereas the *ça* of "La chose freudienne" relies on the Hegelian account of deixis in order to conceptualize the unconscious as a symbolic structure, *das Ding* of *Seminar VII* draws
on the Heideggerian thing as a dimension of existence canceled
by the advent of a representational language, which, in seeking
to refind it, points towards its loss.[18] In *Seminar VII*, Lacan takes
the Heideggerian quadrature of differences opened up by the
jug as a scene of signification: "The vase creates a void [*le vide*],
introducing thereby the very possibility [*perspective*] of filling it
up. The empty and the full are brought by the vase into a world
which, in and of itself, knows nothing of such. The empty and
the full enter as such into the world on the basis of this constructed signifier, the vase" (145). Lacan's vase, a Gallicization
of Heidegger's jug, inaugurates the diacritical structure of signification by manifesting the opposition of full and empty.[19]
The "vide" of the vase, however, is not reducible to the binary
opposition of "vide" and "plein" that it establishes, since it re-

17. Lacan reads Heidegger's quadrature of the thing in terms of the minimum number of elements required for a signifying system (*Seminar VII* 80).
18. Mourning and deixis are essential marks of the real in Kristeva's work
on the pre-Oedipal, the semiotic, and abjection. In her essay "*Le vréel*" (translated as "The True-Real"), Kristeva discusses the function of demonstratives
in the "inscription of the real in the symbolic" during psychotic incursions into
hysterical language. For Kristeva, the deictic borders on and indicates the
presymbolic "unnameable *space of need*," pointing to the "semiotic...the site
of the archaic mother," and what she calls elsewhere the "abject."
19. See the schema of the vase and the inverted bouquet in, for example,
Seminar I, Seminar XI, and "Remarque sur le rapport de Daniel Lagache," in
Écrits F 647–84.

mains without signification, only pointing to the oppositional system to which it remains logically exterior.[20] Rather than being exhausted by the signifiers that represent it, *la Chose* is that deictic kernel "around which," *autour de quoi*, signification unfolds. The Thing as the signifier in its absolute materiality shares in the logic of what Lacan will call S_1, the primary or unary signifier, the unique signifier without signified of primal repression around which all other signifiers—designated as S_2—circulate in the unconscious. *Das Ding* describes the genesis of signification not as a mise en abyme—the infinite regress of rhetorical figuration—but as a *mise en bouteille*, the constellation of signifiers around a thing full of its emptiness, the singularity of zero.[21]

Thus Lacan goes on to insist that the equation of the Thing and the signifier is not metaphorical: "This is the occasion to put our finger on that which is fallacious in the opposition of the so-called concrete and the so-called figurative—if the vase can be full, this is insofar as it is, first, in its essence, empty. And it is in exactly the same sense that speech and discourse can be full and empty" (*Seminar VII* 145). Lacan asserts here that it is not a metaphor to speak of the signifier as a thing, since the vase's thingness—its capacity to be empty or full—is identical with its proto-signifying character, its unfolding of difference. So, too, it is not a metaphor to say that discourse can be empty or full, since emptiness and fullness are not simply "contents" or meanings, but the structure of possiblility, the *Be-ding-ung*, of containment, and hence of metaphor, as such. Finally, empty and full do not exist simply as a binary opposition, whether in things or words; in both cases logical priority is given to *emptiness*, to the void as that which is at once filled, constituted, and left over by its bifurcation into opposites.

Lacan aligns Heidegger's thingly hole with the mustard jar

20. Cf. *Seminar VII* 199–200, in which Lacan distinguishes the structure of opposition as pure *béance* from a signifying system proper.

21. Lacan also associates the Thing and the pure signifier earlier in *Seminar VII* (68). On the distinction between S_1 and S_2, see especially *Seminars XI* and *XVII*.

of his own mythology: "This is what I began to take up at a certain conference in Royaumont, when I insisted on the fact that the essence of the mustard jar, in our daily life, is that it presents itself as an empty mustard jar" (145). Later in the seminar, Lacan multiplies the mustard jar into three: "In drawing here three jars, I want to show you that you have a whole row of them, whether they be mustard or jelly jars.... Note that it is insofar as the jars are identical that they are irreducible. ... This interior, this void of which I no longer know whether I or anyone else came up with it, serves in French at least to designate the notion of the same [*même*]" (233).

By extending Heidegger's singular proto-signifier into a trio of jars, Lacan locates the origin of individuation in repetition: insofar as self-sameness is based on the similarity of (empty) interiors, the void of each jar—and each subject—is as much beyond it as part of it. The similarity of the jars is not based on the specularity of two, but on the deferral of identity in a row or chain indicated by the extension of one to three. Rather than a full-fledged symbolic network based on linguistic substitution, however, the three jars present a pre-symbolic syntax or array of identical—though not self-identical—things.

What interests Lacan in Heidegger's jug is precisely what implicates it in Freud's *Kasten:* its articulation of an emptiness. As if by further association with "The Theme of the Three Caskets," Lacan goes on to read Heidegger's jug in terms of the Judeo-Christian doctrine of creation *ex nihilo* and its classical antithesis, echoed in Lear's "Nothing will come of nothing":

> Nothing comes from nothing.
>   All of ancient philosophy is articulated around this.... Now, if you consider the vase in the perspective which I first offered, that is, as an object made to represent the existence of the void at the center of the real which is called the Thing, this void, such as it is presented in representation, is presented indeed as a *nihil*, as nothing. That is why the potter, just like you to whom I speak, creates the vase around this void with his hand, just like the mythic creator, *ex nihilo*, from out of a hole.
>   (146)

Like the Judeo-Christian god, the potter creates something from nothing by shaping matter around a "hole" or *trou*, which simultaneously informs and is formed by the jug; this hole gives rise to the difference between inside and outside but is not reducible to their logic of difference. What Lacan here calls the "hole in the real" is the void, or the real *as* void, as the hole that emerges at the center of the symbolic differences opened up in the thinging of the Thing. It is the truth of this *trou* that is always refound at the heart of the Lacanian *retrouvaille*.[22]

Lacan here subscribes neither to Aristotelian materialism nor to its Christian negation, but appropriates and revises both through his tacit citation of *Lear*'s "Nothing will come of nothing." If for Heidegger, "the thing things," for *Lear*, "nothing nothings": "nothing"—the tragic negations that form the action of the play—does indeed proceed from Cordelia's "nothing."[23] Rather than creating something in particular out of nothing whatsoever, the Lacanian Thing, in its passage through *Lear*, Freud, and Heidegger, narrates the upsurge of nothing from and as something, some *thing* experienced as "monstrous" and "unnatural," suffering and intrinsically lost.

We can explain not only Lacan's appropriation but also his revision of Heidegger's jug through the intervention of the three caskets, now not in their shape but in their arrangement in a row. In *Seminar VII*, Lacan uses the case of the collector to distinguish object and thing, taking as his example a series of matchboxes arranged in a chain through the interlocking of each box's drawer into the opening of the one in front of it. Lacan analyzes the "excessively satisfying" effect of this collection: "I believe that the effect of shock or novelty produced by this collection of empty matchboxes—this point is essential— was to bring out something we perhaps dwell on too little: a box of matches is not simply an object, but can rather, in the guise or *Erscheinung* in which it was offered up in a truly imposing multiplicity, be a Thing" (136). "Thingness," *choséité*

---

22. Philip Leider pointed out the pun on *trou* and *retrouvaille* to us.

23. On this line as implying "the generativity of nothing," see David Willbern, "Shakespeare's Nothing" 248.

(136), does not lie in any one matchbox but rather in the sublime extension of a series of such boxes. If, as Lacan indicates, sublimation "elevates an object . . . to the dignity of the Thing" (133), such sublimity involves not an ideal quality, but, like Kant's mathematical sublime, a "multiplicity," a quantity in excess of quantification having a "completely gratuitous, proliferating and superfluous, almost absurd character" (136).[24]

Furthermore, although, like Heidegger's jug, each box is empty, its emptiness is always displaced (since each empty drawer is inserted into the next box) and never its own (since the space of each box is partly occupied by the empty drawer of the former). If the sequence of displaced drawers represents the signifying chain in the symbolic order, latent within each box is the void that both causes and is left over by the original act of displacement. The void of the hypothetical first matchbox represents the Thing, the primordial signifier that introduces a hole in the real, which subsequent signifiers both repeat and fill, but only symbolically, with an endlessly deferred lack. The void, however, never exists more than logically "before" the displacement, since the void is as much left by displacement as producing it. Thus the image describes the manifestation of the Thing not as any particular object, nor even as the hollowness of any such object, but as the imbrication of two absences: the opened drawer (symbolic lack) as it passes into and leaves behind the gap caused by the drawer's opening—the hole both in and as the real.[25]

24. For Lacan, the work of art, more than the imitation of a thing or the product of the sublimation of the object to the status of thing, manifests a complicated relation of circumvention and *fort* and *da* of object and thing: "Certainly, works of art imitate the objects they represent, but their purpose is clearly not to represent them. By imitating the object, they make some-thing else [*autre chose*] out of it. Thus they only feign to imitate. The object is instated in a certain relation to the Thing which is designed at once to delimit, to make present, and to make absent" (*Seminar VII* 169).

25. Lacan's apologues of the matchboxes and the three mustard jars in *Seminar VII* anticipate his late interest in Borromean knots from *Seminar XX* on: whereas the matchboxes emphasize the imbrication of the real and the symbolic, and the mustard jars present the relation of the real and the imaginary, the knots interimplicate all three orders, once again around three holes. See especially *Seminar XX* 107–23 and *Seminar XXII*.

Let us return to the honey pot with which Lacan introduces his discussion of the Thing in *Seminar VII*. If the honey pot is a metaphor of metaphor, it is not a metaphor to say so; that is, something *real* is produced in and as the enclosed void that stops the infinite *Eingekasteln* of figures of figuration. We are here rereading Lacan's famous dictum from the conclusion of "L'instance de la lettre dans l'inconscient" that "if the symptom is a metaphor, it is not a metaphor to say so" (*Écrits* E 175, F 528). From the vantage point of Lacan's later discussions of the symptom, we can read past the *literalness* of the symptom as metaphor to its "litter-al" status as *real*, insofar as the symptom's symbolic substitutions gather around a fragment of loss and *jouissance*.[26] Lacan's allusive account of psychoanalytic intertextuality applies to the *Kasten* as well, the oldest of Freudian jugs: "These schemas can be recomposed and transposed in such a way that we will not be putting our new honey in the same old skins" (32). The Lacanian Thing overlays the Heideggerian jug and the Shakespearean "nothing" through the Freudian motif of the *Kasten*. In its status as the figure of absence, and even in its very absence from Lacan's text, the "Theme of the Three Caskets" informs these passages as that which can only be re-found within them. Encountered in the intertextual reticulation of Lacan's discourse, the *Kasten* designates the Thing as that which is always absent from itself, a disappearance not simply represented but also constituted by the objects that figure it. Freud's *Kasten*, we could say, is never "Freud's," since it comes to indicate the limits and conditions of meaning only in its errant paths through Shakespeare and Lacan.

26. In the process, Lacan moves from a rhetorical to an indexical conception of the symptom as sign, shifting from the symbolic *symptôme* to the *sinthome* of *Seminar XXIII*. Lacan there discusses the *sinthome* as a fourth element or order, in excess of the triad of real, symbolic, and imaginary (16 December 1975, 6 and passim). See Zizek's chapter "From Symptom to *Sinthome*" in *The Sublime Object of Ideology*, especially 71–75, J.-D. Nasio, *Cinq Leçons* (15–63), and Nestor Braunstein, *La Jouissance*.

CHAPTER SEVEN

The Tragedy of
Foreclosure

In "classical" Freudian analysis, the treatment of the neuroses, governed by the normative mishaps of the Oedipus complex, follows an Aristotelian plot of discovery grounded in a hermeneutics of recognition, riddles, and primal scenes. Psychosis, the catastrophic refusal of the Oedipus complex brought about by what Lacan calls the "foreclosure" of the "Name-of-the-Father," is situated at the margins of Oedipal interpretation, in a realm where words are treated as things, as fragments, that is, of the real. Whereas neurosis, the normative pathology of "everyday unhappiness," demarcates the operational field of Freudian psychoanalysis, psychosis represented for Freud the limit of psychoanalytic interpretation, indeed of interpretation per se. For Lacan, that limit *as a limit* functions as a pivotal category of both theory and therapy, the psychotic exception that proves the neurotic rule. If neurosis is the object of psychoanalysis, psychosis is its Thing; as Jacques-Alain Miller has indicated, at the empty center of "la Psy-chose Lacanienne" is *la Chose* ("Lacan et psychose" 16). As the pathology whose apocalyptic crises plunge the psychotic into the real and whose recuperative delusions disturbingly mime theoretical speculation, psychosis holds the place of the "extimate" Thing and strange semblant of psychoanalysis.

Lacan's remarks on *King Lear* near the end of *Seminar VII* are almost an afterthought to his fuller readings of *Oedipus at Colonus* and *Antigone*. For Lacan, *Oedipus at Colonus* goes "beyond"

Oedipus Rex by sublating the earlier tragedy's *mythos* of subjection into a drama of ethical subjectification. *Lear*, however, verging on farce in the extremity of its replay of Sophoclean patterns and motifs, is not "beyond" the Oedipus plays so much as "after" them, bathetically repeating without transforming Oedipal tragedy. We argue that in *King Lear*, the *plot of foreclosure*, the cataclysmic rejection of Cordelia as the representative of symbolic law, effects a *foreclosure of plot*. In this reading, the schemes and tropes of Sophoclean drama are systematically repudiated and hallucinatorily retranscribed by *King Lear* in the crossed discourses of tragedy and psychoanalysis, such that the "beyond" of Colonus reappears as the "after" or "over" of Dover Cliffs. The mechanism of foreclosure describes *King Lear*'s paradoxical position in the canon of tragedy as a text that becomes a "classic" precisely in its anamorphic hypertrophy of classical motifs. And even though *Lear*'s themes and mechanisms are easily paired with those of Sophocles' *Oedipus* trilogy, such a coupling, we argue, bears within it the literalizing, dis-figuring, and "cruel" foreclosure of the plots that regulate the classical tradition. This foreclosure takes place not in the intertextual register linking *Hamlet*, Seneca, and *Trauerspiel*, but rather in the canonical conjunction of *King Lear* and Sophocles in the defiles of tragedy. In his essay "La psychose dans le texte," Jacques-Alain Miller cites and glosses a gnomic declaration by Lacan: " 'I am psychotic,' specifying his meaning—'for the sole reason that I have always tried to be rigorous,' thus making psychosis an exercise in rigor" (133). Following Lacan's emphasis on the logic or "rigor" of psychosis, we would argue that construing *King Lear* as a "psychotic" text, far from implying a diagnosis of either the character of Lear or the play's disorderly poetics, serves to articulate the constitutive nodes of intransigent nonmeaning generated by the juxtaposition of *Lear* and Sophocles in the traditions of tragedy and psychoanalysis.

After Beyond Oedipus

In the final section of *Seminar VII*, "The Tragic Dimension of Psychoanalytic Experience," Lacan narrates the denouement

of the Oedipus legend.[1] Oedipus, he tells us, gave up his service
to the state, but not his claims to rank; slighted by the sons to
whom he had relinquished power, he departs for Colonus ac-
companied by his daughters. This selective narration, interweaving ethnographic data with Sophocles' plays, is meant by
Lacan to ring a Shakespearean bell:

> Must I, to make myself clear, evoke another tragic figure, un-
> doubtedly closer to us, namely King Lear?
> I cannot here dwell on the import of this play; I simply want
> to make you understand what the overstepping [*franchissement*]
> of Oedipus is, on the basis of *King Lear,* where we find this
> overstepping in a derisory form.
> King Lear also renounces the administration of the common
> good [*service des biens*], his royal duties—he thinks he is made to
> be loved, the old cretin, and thus hands over the *service des biens*
> to his daughters. But we should not believe that he has really
> renounced anything—for this signals the onset of freedom, par-
> tying with fifty knights, fooling around [*la rigolade*], while he is
> housed alternately by the two shrews to whom he believed he
> could hand over the reins of power.
> Like Oedipus, Lear shows us that whoever advances into this
> zone, whether along the derisory path of Lear or the tragic path
> of Oedipus, must advance alone and betrayed.
>
> (*Seminar VII* 352–53)

Lacan reads *Oedipus at Colonus* as a narrative of the *franchisse-
ment*—the leaping or crossing over—of *Oedipus Rex* and the
pleasure principle for which it stands in Freud's work. For
Lacan, the ultimate ethical act is not giving way on one's desire,
an act achieved by Oedipus at Colonus, who fulfills his life by
choosing his death. Lacan's account of *Oedipus at Colonus* casts
it as the prefiguration of *Lear,* which, Lacan says, is "closer to
us"; echoing Freud's reading of *Hamlet* as a modern *Oedipus
Rex,* Lacan presents *Lear* as a repetition of *Oedipus at Colonus*—
a repetition, that is, of a repetition. The two parts of this double
iteration, however, are structurally distinct: whereas *Oedipus at*

---

1. On Lacan's ethics of psychoanalysis, see John Rajchman, *Truth and Eros.*

Colonus dialectically transumes *Oedipus Rex* as its negating fulfillment, *Lear*, stumbling rather than leaping, fails to transform
what it repeats. The word "derisory" indicates this trajectory
"after" classical tragedy, as its exaggerated shadow and anamorphic projection rather than its dialectical fulfillment and
historical metamorphosis. If, in Shoshana Felman's reading,
Lacan's *Oedipus at Colonus* is "Beyond Oedipus," the *King Lear*
of psychoanalysis is "After Beyond Oedipus." This distinction
between the temporalities of the dialectical "beyond" and the
residual "after"—a distinction that both differentiates and inhabits the two plays—demarcates the temporal rhythm within
Lacanian discourse between an ethics structured by the symbolic and an ethics oriented to the real.

Lacan's discussion of the Oedipus trilogy and *King Lear* is
situated in *Seminar VII*'s larger project of thinking the ethics of
psychoanalysis, the path articulated in Lacan's question, "Have
you acted in conformity with the desire which inhabits you?"
["Avez-vous agi conformément au désir qui vous habite?"] (*Seminar VII* 362) "Desire" must be read here in terms of both
symbolic law and real *jouissance*, each moving beyond the pleasure principle in the service of the death drive. In its symbolic
interpretation, the imperative to act in accordance with one's
desire entails choosing to live with death, the heroic act which
Lacan discerns in the Heideggerian "être-pour-la-mort" of
Oedipus at Colonus (*Seminar VII* 357). Lear, on the other hand,
dies still misrecognizing the path his act has dictated:

> I have shown you the underside and the derisory nature [*déri-
> sion*]—since it is illusory—of this topology, which is in this case
> the topology of the tragic, with this poor Lear who understands
> nothing of it, and makes the ocean and the world resound for
> having wanted to enter into this same region in a beneficial way,
> with everyone's agreement. In the end he appears to us, still
> having understood nothing, and holding, dead in his arms, she
> who is the object, of course misrecognized by him, of his love.
>
> (*Seminar VII* 358)[2]

2. Compare Freud's reading of the *Kasten* motif to Lacan's reading of
Oedipus at Colonus. Freud writes, "Eternal wisdom, clothed in the primaeval

Stuart Schneiderman's gloss of Lacan's imperative implicitly conjoins the narratives of *Oedipus at Colonus* and *King Lear* in a scenario of the death drive conceived as the symbolic deferral of destruction:[3] "The desire to die does not translate into suicide. If, as Lacan put it, one ought to sustain desire and not seek an object that will gratify it and thereby erase it, the desire to die is best enacted when death is kept at a distance.... Lear did not die of wanting to die, he resisted to the end, and Freud's reading of the play in his 'The Theme of the Three Caskets' states that its truth is the submission to death" (23–24). In these terms, to "choose" death is not, in the words of Keats, to be "half *in love* with easeful Death," but rather to *desire* death, to accept its deferral as well as its closure, as in Marvell's phrase, "Make destiny your choice." We would argue, however, that it is this Oedipal subjection to and subjectivization of the death drive at Colonus that Lear's tragic choice "derisorily" repeats rather than tragically works through. In so doing, the postclassical tragedy of *Lear* points to the impasses of the symbolic, which already press *Oedipus at Colonus* back towards the real of *Antigone*.

Thus, in *Seminar VII*, the injunction not to give way on one's desire emphasizes not the alienating desire and displacements of signification determined by the symbolic Other, but rather the real Thing that causes desire, the occasion of loss and *jouissance* that sets both desire and prohibition into motion. In *Seminar VII*, Lacan uses *Antigone* to stage the congruity of psychoanalytic and tragic ethics through the heroine's refusal to substitute the object in desire—Haemon, the good of the community—for the intransigently nonsubstitutable Thing-of-

---

myth, bids the old man renounce love, choose death and make friends with the necessity of dying" (*SE* 12:301.) Lacan writes, "That is the preference with which a human existence, that of Oedipus, must end, so perfectly completed that he does not die from the usual sort of death, that is, an accidental death, but rather from true death, wherein he himself erases his own being" (*Seminar VII* 353).

3. For a similar account of the death drive and narrative, see Peter Brooks, *Reading For the Plot* 90–112.

loss, an ethics borne out in *Antigone*'s incorporative poetics. In Zizek's tendentious gloss of Lacan's *Antigone*,

> [W]e could perhaps risk a small rectification of the Lacanian maxim of the psychoanalytic ethic "not to cede one's desire": is not desire as such already a certain yielding, a kind of compromise formation, a metonymic displacement, retreat, a defence against intractable drive? "To desire" *means* to give way on the drive—insofar as we follow Antigone and "do not give way on our desire," do we not precisely step out of the domain of desire, do we not shift from the modality of desire into the modality of pure drive?
>
> (*Looking Awry* 172)

Read through *Antigone* rather than *Oedipus at Colonus*, "not giving way on desire" radicalizes desire into drive: both the drive as death drive, incarnated in the heroine driven to her death by interminable mourning, and the drive as the visceral, almost protoplasmic *jouissance* that resounds in the *asēma* cries of the birds glutted on carrion (*Antigone* 1016–22). Whereas the symbolic reading of Lacan's imperative would emphasize Antigone's insistence on the rites and rights of mourning that constitute the object in desire, Zizek's reading of this ethic in terms of the real isolates Antigone's resolute movement towards the radical failure of symbolic displacement in the (sur)real crypt of live burial. Thus, *Oedipus at Colonus* allegorizes the symbolic trajectory of *Antigone* in psychoanalysis, but *Lear*'s residual, "derisory" repetition of *Oedipus at Colonus* indicates *Antigone*'s drive toward the real.

The ethics of psychoanalysis approached in *Seminar VII* bears witness to Lacan's ongoing reinterpretation of the Freudian imperative, "Wo Es war, soll Ich werden," translated in the *Standard Edition* as "Where id was, there ego shall be" (*SA* 1:516; *SE* 22:80). Ego psychology traditionally understands this apothegm to imply the ego's colonial expansion into the undiscovered country of the id: what was id shall be ego. In *Seminar II* and "La chose freudienne," Lacan, reversing the direction of the phrase, converts the appropriation of id by ego into the expropriation of the ego by the id: what was ego shall come to be the subject of the unconscious. *Oedipus at Colonus,* in Shoshana Felman's reading, fulfills this early Lacanian injunction to symbolize the imaginary: dying into his past at Colonus, Oedipus is *"born,* through the assumption of his death... *into the life of his history"* ("Beyond Oedipus" 134). For Oedipus—and for the moment of Lacan's appropriation by American criticism represented by Felman's essay—the "Es" indicates the unconscious as a symbolic formation. For the *Lear* of the later Lacan, however, "Es" has become *das Ding,* the "misrecognized object" that Lear carries dead in his arms. Thus, in *Seminar XI,* Lacan reinterprets the *Es* of Freud's injunction: "But the subject is there to rediscover *where it was*—I anticipate—the real" (E 45, F 45). In these terms, to choose the third casket would mean coming to be in the place where "it," the thing, the cause "was," but as the index of a trauma that by definition cannot be historicized. In his 1966 essay "Science and Truth," Lacan writes, "the *soll Ich*... of Freud's expression... brings forth the paradox of an imperative that presses me to assume my own causality" (13; *Écrits* 865). This imperative entails not simply that the subject go "beyond" itself by dialectically subjectivizing the history that expropriates it, but rather that the subject can only do so by coming to be in the intractably nondialectical and ahistorical place of the Thing, the "after"—the cause and residue—of the beyond.[4]

For psychoanalysis, ethical action entails neither blind submission to the symbolic order (the state of the unanalyzed neurotic) nor rejection of the symbolic order (the state of the psychotic), but rather coming to be in the place of the *Es,* the It or Thing residual to the symbolic as its inconsistency. In "Seminar XV," "L'Acte psychanalytique," Lacan once more distinguishes the two valences of the *Wo Es war* in his work:

> You can see it, you can put your finger on it: there are two *Wo es war*'s, two "there where it was" 's, which correspond moreover

4. Cf. Zizek's defense of the ahistoricism of psychoanalysis, "With an Eye to Our Gaze" 50–51.

to the distance that separates the unconscious from the 'Id' [*Ça*] in psychoanalytic theory. There is the "there where it was" inscribed at the level of the subject, and which, as I have said already—I repeat it so that you will not let it go by unnoticed—remains attached to this subject as lack. There is another "there where it was" which has an opposite place: the one that remains attached to the "I am not" of the unconscious as object, object of loss [*objet de perte*].

The initial lost object of all analytic genesis, the one Freud insistently talks about during the entire time of the birth of the unconscious, is the cause of desire. We will see it as the crux of the act.

(10 January 1967, 86)

Lacan distinguishes here the symbolic "Wo Es war" associated with the unconscious structured by linguistic lack from the "Wo Es war" of the real, whose *Es* indicates the *ça* or "it" of traumatic loss. Whereas the first narrates the alienation and division of the subject, the second isolates the separating out of a real object as the derivative of the subject's splitting and the Other's de-completion. Moreover, Lacan links this object of loss to "the act" that defines the ethics of psychoanalysis. In Lacan's discourse, the word "act" connotes neither a free choice (which implies imaginary autonomy and the reign of the ego) nor a subjection to fate (the inexorable law of the signifying chain) but a transgression of the symbolic order delimited though not determined by its commandments. As Lacan says in *Seminar VII*, "My thesis is that moral law, moral commandment, the presence of the moral agency, is that through which, in our activity insofar as it is structured by the symbolic, the real presents itself—the real as such, the weight of the real" (28). Here Lacan specifies the symbolic as the structure through which the real precipitates in and as the field of ethical action. Thus Antigone transgresses the law as symbolic limit precisely in her insistence on its material letter.[5]

5. Another example is Caesar's crossing of the Rubicon: "Crossing the Rubicon did not have a decisive military significance for Caesar, but on the contrary, to cross it was to return to the mother-land—the land of the republic,

For Lacan, *King Lear* constitutes an "inverse" or "derisory" version of this tragic ethics: although Lear, like Antigone and like Oedipus at Colonus, chooses death, he continually misrecognizes his desire by confusing the trauma of *das Ding* with the *Traum* of infantilization. In this scenario, Cordelia functions as Lear's "misrecognized object" (*Seminar VII* 358)—the object that occupies the place of the Thing. The misrecognition of Cordelia is not accidental but necessary, since every object is constituted in the simultaneous representation and occlusion of the Thing. The concept of misrecognition has shifted in Lacan's work from the shaping of the ego in the alienating image of the object to a twist within the object itself, whose shimmering surface at once covers and constitutes a fragment of the real. If *Hamlet* and *Oedipus Rex* primarily enact the splitting of the subject, *Lear* and *Antigone* dramatize the torsion within the object. In this, Lacan echoes Freud, who had also emphasized the vicissitudes of the object in misrecognition as the tragic impetus of *King Lear:* "[Lear] should have recognized [*erkennen*] the unassuming, speechless love of his third daughter [*Dritten*] and rewarded it, but he misrecognizes [*verkennt*] it" (*SE* 12:293; *SA* 10:185; translation altered). For Freud and Lacan, the ethical imperative of the play is not that Lear should simply have acknowledged Cordelia as his "best object," as loyal, appropriate, praiseworthy receiver of love in an imaginary economy of value, but rather that he should assume (not reject) her as "a thing so monstrous," as the necessarily "speechless," deathly, and intrinsically misrecognized Third (sister, casket, order).

To combine Freud and Lacan's ethical *sententiae,* the imperative not to give way on one's desire requires coming to be in the place of the *Es* as the traumatic thing or foreign body that intrusively yet intimately "inhabits" the subject. Lacan's final comments on *Lear* pointedly echo Freud's last words in "The Theme of the Three Caskets," since both accounts end with the image of Cordelia dead in Lear's arms. Through the act of

---

the land that one would rape were one so much as to approach it" ("Seminar XV," 10 January 1967, 80).

homage that allusion performs, Lacan bears Freud dead in his arms, as psychoanalysis comes to be there where *Lear* was. If Cordelia is the Thing of *King Lear,* "The Theme of the Three Caskets"—the Freudian allegory of the signifier as thing—is the textual Thing of *Seminar VII,* the unnamed motif realized as a motif of the unnameable through the *Seminar*'s reiterated figures of hollowness and its dis-contents.

La Psy-chose Lacanienne

Lacan's articulation of a psychoanalytic ethics of the real passes, both historically and theoretically, by way of psychosis, since it was in terms of psychosis that Lacan began to radicalize the status of the real. Whereas *Seminar I* and *Seminar II* emphasize the imaginary and symbolic orders, it is no accident that Lacan's *Seminar III,* on psychosis, predicts his later approach to the real.[6] Moreover, in *Seminar III,* when enunciating the psychotic foreclosure of the paternal metaphor, Lacan also introduces the *point de capiton,* the master signifier that retroactively interpellates the subject into the symbolic order. So too, we could say, in *Seminar III* Lacan buttons or upholsters neurosis—the order of symbolic substitutions and displacements—to psychosis as both the radical denial and the infantile kernel of Oedipal representation.

In his analysis of Schreber's autobiography, Freud tried to account for the specificity of the psychotic's defense mechanism, its difference, that is, from the "return of the repressed," which characterizes neurosis: "It was incorrect to say that the perception which was suppressed internally is projected out-

6. In the opening session of "Seminar V," Lacan reviews the progression of his seminar in these terms (6 November 1957, 6–7). On the Lacanian account of psychosis, see François Ansermet, Alain Grosrichard, and Charles Méla, eds., *La psychose dans le texte;* Hervé Castanet, *L'experience clinique des psychoses;* Maurice Dayan, *Les relations;* Gerard Pommier, *Le dénouement d'une analyse;* Sol Aparicio, "La forclusion"; Éric Laurent, "Structures Freudiennes"; and Rosine Lefort, "Le S_1." For work in English, see David Allison et al., *Psychosis and Sexual Identity;* Evelyne Keitel, *Reading Psychosis;* and Michael Walsh, "Reading the Real."

ward; the truth is rather, as we now see, that what was abolished [*das Aufgehobene*] internally returns from without" (*SE* 12:71; *SA* 7:194). In his later analysis of the "Wolf-Man," Freud designates the absolute rejection of castration as *Verwerfung*, repudiation. In *Seminar III*, Lacan combines these senses of sublation and refusal, of dialectics and its refuse, in the term "foreclosure," in order to rephrase Freud's formula in Lacanian terms: that which is rejected or foreclosed from the symbolic reappears in the real (21). In *Seminar VII*, which renovates the question of the real by way of the Thing, Lacan presents psychotic paranoia as the "rejection of a certain prop in the symbolic order, that specific prop around which can occur . . . the division of the relation to *das Ding* into two sides" (67). With the rejection or foreclosure of the symbolic bar that divides the real Thing from the object of representation, the maternal Thing threatens to emerge in the unbearable and nonsymbolized real of hallucination, in what Melanie Klein calls the "unreal reality" of infantile psychosis.[7]

The Thing laid bare in *la psy-Chose*, however, paradoxically links as well as opposes primal repression and foreclosure.[8] The logic of psychoanalysis repeatedly arrives at a zero degree—in the language of *Lear* a "nothing"—in which foreclosure, the absolute denial of the symbolic order and the precondition of psychosis, is indistinguishable from primal repression, the absolute foundation of the Oedipal law, which governs neurosis. Foreclosure, as the strange double of primal repression, is indeterminately both inclusion and exclusion. At once "anti-" Oedipus, as its antithesis, "beyond" Oedipus, as its synthesis, and "after" Oedipus, as its residuum, foreclosure determines the rule of Oedipus through the possibility of its

7. Klein writes, "We see that the child's earliest reality is wholly phantastic; he is surrounded with objects of anxiety, and in this respect excrement, organs, objects, things animate and inanimate are to begin with equivalent to one another. As the ego develops, a true relation to reality is gradually established out of this unreal reality" (in *The Writings of Melanie Klein* 1:221). Lacan cites the expression, in English, in *Seminar I*.

8. In "Seminar XIV," for example, Lacan connects "l'objet perdu comme tel" with that which "surgit sous la rubrique de l'*Urverdrängung*" (15 February 1967, 131).

radical exception. In an exchange with Jean Hyppolite concerning the French translation of Freud's term *Verwerfung* in *Seminar I*, Lacan first describes the mechanism that will soon be called "foreclosure" exactly as a kind of primal repression:

> This important articulation [of the distinction between *Verdrängung*, repression, and *Verwerfung*, foreclosure] shows us that originally, for repression to be possible, there must be a beyond of repression, something final, already primitively constituted, an initial nucleus of the repressed, which not only is unacknowledged, but which, for not being formulated, is literally *as if it didn't exist*—I'm just following what Freud says [*je suis là ce que dit Freud*]. And nevertheless, in a certain sense, it is somewhere, since, as Freud everywhere tells us, it is the centre of attraction, calling up all the subsequent repressions.
> I'd say that that is the very essence of the Freudian discovery.
>
> (E 43, F 54)

Whereas Lacan's notion of foreclosure is usually understood as the rejection of primal repression, here the two concepts are fundamentally knotted together.[9] As repression's "refusal," foreclosure is both "something final," its repudiation, and something "initial," its origination. Moreover, this alterity of and within repression lies at the heart not only of the unconscious, but of *psychoanalysis itself*, since Lacan defines the "very essence of the Freudian discovery" as its primal deviation from its own central, constitutive theory.

In *Seminar III*, Lacan lays out the normatively ex-centric status of foreclosure as the primal rejection that logically precedes neurotic repression:

> Prior to all symbolization—this priority is not temporal but logical—there is, as the psychoses demonstrate, a stage at which it

---

9. Zizek points out that Lacan and J.-A. Miller expand the notion of foreclosure to include "a certain foreclosure proper to the order of signifier as such; whenever we have a symbolic structure it is structured around a certain void, it implies the foreclosure of a certain key signifier" (*The Sublime Object of Idelology* 72–73). See also the anonymous essay in *Scilicet*, "Le sujet et l'acte sexuel: une affaire de réel."

is possible for a portion of symbolization not to take place. This
initial stage precedes the entire neurotic dialectic, which is due
to the fact that neurosis is articulated speech, in so far as the
repressed and the return of the repressed are one and the same
thing. It can thus happen that something primordial regarding
the subject's being does not enter into symbolization and is not
repressed, but rejected.... At the level of this pure, primitive
Bejahung, which may or may not take place, an initial dichotomy
is established—what has been subject to *Bejahung,* to primitive
symbolization, will have various destinies. What has come under
the influence of the primitive *Verwerfung* will have another.

(94, 95; trans. Russell Grigg)

Lacan's account here is based on his reading of Freud's essay
"Die Verneinung," in which the first relation to externality
(*einem Ding*) results in a simultaneous inclusion and exclusion:
"The original pleasure-ego wants to introject into itself everything that is good and to eject from itself [*von sich werfen*] everything that is bad" (*SE* 19:237; *SA* 3:374). This absolute rejection,
which according to Lacan precedes and opposes the "neurotic
dialectic," also founds it, insofar as foreclosure constitutes the
initial possibility of negation that conditions all future ones.[10]

Whereas in neurosis, the past returns symptomatically in
tropes that both require and satisfy interpretation, in psychosis,
the past, literalized and disfigured, remains scattered and mul-
tiplied across the surface of discourse. Thus at the beginning
of the Schreber case, Freud, defending his analysis of a written
document, writes, "The psycho-analytic investigation of paranoia would be altogether impossible if the patients themselves
did not possess the peculiarity of betraying (in a distorted form,
it is true [*allerdings in entstellter Form*]) precisely those things
which other neurotics keep hidden as a secret" (*SE* 12:9; *SA*
7:139). A neurotic model of textuality tracks meaning through
the distinction and movement between surface and depth
mapped in the metaphor of the hidden secret. A psychotic
model of textuality, however, would have no secret meaning

10. Jacques-Alain Miller suggests that all psychosis is triggered in a quasi-
Oedipal situation ("Lacan et psychose" 27).

to reveal, and would read *superficially*, across the distortions and deformations of the textual tegument rather than beneath it. The point of such a practice of reading, however, is not to diagnose texts as neurotic or psychotic, but rather to use the concept of foreclosure to approach those discursive moments of radical exclusion that at once stall and install the symbolic structures of tragic drama and its Oedipal interpretation.

Freud's late essay "Constructions in Analysis" (1937) specifically maps modes of psychoanalytic reading onto the nosological distinction between neurosis and psychosis, a move that sublates psychosis from a particular disorder to a principle of textual functioning and psychoanalytic practice.[11] Freud distinguishes the everyday work of "interpretation" from the punctual interventions of "construction," in which the past is not explained or deciphered as much as fictionalized and even fabricated. In construction, the analyst is concerned less with the empirical truth or falsehood of the aetiological narrative that he or she proposes than with its effects on the analysand's symptoms. Quoting Polonius, Freud writes that, in construction, "our bait of falsehood had taken a carp of truth" (*SE* 23:262); Freud's citation shifts his literary point of identification from Hamlet, the obsessional interpretive detective, to Polonius, the aging, paranoid constructor of erotic fictions. Later in the essay, Freud reworks another favorite line of Polonius: "There is not only *method* in madness, as the poet has already perceived, but also a fragment of *historical truth* [*ein Stück historischer Wahrheit*]" (*SE* 23:267; *SA Ergänz.* 404–5). The declension of Freud's line from the *method* of interpretation to the *fragment of historical truth* repeats the rhythm that links and separates *Hamlet* and *Lear*, the symbolic and the real, in psychoanalysis. The logic of the citations, moreover, suggests a larger turn in psychoanalytic attention from neurosis, as the exemplary object of analytic hermeneutics, to psychosis as its strange and estranged other at the limits of psychoanalytic interpretation.

Concluding his essay with an extended comparison between

---

11. For a more extended account of construction, see Kenneth Reinhard, "The Freudian Things: Construction and the Archaeological Metaphor."

psychoanalytic constructions and psychotic delusions, Freud
suggests that both contain a "fragment" or "kernel" of reality.
Freud writes,

> The delusions of patients appear to me to be the equivalents of
> the constructions which we build up in the course of an analytic
> treatment—attempts at explanation and cure, though it is true
> that these, under the conditions of a psychosis, can do no more
> than replace the fragment of reality [*das Stück Realität*] that is
> being disavowed [*verleugnet*] in the present by another fragment
> that had already been disavowed in the remote past. It will be
> the task of each individual investigation to reveal the intimate
> connections between the material [*Stoff*] of the present disavowal
> and that of the original repression. Just as our construction is
> only effective because it recovers a fragment of lost experience
> [*ein Stück vorlorengegangener Lebensgeschichte*], so the delusion
> owes its convincing power to the element of historical truth
> which it inserts in the place of the rejected reality.
>   (*SE* 23:268; *SA Ergänz.* 405–6)

The fragment of reality that joins construction and delusion
in Freud's analogy functions neither as a historical narrative
nor as a repressed element in the symbolically distorted com-
promise-formations that return in the symptoms of neurosis,
but rather as "etwas Schreckliches" (405), literally "something
terrible," a traumatic incursion that, disavowed or repudiated
[*verleugnet*], is preserved as a denied fragment lodged in the
symbolic chains that constitute the subject's history. Thus the
phrase "a fragment of historical truth" should be read—perversely or perhaps psychotically—as referring to precisely that
catastrophic piece of the real which, in exceeding historicization, thereby causes the retroactive attempt to accommodate
that excess. This is the traumatic reality that in the earlier essay
"Negation" (1925), textual fragments of which are literally incorporated into "Constructions in Analysis," Freud had called
das Ding, the intimate exteriority which in psychosis danger-

ously merges with the master signifiers assumed to cancel it.[12] At the end of the 1937 essay, Freud implicates this fragment of the real in the complexities of the *Krankheitsverursachung,* "the causation of the illness" (*SE* 23; *SA* 406); embedded in this compound is *Ursache,* "cause," literally "primal object," which casts the cause of both illness and subject as the primal lost Thing (*Ur-Sache*) of the real.

On the one hand, psychoanalysis involves interpretation, the traversal and articulation of "surface" and "depth"; if the work of interpretation traditionally strives to move from signifier to signified, structuralist projects of interpretation emphasize the dynamics of that movement. On the other hand, psychoanalysis entails construction: the psychotic foreclosure of structure that distributes the signifiers of interpretation across the textual surface in paranoid delusions and contrafactual hallucinations. Construction—conceived as a critical and poetic as well as analytic possibility—would thus isolate the glittering veneer of language in order to object-ify the generative inconsistencies within symbolic interpretation. By itself, interpretation can do no more than subject the subject to the automatic functioning of the signifying chain. By itself, construction would be only "wild," or rather "crazy," analysis, that is, nothing more nor less than psychosis. In "The Loss of Reality in Neurosis and Psychosis" (1924), Freud writes that "neurosis does not disavow the reality, it only ignores it; psychosis disavows it and tries to replace it. We call behaviour 'normal' or 'healthy', if it combines certain features of both reactions—if it disavows the reality as little as does a neurosis, but if it then exerts itself, as does a psychosis, to effect an alteration of that reality" (*SE* 19:185). So, too, the ethics of psychoanalysis, and of psychoanalytic reading, would punctuate the ongoing interpretation of psychic reality with constructions that reconfigure the subject's fundamental fantasy through the "altered" reality of hallucination.

12. See, for example, Rosine Lefort's suggestion that in psychosis, the S_1 or master signifier functions as the *objet a,* the fragment of the real outside signification ("Le S_1," 55, 56).

Construction, we could say, does not reduce the analysand's linguistic production to the mechanical *insistence* of the signifying chain, but rather hits upon the visceral *persistence* of nodes of *non*-sense, which traumatize the subject. In the project of Lacanian analysis, the aim of construction would not be to signify those nodes but to re-constellate them in order to attenuate the subject's alienation in the symbolic order.

In "Séminaire XIV" and "Séminaire XV," Lacan calls this reorganization of the analysand's fundamental psychic coordinates "traversing the fantasy," the "ethical" event that signals the end of analysis. In Gerard Pommier's account,

> The end of analysis involves fantasy, such as it is constructed during the analytic task: he who suffers from a symptom enters into analysis in order to get rid of it, and its literal reading opens up an empty space [*vide*] where fantasy can be constructed. At the moment of the denouement, if it takes place, the analysand recognizes his divided place in that which is contradictory in this fantasy, which is thus traversed by that cleavage itself. This moment is ethical because it requires that a contradiction be maintained, and the latter cannot be maintained unless a shift takes place towards the function of the analyst, or at least towards the equivalent of such a function.
>
> (*Le dénouement* 261)

Pommier marks three moments in psychoanalytic work: the *interpretation* or "literal reading" of the symptom, whose alteration opens up a space for the *construction* of fantasy, which is in turn *traversed* or passed by the analysand, as he or she enters the position held by the analyst. As Lacan puts it, " '*Là où c'était* …*'* traduisons: '*je dois devenir*', continuez, '*psychanalyste*' " [" 'There where it was … ' let us translate: 'I must become,' and continue, a 'psychoanalyst' "] ("Seminar XV," 10 January 1967, 81). Implicit here is the recasting of the position of the analyst from the Other "supposed to know" the analysand's desire to the *objet a*, the cause of desire. To traverse the fantasy is to assume one's causality, understood here as the point of contradiction and division—the lack of reciprocity between subject and object embodied in, for example, the scandal of castration, or the impossibility of a sexual relation—which the fantasy contains and veils.[13] In the formula for fantasy ($ ◊ a), the *objet a* both masks that impossibility through the (imaginary) lures of the fantasy of which it is an element, and *is* the (real) non-relation between the two poles. Hence, in Pommier's formulation, at the end of analysis, the fantasy is traversed by its own cut, in the sense that the *objet a* is assumed not as the panacea of division, but as division itself.

Insofar as this object, in both Freud's and Lacan's accounts, is initially constituted through the mode of hallucination, it remains infused with the strange light of infantile psychosis.[14] The object of psychoanalysis is a fundamentally *lost* object, constituted through hallucination in the default of satisfaction; the object emerges in the place of the Thing, the upsurging of quantity that renders the condition of the *infans* inherently psychotic. The hallucinatory foundations of the object anatomize the real of the *objet a* as neither an empirical phenomenon nor as the noumenal *Ding an sich*, but as pure semblance, as sheer appearance without meaning or referent. This initial positing of the object as hallucination lodges a psychotic kernel of the real in the scene of fantasy. In Pommier's account, "There exists, at the very heart of that which is hallucinated, a pivot point where hallucination turns into fantasy" (*D'une logique de la psychose* 88). This turning point, internal to hallucination, is

13. Our understanding of the traversing of fantasy derives from Bruce Fink's account: "*La traversée*—the traversing, transversal, crossing, or flip-flopping—of the fundamental fantasy is presented as the result of the analyst's action in the course of analysis in pushing the patient ever closer to a truth—that there is no such thing as a sexual relationship, that there is no possible *relation* between the sexes—which is beyond knowledge and meaning. The traversing involves a 'repositioning of the ego as subject in this *a* which *I* was for the Other's desire,' i.e., a repositioning of the subject as object *a* in relationship to the Other" ("Alienation and Separation" 112).

14. In *Seminar III*, Lacan writes, "Reality, in as much as it is supported by desire, is initially hallucinated. The Freudian theory of the birth of the world of objects . . . implies that the subject remains suspended at the point of what makes his fundamental object the object of his essential satisfaction. . . . [T]he subject does not have to *find* the object of his desire, he is not led, channeled there, by the natural rails of an instinctual adaptation. . . . He must on the contrary *refind* the object, whose emergence is fundamentally hallucinated" (98; trans. Russell Grigg).

what Lacan calls "the lack in the Other," at once the absence
of the mother, which causes the hallucination of her presence,
and the mother's unknown desire, which demands the child's
fantasy of fulfilling her. This overlapping *loss of* and *lack in* the
(m)Other forms the neurotic pivot that turns hallucination into
fantasy, demand into desire, the Thing into object.

"The subject," declares Lacan, "is immanent in his verbal hallucination" (*Seminar XI* 258). If the object of fantasy is founded
on an originary hallucination, it would follow that the notion of
traversing the fantasy itself *traverses the hallucination,* in terms of
both psychoanalytic work and the process of its theorization.
The coinage "traversing the hallucination" serves to bring into
focus the role of psychosis as a necessary bend or swerve within
the ethical project, historical unfolding, and peculiar epistemology of psychoanalysis.[15] "Traversing the hallucination" should
not be taken as either a clinical diagnostics ("You are hallucinat-
ing") or as a cultural program ("Let's hallucinate!"), but rather
as a *construction* of the historical, theoretical, and technical contingencies by which psychoanalysis could only formulate the analytic act of traversing the fantasy through the analysis and
theorization of psychosis and the real. As a construction rather
than an interpretation, the phrase "traversing the hallucination" is designed to (re)psychoticize the formula for fantasy, by
isolating the ahistorical elements of the real embedded in scenes
of symbolization, historicization, and canonization.

The Case of Eyes

Thus both in and between Freud and Lacan, the foundation
of the Oedipal era, psychically and theoretically, depends on

15. In "Seminar XIV," Lacan asks, "How is it that analytic knowledge
manages to pass into the real" ["comment il se fait que le savoir analytique
vienne à passer dans le réel"]: "The path by which what I teach passes into
the real bizarrely enough is no other than *Verwerfung,* the actual rejection which
we see occur at a level of the generation of the psychoanalyst's position, insofar
as that position wants to know nothing about what is nonetheless its only
knowledge. What is rejected in the symbolic must be focalized in a subjective
field somewhere, in order to reappear at a correlative level in the real" (15
February 1967, 128).

its potential failure. *King Lear*, we argue, is the tragedy of the foreclosure of tragedy: it unfolds in and as the refusal to enter into the Oedipal *mythos* of recognition and reversal, which nonetheless continues to (mal)function as its generic ideal. If *Oedipus Rex* and *Oedipus at Colonus* together enact a dialectic of misrecognition, recognition, and their synthesis in historical symbolization, *Lear*, as Lacan suggests in *Seminar VII*, is a "derisory" tragedy in which recognition itself, as a structural principle, is insistently misrecognized. Rather than repressing the Oedipal narrative of blindness and insight, by, for example, condensing and displacing its *topoi*, *Lear* forecloses *Oedipus* in the canon of tragedy: Shakespeare's play reproduces Sophoclean conventions not as symbols but as letters. In Kent's phrase, the motifs of classical tragedy function like a "whoreson zed," an "unnecessary letter" (II.ii.61), deprived of their significative and performative efficacy while suffered to circulate with the unreal reality of hallucination.

Most fundamentally, *Lear* is a play without a fundament: its tragic action is set into motion by the catastrophic foreclosure of Cordelia, a rejection, linguistic in nature, that is both triggered and emblematized by the word "Nothing" and its vicissitudes in the play. Cordelia's "Nothing" initially legislates the necessity of symbolic castration, the renunciations entailed by marriage—a valence supported by the Elizabethan sense of "nothing" as the lack of the phallic "thing."[16] Rejected by Lear, Cordelia's "Nothing" divides into and superimposes the gaps named by the symbolic "no" and the real "thing." Rather than accepting the necessity of substitution, Lear's demand for pre-Oedipal union forecloses the tragic flaw of the symbolic, which reappears in the real: in the form of Lear's hallucinations, the "kind o'thing" of the fool (I.iv.182), the play's *fort-da* game with Dover cliffs, and the vertiginous multiplication of defective recognition scenes that gather at its edge.

The syllable "cast-," threaded between "castration," "incest," "*Kasten*," "Jocasta," and "casting out," operates as a master signifier that represents *King Lear* in and to the discourses of

16. See Willbern, "Shakespeare's Nothing" 245–47.

psychoanalysis and classical tragedy.[17] Railing against Goneril, Lear enunciates the Sophoclean theme of blindness under the rubric of "casting out" his eyes, an apotropaic defense against the loss of manhood signified for him by his tears:

> Life and death! I am asham'd
> That thou hast power to shake my manhood thus,
> That these hot tears, which break from me perforce,
> Should make thee worth them. Blasts and fogs upon thee,
> Th'untented woundings of a father's curse
> Pierce every sense about thee! Old fond eyes,
> Beweep this cause again, I'll pluck ye out,
> And cast you, with the waters that you loose,
> To temper clay. Yea, is't come to this?
> Ha! Let it be so: I have another daughter,
> Who, I am sure, is kind and comfortable:
> When she shall hear this of thee, with her nails
> She'll flay thy wolvish visage. Thou shalt find
> That I'll resume the shape which thou dost think
> I have cast off for ever.
>
> (I.iv.294–308)

The word "cast" had first been used in the play to describe Lear's rejection of Cordelia: France had said, "Be it lawful I take up what's cast away" (I.i.252), and Goneril noted "with what poor judgment he hath now cast her off" (I.i.289–90).[18]

17. On "cast-" in Sophocles and psychoanalysis, see Stephen Bröser, "Kästchen, Kasten, Kastration." We would argue that the linguistic economy of "cast-" in the play can be used to allegorize Lacan's typologies of the three orders, and the three *dis*orders correlative with them, in terms of Freud's caskets. Neurosis, the symbolic disorder governed by *castration*, occupies the place of the second casket; psychosis, the *casting out* of castration into the real, holds the place of the third casket; perversion, insofar as it pursues the regressive dream of imaginary *incest without castration*, is marked by the first casket. Furthermore, each disorder founds itself on the exclusion of the others: if psychosis casts out castration, neurosis casts out the *Kasten* which exceeds its law, and perversion is literally the *un-cast* (unchaste), neither the lack legislated by castration nor the loss incurred by the *Kasten*, but rather the act of denegation that fetishizes their nonintersection.

18. See also V.iii.5, Cordelia to Lear: "For thee, oppressed king, I am cast down."

By insisting here that he has not "cast off for ever" the phallic shape of king, Lear again casts out the castration that Cordelia's "Nothing" had pronounced in forbidding Lear's pursuit of incest (from Latin *incastus,* unchaste).[19] Thus, although the passage seems to enunciate the Sophoclean theme of blindness and insight, Lear's desire to "cast out" his eyes repeats rather than cancels the rejection of Cordelia.

In *King Lear,* the Oedipal symbolics of castration reach their climax with the blinding of Gloucester, a scene whose staging of recognition has helped assure *Lear*'s place in the canon of tragedy by appearing to replicate the act of submission to the law which the blinding of Oedipus has come to represent in tragic discourse. Shakespeare's theatrical emphasis, however, on the physical invasion of the bodily envelope, epitomized by Cornwall's savage apostrophe, "Out vile jelly!," more closely approximates the traumatic confrontation between symbolic and real concretized in the piercing of Oedipus's ankles. In the Oedipal myth, the exposure of the *infans* signifies not the symbolic subjection that dissolves the Oedipus complex but rather the primal repression that institutes it, in which the real materiality of a primal signifier (S_1)—the name of Oedipus as "swollen foot"—cruelly buttons, sews, or interpellates the subject of culture into the symbolic order. Moreover, the symbolic imposition of the name through primal repression is coterminous with the foreclosure of the infant Oedipus from the family and community, as the father attempts to escape the tragic *mythos* established by the oracle. As Gerard Pommier writes, "The term 'real' does not simply describe what words are unable to name, but also what words produce when their ambition to speak fails" (*Le dénouement* 30). In the myth of Oedipus, the real does not encompass the *unnameable* as a ground beneath and before language, but rather the *proper name,* the pure signifier, which stands in for language's failure to signify.

The subject is precisely such a failure—a botched signifi-

19. On the familial and linguistic economy of incest in Shakespeare, see Marc Shell, *The End of Kinship.*

cation that paradoxically inscribes the subject into the ideologies of culture at the real "nothing" where primal repression and foreclosure asymptotically converge.[20] In the Oedipal myth, the name "Oedipus" staples a unary signifier (S$_1$) onto the swollen flesh whose anamorphic distension both precedes the name as its real referent (*das Ding*) and swells around the signifier as its inflamed aftereffect (*objet a*). In *King Lear,* Gloucester's blinding retroactively pins the symbolic *drama* of Oedipal recognition onto the real *trauma* of Oedipus's exposure.[21] In the process, the Shakespearean scene of blinding rewrites Oedipus's self-blinding from a moment of symbolic "castration" or "recognition" to one of real mutilation, itself a repetition of the pierced ankles. Thus the pairing of the two scenes, canonical rather than intertextual, implicates psychosis as a normative position of the *infans* in the symbolic constellations of desire that hystericize and Oedipalize the speaking child.[22]

In the *Oedipus Rex* of classical psychoanalysis, blinding not only symbolizes castration, but symbolizes castration *as symbolization*, as the recognition, transcription, and assumption of and by one's history in its alterity, the coming to be there where one's past was. Blindness as figure, however, casts out—is itself blind to—blinding as both disfiguration and defiguration. As the literal and literalizing defacement of the site of symbolic integration, blinding is the act that leaves over what the mutilated Gloucester calls "the case of eyes" (IV.vi.147). *Lear* unfolds between the consolidation or symbolic "jelling" of the subject and its material residuum, the "vile jelly" of Gloucester's

20. As Jacques-Alain Miller writes, "Let us say that the most radical and surprising definition of the subject which Lacan proposed . . . is that it is no more than a 'discontinuity in the real' " ("Les réponses du réel" 13).

21. On the relation between trauma and drama in *King Lear,* see Timothy Murray, "Drama Trauma."

22. On the "paranoid-schizoid" position of infancy, see Melanie Klein, "Notes on Some Schizoid Mechanisms" and "Mourning and Its Relation to Manic-Depressive States," in *The Writings of Melanie Klein,* vol. 1. Juliet Mitchell sketches "the links between the psychology of the actual neurosis and the psychosis" in Klein's work ("Introduction" 87). See also the insistence by both Freud and Lacan that reality is originally experienced as hallucination.

punctured eyes.[23] Whereas for Oedipus, blindness and insight are structurally linked in the scene of discovery, for Gloucester, the two events are simply metonymically contiguous, *post hoc* rather than *propter hoc,* bound not by the machinery of plot but by the incidental ligatures of theme. In *Lear,* blindness does not signify insight, but, as in Lear's desire to cast out his eyes rather than weep like a woman, functions as an index of the scotomization that mimes symbolic recognition in the mode of hallucination.

The classical *mythos* or plot of recognition, foreclosed from the symbolic order of *King Lear,* reappears in the real of theatrical spectacle as the materiality of *lexis, opsis,* and *melopoeia,* the residual categories of the Aristotelian dialectic of *mythos* and *ethos.* In *King Lear,* the onstage presentation of Gloucester's blinding demonstrates the monstrosity of the theatrical *realia* whose indecorous transgression of the Aristotelian protocols of representation manifests the violence that occasions them. This is the violence of *Lear*'s "Theater of Cruelty," which entails not only the representation of violence, but also violence to representation: in this scenario, the imaginary function of the eye as the guarantee of the autonomous self is collapsed into the "vile jelly" of the imploded eyeball, a reduction to pure *organ,* which effectively forecloses the symbolic *organ*-ization represented by Oedipal blinding.[24] As Kent says, "See better, Lear; and let me still remain / The true blank of thine eye" (I.i.157–58); the valence of the phrase "true blank" switches between the projective mirror of the iconic on the one hand, and the regulatory "blanks" or lacks of the linguistic, on the other— the vectors of imaginary insight and symbolic blindness, which

23. For a different reading of the literalness of blinding in *King Lear,* see Paul Alpers, "*King Lear* and the Theory of the Sight Pattern." Stanley Cavell discusses Alpers's essay in *Disowning Knowledge* 44ff.

24. The eye as disembodied organ is the other side of Artaud's notion of "the body without organs" taken up by Gilles Deleuze and Félix Guattari, for whom it marks the "primary repression" which opposes the "desiring-machines" of schizophrenia (*Anti-Oedipus* 9). On Artaud and the Theater of Cruelty see Derrida, *Writing and Difference.*

are bound together in the Oedipal *mythos* of recognition. At the same time, the "true blank" also uncannily precipitates the visceral and vitreous white of the eye as the thing-like gaze: the intrinsically nonseeing part of the optical apparatus, which supports the work of representation as neither a screen nor a lack, but as a smear or glaze floating on its surface.[25]

In act 4, Kent asks the Gentleman about the effects of his earlier letters on Cordelia: "Did your letters pierce the queen to any demonstration of grief?" (IV.iii.9–10). Here, the play's language of invasive perforation has shifted to the agency of the letter itself. This piercing by the letter, like the piercing of Oedipus's ankles by and as his name, indicates again that *King Lear* does not replace the symbolic castration of *Oedipus Rex* with literal blinding, as Paul Alpers has argued, but rather with the literalization of the symbolic, its piercing by the letter as real. It is not simply, that is, that the eyes of Gloucester are poked out by the character Cornwall, but that the text of *King Lear* is pierced by the real-ized motifs of *Oedipus Rex* in the psychoanalytic discourse of tragedy.[26]

If the simultaneous citation and deflation of Sophoclean anagnorisis indicates *King Lear*'s foreclosure of the Oedipus plays, where does such a foreclosure take place? It cannot be strictly intertextual, since Shakespeare most likely did not read Sophocles. The plays are joined not by the connections of influence, but by their arrangement in the canon, and it is only within this order that the foreclosure of *Oedipus* by *Lear* can be said to occur. Intertextuality is a function of the Shakespearean universe of discourse, "what Shakespeare read"; canonicity, insofar as it is distinct from intertextuality, is produced through

25. We are indebted here to Harry Berger, Jr., for this gloss of these lines: "Editors tell me 'blank' means the center of a target, but the genitive, 'of,' arrows back from object to part and turns 'blank' into the center of a sightless eye. . . . Kent's feathered phrase flies through the text and pierces other blanks" ("'Some Squeaking Cleopatra' " 2).

26. The entire scene between Kent and the Gentleman, including the Gentleman's highly emblematic answer to Kent's question, is missing from the Folio, probably because of the scene's nondramatic, expository character. On the argument that the Folio omissions represent a more "dramatic" text, see Gary Taylor and Michael Warren, eds., *The Division of the Kingdoms*.

the retroactive selection and ordering of texts in the libraries and syllabi of Literature. Intertexuality is primarily symbolic—founded on the transformative agon of texts within the tradition—whereas canonicity is primarily imaginary, based on a fantasy of "the Great" or "the Tragic," which triumphantly unites texts across time and space in the pedagogic service of reproducing Western values. The repressive and sublimatory dialectic of the two constitutes the literary tradition, in which the projected ideals of the canon both screen and manifest the intertextual conditions and contradictions of culture. Thus Shakespearean drama can be linked *canonically* to Greek tragedy not only by virtue of, but more important, through the active exclusion of, the manifold *intertextual* links with "minor" Latin, medieval, or popular works.

This distinction between intertextuality and canonicity parallels the Freudian apposition of interpretation and construction: the interpretive work of analysis, involving the ongoing recollection and symbolic reinscription of repressed representations, is interrupted by moments of construction, the analyst's speculative syntheses, which Freud compares to the delusions that fill the vacuum left by psychotic foreclosure. Like interpretation, intertextuality unfolds through the metaphoric condensation and metonymic displacement of one text by another. Like construction, canonicity is constituted through the nonhistorical conjunction of texts according to the fundamentally imaginary ligatures—pedagogical more than philological—of character, theme, and motif.

Given the dialectical distinction between the canonical and the intertextual, two critical possibilities arise in response to the anachronistic conjunction of *King Lear* and *Oedipus*. The first would be the imperative to symbolize the imaginary by historicizing the connections between the two plays. Such a project might include determining the ideological parameters and contingencies of the dramas' yoking, or rejecting the coupling altogether in favor of intertextually based pairings such as *Hamlet* and Seneca, or *King Lear* and the Book of Job. The second possibility, however, would involve dwelling on the plays' conjunction precisely as ahistorical, as "pure construction," in or-

der to locate the psychotic moments that found—and poten-
tially reconfigure—the order of literature. Whereas the imperative to symbolize the canon by asserting the necessity of
intertextuality involves *interpretation*, the imperative to realize
the canon around its moments of impossibility entails *construction*. Accordingly, we construe *King Lear*'s textuality through
the logic of "canon construction," a phrase that indicates both
the ideological stapling of texts that conserves the tradition,
and the psychotic quantum of those junctions, which threatens
to pervert the discourse of the tragic from within. Such canon
construction requires that we encounter the order of literature
as both "merely" and profoundly constructed; thus in this chapter we delimit the traumatic perforations disclosed by the institutional alignment of *Oedipus* and *Lear*. In addition, however,
canon construction also designates the schizoid reconstruction
of the canon through scandalous cuts and absurd additions of
old and new texts, which are maintained as *Ding*-like, at once
inside and outside the literary tradition. If both canonicity and
intertextuality involve a fundamental (Oedipal) fantasy of literary history, canon construction would be an attempt not to
reinterpret or reevaluate that fantasy, but to alter it, to shift
and traverse its coordinates by psychotically repunctuating it.

In *Kafka: Toward a Minor Literature*, Gilles Deleuze and Félix
Guattari write that "minor no longer designates specific literatures but the revolutionary conditions for every literature
within the heart of what is called great (or established) literature. . . . There is nothing that is major or revolutionary except
the minor" (18, 26). Only "minor" texts, Deleuze and Guattari
suggest, can become truly "major," but with the consequence
that the local transactions and resistances that define the "mi-
nority" of such texts disappear into the master plan whose
landmarks they constitute. "Becoming-minor," as both a critical
and a cultural imperative, implies reactivating or "deterrito-
rializing" those moments of the canon which, although integrated into its narratives, remain foreign to it. Typical of their
"anti-Oedipal" position, Deleuze and Guattari write of psychoanalysis here that it has "only one single dream: to assume a

major function in language, to offer [itself] as a sort of state language, an official language" (27). Psychoanalysis too, however, only became "major" by first "becoming-minor": like Kafka in Prague, Freud found in a provincial and anti-Semitic Vienna an *unheimlich* home for psychoanalysis, which was thus cast from the beginning as a discourse in and of exile. Psychoanalysis has remained residual to its institutional places of residence, a discipline "extimate" to both the human and the natural sciences. Moreover, psychoanalysis in the United States today has once again been marginalized in both therapeutic and academic communities. Perhaps it is from this position "after Oedipus" that a "minor" psychoanalysis, a psychoanalysis-after-Psychoanalysis, can emerge and articulate not only the necessity but the *impossibility* of Oedipus, its constitutive impasses in the vicissitudes of literary history.

If, as the title of this half of the book indicates, "LEAR" and "REAL" are anagrams of each other, a longer, more paranoid palindrome suggests itself here: "LEAR'S IN ISRAEL." The rules of the palindrome demand the production of a certain minimum quantum of sense that precipitates out of and holds together the systematic unfolding of the palindrome's letters. The "sense," however, that clings to the palindrome's paranoic, self-mirroring consistency is the sense of *joui-sense,* a sense in non-sense, an enjoyment of the material properties of language. To write LEAR'S IN ISRAEL is to conjoin historically disparate discourses in a rigorously logical yet virtually absurd construction which reconstellates the symbolic intersections of Shakespeare and psychoanalysis around the non-converted, non-integrated reality of the Jew. Thus this palindrome serves to designate, for example, the boxing up of *The Merchant of Venice* and *King Lear* in Freud's essay "The Theme of the Three Caskets," as well as the abscessive poetics that tatoo the "Old Testament" text of Job onto *King Lear*'s Christian eschatology. Moreover, the phrase violently yokes the identifications of the "excommunicated" Lacan with the rejected Lear—an analogy noted by Stuart Schneiderman—and the Jewish Spinoza, whose subjection to the exclusionary rites of *kherem* and *chammata* are

taken by Lacan as the historical type of his own expulsion from
the International Psychoanalytic Association (*Seminar XI* 3–4).[27]
Although the sheer absurdity of the palindrome absolutely resists "interpretation," its nonsensical logic of the letter allows us
to *construct* a paranoid frame that reorganizes *King Lear* and psychoanalysis around such a piece of verbal litter. To pursue the
path indicated by the palindrome without succumbing to the
lures of "wild analysis" ("That way madness lies"), however, we
will follow *King Lear* across the topography of two alternate
tragic trajectories: the psychotic road to Dover and the neurotic
road to Colonus.

Lear at Dover

The interaction between Edgar and Gloucester at "Dover
Cliffs" stages a scene of therapy, but a therapy of construction
rather than interpretation, insofar as the guided delusion
through fabricated space into which Edgar plunges his father
enacts a psychodrama of cruelty. Whereas the interpretive work
of psychoanalysis is epitomized by the riddling ironies of Tiresias or the play-within-a-play of *Hamlet,* both of which "discover" prior events through the play of language, the Dover
Cliffs scene constructs a purely fictional narrative, which, in
staging the coordinates of representation as perspectival illusion, materializes the constitutive contradictions and residua of
that Renaissance humanist discourse.

Gloucester, in search of death at Dover, is led by Edgar (in
his role as deceiving crutch, a kind of anti-Antigone) to a "Dover
Cliffs" constructed out of words:

Come on, sir; here's the place: stand still. How fearful
And dizzy 'tis to cast one's eyes so low!

27. See Stuart Schneiderman, *Jacques Lacan* 17. On "becoming-Jewish," see
Deleuze and Guattari, *Anti-Oedipus* 291–92. Their formulation that "a Jew
becomes Jewish, but in a becoming-Jewish of the non-Jew" would be especially
useful in analyzing the Jewish atheism of Freud, in, for example, *Moses and
Monotheism.* "Lear's in Israel" appears in John Pool's *Lid off a Daffodil* (no
pagination).

The crows and choughs that wing the midway air
Show scarce so gross as beetles; half way down
Hangs one that gathers sampire, dreadful trade!
Methinks he seems no bigger than his head.
The fishermen that walk upon the beach
Appear like mice, and yond tall anchoring bark
Diminish'd to her cock, her cock a buoy
Almost too small for sight. The murmuring surge,
That on th'unnumber'd idle pebble chafes,
Cannot be heard so high. I'll look no more,
Lest my brain turn, and the deficient sight
Topple down headlong.

(IV.vi.11–24)

As commentators have pointed out, Edgar's speech tries to reproduce in words the recession of space revolutionized by the visual technologies of Renaissance art and subjectivity.[28] Jonathan Goldberg in particular has linked the vanishing point into which Gloucester falls with the Lacanian real (258). Elaborating his argument, we would distinguish two visual logics realized in this constructed space: the "nothing" marked by the vanishing point of perspectival representation, and the middle ground of the sampire gatherer whose mirage-like "hanging" smudges or clouds that space. In the passage, the fetishistic "cock," which presents a point "almost too small for sight," anchors representation and its illusions around the vortex of a "nothing"; in Lacanian terms, this vanishing point is coordinate with the S_1 or master signifier of primal repression. Like the piercing of the ankles of Oedipus by the name, this punctiform mark, itself insignificant, makes possible the mimetic signification of space and the infinite recessions of representational desire—the S_2 which designates the signifying chain. Thus, in Lacan's analysis of perspective in *Seminar XI*, the vanishing point correlative with the eye of the beholder not only

28. On Renaissance perspective and Lacan, see Barbara Freedman, *Staging the Gaze;* on the visual parameters of the Dover Cliffs scene, see John Bender, *Spenser and Literary Pictionalism* 95–98. See Zizek's *Looking Awry* for an account of the real and anamorphosis in Shakespeare.

provides the viewer with assurances of property and self-consciousness, but does so through the negative sublime of its infinitesimal calculus: "When carried to the limit, the process of this meditation, of this reflecting reflection, goes so far as to reduce the subject apprehended by the Cartesian meditation to a power of annihilation" (81). In the Dover Cliffs scene, perspectival recession violently foreshortens and finally annihilates the objects in the visual field, so that men become mice and the ship, "diminish'd to her cock," is finally reduced "almost too small for sight." This drastic attenuation of the object to an evanescent mark constitutes the subject of representation and organizes the visual field; it is precisely in being unable to see the ship's buoy and unable to hear the "murmuring surge" that Gloucester is made to believe in their vanishing reality.

In the middle ground of Edgar's verbal picture, however, "Hangs one that gathers sampire, dreadful trade!" The figure of the sampire gatherer scales the recession of space according to the measure of man—"Methinks he seems no bigger than his head." "Hangs" points to another effect of this figure, which is to delimit a visual disturbance within the geometric space of the image. The sampire gatherer hanging in the receding vista is not only geometrically reduced but also spatially dislodged or unfixed from the perspectival grid. Like the anamorphic death's head, which, in Lacan's account, "floats" in the foreground of Holbein's *Ambassadors* (*Seminar XI* 92), the sampire gatherer, reduced to his head, leaves a stain or blur on the skin of representation. This floating head, we would argue, "surfaces" within the representation of depth and threatens to level its carefully constructed illusion, just as the actual flatness of the stage sensed by Gloucester ("Methinks the ground is even" [IV.vi.3]) collapses the perspectival depths constructed by Edgar. In Edgar's speech, the reduction of the body to the size of its head through the movement towards the vanishing point also inflates the head to the size of its body in a representational hydrocephalism that bloats and twists the humanist measure of perspective from within. In Lacanian terms, the vanishing point marks the place of the primal signifier (S_1), which orders

and flaws representation (S₂); the hanging blot, which ana-
morphically distorts that picture as the optical afterimage of
its representational structure embodies the *objet a,* "the shimmering of a surface that is not, in advance, situated for me in
its distance" (*Seminar XI* 96).

The general movement of Edgar's verbal construction is to
mime the vertiginous effects of a fall into the converging lines
of representational space, a plummet which is arrested by a
"hanging," a momentary, derealizing suspension of and torsion
within the perspectival illusion. So, too, Gloucester, the anni-
hilative subject of the tunnel of vision into which he falls, is
also left hanging within it, not yet dead but also no longer fully
alive. This condition is maintained by the suspension of anagnorisis between father and son in the scenes that follow; as
soon as Edgar finally reveals himself, the father, realizing that
he is dead, in fact dies (V.iii.194–98). This motif of an *arrested
fall* displays the topologic of what Lacan calls in *Seminar VII* the
"between-two-deaths," the upsurge of the real as the interval
between biological death and its symbolization. Whereas the
law of mourning prescribes the cultural signification of biological death through funeral rites, the Sadean articulation of the
"second death" emphasizes—like Hamlet contemplating the
murder of Claudius at prayer—the eternal damnation of the
soul in an absolute refusal of symbolic consolations (*Seminar
VII* 293–94). For Lacan, the "between-two-deaths" that characterizes the temporality of tragedy suspends the Sadean *death
to the symbolic* effected by psychosis within the *symbolization of
death* performed by Oedipal mourning. In the scene at Dover
Cliffs, we could say that Artaud's Theater of Cruelty converges
with the Sadean ethics of the second death within and through
the competing protocols of Renaissance representation. Like
Artaud's utopic dramaturgy, Edgar's theater reduces dramatic
representation to the pure signifiers of spectacle. Like Sade's
ethics of *jouissance,* Edgar's refusal to identify himself sustains
visceral life through the refusal of life's cancellation by symbolic
rites and tragic recognition. Gloucester's arrested fall into the
space of a representation "constructed" around points and

stains of the real materializes the scene's larger gesture of de-
laying anagnorisis in order to suspend the symbolizing closure
of the second death.

The scene of Gloucester's blinding begins with the pron-
ouncement of two divergent fates for the old man:

> *Regan:* Hang him instantly.
> *Goneril:* Pluck out his eyes.

(III.vii.4–5)

The second plan stitches Oedipal recognition onto the corporeal piercing performed by the name of Oedipus; Gloucester's imagined fall into the geometrical apex of his own
blindness brings to a point this hallucinatory literalization of
the Oedipal *mythos* in *King Lear*. The "hanging" or suspending
of Gloucester in the unreal reality of the between-two-deaths,
however, completes the trajectory of the first suggestion,
"Hang him instantly." Following the psychotic logic of canon
construction, Gloucester's suspended falling reroutes the
tragic trajectory of *King Lear* from the blinding of Oedipus
through the "hanging" that knots Jocasta, Antigone, and Cordelia in a single fate.

Gerard Pommier defines analytic construction as the formalization of the analysand's fantasy into Lacanian mathemes
(S_1, a, Φ, and so on) in order to mark the limit points of the
fantasy in the real (*Le dénouement* 156–58). Such mathemes,
Pommier specifies, are not signifiers in the way that dreams
and *lapsae linguae* are, but rather "mute points of structure"
(152), which can be discerned but not discovered or interpreted
in the analysand's linguistic productions: "He learns to find its
mute presence through the multiplicity of its presentations;
and little by little he will grasp its contours, even though its
ultimate meaning continues to escape him" (156). Edgar's mapping of Dover Cliffs is a "construction" not only in the Freudian
sense of a fictional account motivated by fragments of truth,
but also in Pommier's Lacanian sense of a formal reduction;
thus the scene graphs representation around both the anchoring point and the derealizing suspension of perspectival space.

So too, our reading of Dover Cliffs as construction *is itself such a construction,* insofar as it substitutes both a Lacanian algebra (S_1, S_2, a) and the "tragemes" of Sophocles (the pluckings, piercings, and hangings of the Oedipus trilogy) for the points, lines, and planes of Edgar's vision. Such a translation is, we might say, *topological* rather than *tropological,* insofar as it involves the anamorphic mapping of points from the tilted plane of one discourse onto that of another. Our reading thus interprets the Dover Cliffs scene by constructing it, by locating the limits of representation in the encounter of tragic and psychoanalytic discourses.

The Promis'd End

King Lear's cruel stitching of *Oedipus Rex* and *Antigone,* of blinding and hanging, of castration and *Kasten,* impedes and suspends the play's more strongly pronounced symbolic itinerary from *Oedipus Rex* to *Oedipus at Colonus.* This interruption of *Lear*'s Oedipal dramaturgy by the extimate logic of *Antigone* participates in the general deformation of anagnorisis in the final acts of the play. In *Lear,* recognition scenes, coming too soon or too late, are avoided, aborted, or ineffectual; these scenes, moreover, collect at the "extreme verge" of Dover cliffs (IV.vi.26), the play's delusory "promis'd end" (V.iii.262). These scenes exceed and condition the Oedipal dialectic of recognition and misrecognition insofar as the symbolic structures of tragedy, ejected by *King Lear*'s plot of foreclosure, can only return in the monstrous real of hallucination.

Thus in the reunion between father and daughter in act 4, Lear, roused from his "wheel of fire" (IV.vii.47), is awakened from a burning dream into a dream-like reality dominated by the specter of the child around whom his conscience and consciousness is gradually restored, a process that culminates in his acknowledgment of Cordelia. In a typically and profoundly Shakespearean device, the scene operates by repeating the disastrous formulas of the drama's cataclysmic opening:

> *Lear:*   For, as I am a man, I think this lady
>   To be my child Cordelia.
> *Cordelia:*   And so I am, I am.
> *Lear:*   Be your tears wet? Yes, faith. I pray, weep not:
>   If you have poison for me, I will drink it.
>   I know you do not love me; for your sisters
>   Have, as I do remember, done me wrong:
>   You have some cause, they have not.
> *Cordelia:*   No cause, no cause.
> *Lear:*   Am I in France?
>
> (IV.vii.68–76)

Even after "recognizing" Cordelia, Lear says, "I know you do not love me," continuing to avoid his youngest daughter's love. So, too, Cordelia's response, "No cause, no cause," repeats and recasts her initial "Nothing." Cordelia's "cause" retranslates "thing" across the French word "chose," derived from the Latin *causa;* returned from France, she repeats in a foreign tongue her emblematic "nothing," which had "caused" the tragic foreclosures that form the action of the drama. As if registering this translinguistic operation, Lear queries, "Am I in France?"[29]

The encounter follows the logic of repetition exploited in Lady Macbeth's sleepwalking scene, in which the play's prior signifiers—the "damned spot," the language of doing and undoing, the "knocking at the gate"—are redeployed in the theater of hallucination (V.i). Indeed, to pursue the analogy with *Macbeth*, the Cordelia of the reunion scene functions like the knocking brought out in Thomas De Quincey's 1823 essay, "On the Knocking at the Gate in *Macbeth*." De Quincey writes, "The knocking at the gate is heard, and it makes known audibly that the reaction has commenced... the reestablishment of the goings-on of the world in which we live first makes us profoundly sensible of the awful parenthesis that had suspended them" (328). The knocking is that little bit of reality that both signals the restoration of the quotidian world and retroactively makes us aware that the everyday had been momentarily de-

---

29. We thank Wendy Hester for pointing out the "France" reference.

realized. In *Seminar XI*, Lacan comments on the phenomenology of awakening in terms strikingly reminiscent of De Quincey's analysis:

> The other day, I was awoken from a short nap by knocking at
> my door just before I actually awoke. With this impatient knock-
> ing I had already formed a dream, a dream that manifested to
> me something other than this knocking. And when I awake, it
> is in so far as I reconstitute my entire representation around
> this knocking—this perception—that I am aware of it. . . . When
> the knocking occurs, not in my perception, but in my conscious-
> ness, it is because my consciousness reconstitutes itself around
> this representation—that I know that I am waking up, that I
> am *knocked* [last word in English in the original].
>
> (E 56, F 55–56; translation altered)

In De Quincey's *Macbeth* and in Lacan's dream, the "knocking"
is a piece of reality equally foreign both to the dream work,
which weaves it into its fabric, and to consciousness, which only
gradually reorganizes itself around the kernel of perception.[30]
Thus consciousness emerges as the retroactive representation
of a perception that always remains alien to it, both missed in
time and in a different register. Moreover, the word "knocking," spoken in English in Lacan's seminar, is precisely such a
foreign piece of Romantic-Shakespearean language around
which psychoanalytic discourse situates itself.

So, too, Cordelia's manifestation to the delirious Lear relo-
cates him "in reality," but only across the distended period of
the waking dream: the time, that is, between Lear's initial
arousal and his acknowledgment of Cordelia, and also, more
broadly, the time that has lapsed between Cordelia's "Nothing"
in act 1 and its translation into the punctual repetition of "No
cause, no cause" in act 4. In *Lear*, the reunion scene, rather
than simply recalling the madman from his dream, fragilely
reconstructs the everyday reality of representation around the
unreality of hallucination, as pure quantity unassimilated by

---

30. Cf. Freud's dream of the burning child, which Lacan goes on to read
in these terms.

consciousness. Thus the Doctor advises against filling in the gaps of memory ("And yet it is danger / To make him even o'er the time he has lost" [IV.vii.79–80]), counseling the maintenance of amnesia as the only foundation for Lear's return to reality. We could say that through the scene, the play "traverses the hallucination" by coming to be where its trauma was, by assuming the repudiated "Nothing" as its "(no) cause." In becoming the "child-changed father" of his infantile fantasy, Lear has tragicomically come to be in the position of the Thing lost as such, in Cordelia's phrase, the "poor *perdu*" (IV.vii. 17, 35).

The play can be said to "traverse the hallucination" at Dover, but it does not "traverse the fantasy," because, as the following scenes exhibit, the play's fundamental fantasy of incest without castration has not been altered. Like Gloucester, Lear remains suspended in the imaginary; led off with Cordelia to prison, he continues to inhabit the *incastus* union of two: "Come, let's away to prison; / We two alone will sing like birds i' th' cage" (V.iii.8–9). The image of the bird cage encloses or encases the "kind nursery" of Lear's initial demand for love; insofar as Lear's demand still refuses the dialectical mediation of desire, it points to the hallucinatory kernel of all fantasy from within the prison of the imaginary.

If Cordelia living appears to Lear as dead ("You are a spirit, I know; where did you die?" [IV.vii.49]), in Lear's last words, Cordelia dead appears to him as living: "Look on her, look, her lips, / Look there, look there!" (V.iii.309–10). Timothy Murray has noted the specifically anamorphic nature of Lear's final vision of Cordelia through the looking glass, a side view that materializes her strange condition as living/dead in "the stain of indirect representation, the mist of the mirror" ("Drama Trauma" 22). The "recognition" of Cordelia by Lear, and of Edgar by Gloucester, mimes the passage from unconscious to conscious, from blindness to insight, from latent to manifest, but it only does so in the delusional, literalizing, and superficial mode of hallucination. For both Gloucester and Lear, the logic of psychosis forces an encounter with the real, but at the same time precludes symbolizing that encounter, since the real appears only in the mode of delusion. In the drama of psycho-analysis, *Lear* stages both a salutary and a derisory appointment with the real: salutary because it dramatizes the emergence of the Thing, and derisory because that Thing remains uncan-celed by language, hence a hallucination that cannot be as-sumed as the cause of desire.

Lear's final misrecognition of Cordelia is glossed by a pair of questions that the play leaves unanswered:

> *Kent:*   Is this the promis'd end?
> *Edgar:* Or image of that horror?
>
> (V.iii.262–63)

"Promis'd end" can be read either as the apocalyptic destruction of the symbolic order, the Schreberian "end of the world" caused by *Verwerfung*, or as the symbolization performed by dramatic closure as it comes to be where primal repression was, the dying into history achieved by Oedipus at Colonus. This dichotomy within "promised end" is reproduced and modified in the questions as a pair: "promised end" indicates the death of the symbolic in apocalypse (psychosis); "image of that hor-ror" describes the symbolization of death in the Christian econ-omy of historical prefiguration (neurosis). These are not posed as "rhetorical questions," but, we would insist, as "real ques-tions," as questions *concerning the real*, questions that suspend *King Lear* between the collapse of representation, the "promised end," and the representation of collapse, "the image of that horror."

In Stephen Booth's apt characterization of the play's un-ravelling of *mythos*, "Not ending is a primary characteristic of *King Lear*" (*"King Lear, "Macbeth," Indefinition, and Tragedy* 15). As Jonathan Goldberg has argued, "Dover" is a principle not of Christian transumption but of unrelenting deferral in the play.[31] The incantatorily repeated "Dover," ringing with the promise of the word "Dove"—a christological beyond of

---

31. In "Perspectives: Dover Cliffs and the Conditions of Representation," Jonathan Goldberg reads the vanishing point in Edgar's perspectival repre-sentation of the imaginary Dover cliffs in terms of Lacan's "Real."

peace and reconciliation—repeatedly reveals itself only as an
"over" or "after," a site of deception and defeat, which, in
"un-promising" the end it had appeared to offer, constitutes
the "D/over-turning" of Colonus.[32] This reading of Dover in
terms of the endless deferral of desire, however, is in turn
checked or suspended by the "hanging" of the play in the
between-two-deaths. This arrest marks Lacan's rewriting of
his conception of the death drive from the mechanistic insistence of the signifying chain to the traumatic irruption of
pure drive, undialecticized demand, that bungles the orderly
displacements of signification.[33] The "between" of the between-two-deaths—which is also the "between" of *between-two-
death-drives*—does not delineate a threshold space of symbolic
mediation or imaginary reconciliation, but rather, following
the topology of the *Kasten,* the extimate surface of the real.
So, too, if the ethics of psychoanalysis is oriented by this
suspended trajectory, the suspension at stake involves not
endless undecidability but rather a "stretched truth," the twists
and knots within the discourse of science that mark the impasses of its structure.[34]

Both *Lear* and *Oedipus at Colonus* enact the injunction of
Freud's "Wo Es war, soll Ich werden," but the achievement of
Oedipus guarantees symbolization, whereas its derisory inver-
sion in *Lear,* entering "like the catastrophe of the old comedy"
(I.ii.131–2), points to the foreclosure of symbolization. *Oedipus
at Colonus* and *King Lear,* neurosis and psychosis, represent the
counterplots of mourning that converge in *Antigone,* the play
that founds successful symbolization at Colonus in the possibility of symbolization's failure at Dover. *King Lear,* whose "traversal of the hallucination" derisorily warps the transumptive
itinerary of Oedipus, unwittingly points towards the analytic
path of traversing the fantasy which it nonetheless fails to

32. "Dover" is repeated eleven times in the play, with especial insistence
during the scene of Gloucester's blinding (III.vii.49–92).
33. On Lacan's changing conception of the death drive, see Zizek, *The
Sublime Object of Ideology* 131–36.
34. On the distinction and relation of science and truth in psychoanalysis,
see Lacan's essay "La science et la vérité," *Écrits* 855–77.

achieve. Rather than traversing its fantasy, coming to be in the place of the *objet a, King Lear* has only "traversed its hallucination" by pathetically coming to be in the place of the Thing uncanceled by repression. Jacques-Alain Miller writes of Lacan's early study, *Les complexes familiaux,* that "Psychosis is there, already situated as a kind of parody" ("Lacan et psychose" 29). So, too, we could say that the itinerary of *Lear* enacts a psychotic parody "already situated" within the family complexes dramatized in the Oedipus trilogy. In so doing, *Lear's* hallucinatory traversal isolates the mortifying moment of the real, hung—like Jocasta and Antigone—within the Oedipal scene of symbolization. In its traversal through and by psychoanalysis, *King Lear* leaves us between two readings, the "promised end" and the "image of that horror." To be hung between two readings is not, however, to be caught in the supposed "interminability" of analysis, but rather to be on the way to symbolization through the detour of the real—on the road to Colonus, by endless way of Dover.

A F T E R - W O R D

Full fadom five thy father lies,
  Of his bones are coral made:
Those are pearls that were his eyes:
  Nothing of him that doth fade,
But doth suffer a sea-change
Into something rich and strange.
                              —Shakespeare, *The Tempest*

If the symptom is a metaphor, it is not a metaphor to say
so, any more than to say that man's desire is a metonymy.
For the symptom *is* a metaphor whether one likes it or
not, as desire *is* a metonymy, however funny people may
find the idea.
                              —Lacan, *Écrits*

The coupling of these passages from Shakespeare and Lacan,
each of which insists on the performative, actualized status of
the rhetorical transformations it analyzes, raises the question
of the precise relation between the two discourses at stake in
this book. In *After Oedipus* we track and stage the temporal logic
that links *Hamlet* and *Lear* in the unfolding of psychoanalytic
discourse. Like the Inter-Section, this "*After*-Word" maps the
movement of the two halves of the book onto another set of

Lacanian diagrams. Such a graphic translation of literature into theory may appear "merely" allegorical. We argue, however—paraphrasing Lacan's formulation about the rhetoric of desire and the symptom—that, if Shakespeare is an allegory of psychoanalysis, it is not an allegory to say so. As Joel Fineman has argued in "The Structure of Allegorical Desire," allegory combines metaphor and metonymy, condensation and displacement, or, in the language of *The Tempest,* "coral" and "bones." Insofar as the relation between Shakespeare and psychoanalysis is produced precisely through such rhetorical sea changes, their intersection is structurally allegorical. It is, however, not an allegory to say so, since the conjunction and disjunction of Shakespeare and psychoanalysis symptomatically exemplify the allegorical status of all criticism as rhetorical, as occuring in language as well as describing it. To say that "it is not allegorical to say so," is not, then, to claim a critical position based in some reality outside of allegory, but rather to define allegory *as* the reality of cultural representation.

Moreover, if allegory defines linguistic *reality*, the world of imaginary and symbolic representations, a second gloss of the phrase would isolate a modality of the *real* left over by allegorical signification as such. In Lacan's various sets of diagrams, the mathemes—*objet a*, Φ, S_1, and so on—are themselves, according to Lacan, material remnants of the structural transformations they constellate. In this sense, these elements function as nonsynthetic nodes or interstices between the symbolic and the real, obdurate bits of bone adhering to the elegiac metaphors of pearl and coral. Mapping literary texts onto Lacan's graphs at once places the works of the tradition in structural relation to each other *and* points to their irreducibility vis-à-vis those structures. Insofar as *Hamlet* and *Lear* constitute points of impasse within the theoretical narratives of literary history which they generate and inhabit, the plays not only "take the place of" the Lacanian mathemes in a mode of rhetorical substitution, but also materialize such intransigent knots or navels within representation. In this second sense, it is not an allegory to say that Shakespeare is an allegory of psychoanalysis, since the substitutions on which allegorical *signification*

depends have ceded to the allegorical *signifier* in excess of se-
miological production. Such a claim for the residual status of
the Shakespearean text cannot, of course, be thought apart
from its position in literary tradition. If the *symbolic* place of
Shakespeare in the order of Western literature and theory manifests the intertextual "richness" of Shakespearean discourse,
the *real* around which that discourse accretes testifies to the
"strangeness," the radical otherness, of the signifier.

To Open the Question Mark

Lacan's extended reading of *Hamlet* is the centerpiece of his
exposition of the graphs of desire, the "Che vuoi?" schemata,
presented in his fifth and sixth Seminars (1957–59) and published in his essay "The Subversion of the Subject and the
Dialectic of Desire."[1] In these diagrams, Lacan charts subjectivity as an effect of the temporal process of signification, the
penetration and constitution of the subject by the signifier. It
is through such a process that psychoanalysis has been articulated by its relationship with Shakespeare, in the rhythm that
counterpoints *Hamlet* and *King Lear* within the larger temporal
movement coupling ancient and modern tragedy in the history
and theory of literature. The "Che vuoi?" diagrams not only
allow us to map *Hamlet* and *Lear* onto the psychoanalytic conception of desire, but also to recapitulate emblematically our
larger argument that psychoanalysis is an effect of its traversal
by and through literature.

Lacan's first graph of desire charts the splitting of the subject
($) by the transcription of primal need ($\triangle$), the mythical inten-
tionality of the pre-subject, into the linguistic register of demand (the statement S→S'), which forever alienates the subject
from instinctual satisfaction (Fig. 6). The subject is divided both
by the synchronic structure of language as Other, the battery
of signifiers (designated "A" for *Autre*), and by the temporal

1. Our versions of the diagrams are simplified and at points modified.
See also Slavoj Zizek's chapter "Che vuoi?" in *The Sublime Object of Ideology*.

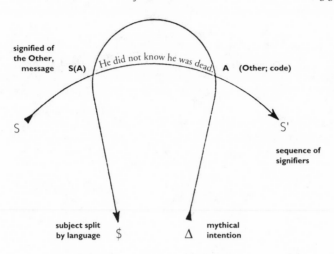

signified of
the Other,
message   S(A)   He did not know he was dead.   A   (Other; code)

S

S'

sequence of
signifiers

subject split
by language $ Δ   mythical
intention

Figure 6

dialectic between the sequence of signifiers (S–S') and the meaning they retroactively produce, labeled s(A), "signified of the Other." Lacan appropriates Roman Jakobson's distinction between metaphor and metonymy to show the meaning of the sentence unfolding in time across a metonymic series of words, signifiers that have been selected according to the logic of metaphor from a synchronic vocabulary. The first word of a sentence, that is, becomes meaningful only after the last word has been enunciated, "a retroversion effect by which the subject becomes at each stage what he was before and announces himself—he will have been—only in the future perfect tense" (*Écrits* E 306, F 808). Lacan takes his example from Freud's essay, "Two Principles of Mental Functioning," which recounts a young man's dream of his father:

> His father was alive once more and . . . was talking to him in his usual way. But he felt it exceedingly painful that his father had really died, only without knowing it. The only way of understanding this apparently nonsensical dream is by adding "as the dreamer wished" [*nach seinem Wunsch*] or "in consequence of his wish" after the words "that his father had really died," and by further adding "that he [the dreamer] wished it" to the last words.
>
> (*SE* 12: 225; *SA* 3:24)

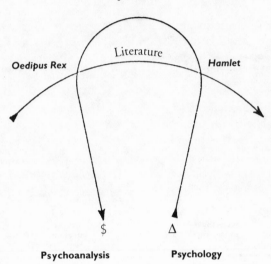

Oedipus Rex   Literature   Hamlet

$ Δ

Psychoanalysis   Psychology

Figure 6a

Lacan formalizes the dream as the statement "He did not know that he was dead," a sentence which does not "know" death until its cadential conclusion. Furthermore, the meaning of the sentence is constructed in relation to a code, "a synchronic and enumerable collection of elements in which each is sustained only by the principle of its opposition to each of the others" (*Écrits* E 304, F 806). The presence of any one signifier is thus a function of the absence of another, as in the *fort-da* game of signification enacted both structurally and thematically by the sentence "He did not know [*da*] he was dead [*fort*]."[2]

In Figure 6a, we plot the relationship of psychoanalysis and literature onto Lacan's graph of subjectivity and language: psychology (the doctrine of the autonomous self, corresponding to the moment of mythical intention on Lacan's diagram) becomes psychoanalysis (the theory of the split subject) by passing through literature. The sequence of literary texts selected by psychoanalysis functions retroactively, since it is only in the movement from *Oedipus Rex* to *Hamlet* and back that the meaning of *Oedipus*, and with it the project of Oedipal interpretation,

2. See "Seminar VI," 12 November 1958, 11, and 19 November 1958, 24.

will have been determined. *Hamlet's* position "after Oedipus" in psychoanalysis is structural as well as historical, insofar as it operates as the earlier play's *nachträgliche* interpretation. It is no accident that the two plays dramatize the two halves of Lacan's exemplary dream thought: if *Oedipus Rex,* as a play of recognition or *anagnorisis,* emphasizes the drama of "he did not know," *Hamlet,* unfolding in the aftermath of classical recognition, displays the theater of the dead father. In the movement from one to the other that psychoanalysis enunciates, *Oedipus Rex* becomes Oedipal in relation to a *Hamlet* that functions as its code, as the set of repressed or distorted interpretive protocols that retroactively project the earlier drama as their meaning, and as meaning more generally: both the Oedipal plot of hermeneutic discovery that governs interpretation ("he did not know"), and the message discovered by psychoanalysis in every cultural artifact ("the father is dead").[3]

The conjunction of *Oedipus Rex* and *Hamlet* is, of course, specific to psychoanalysis; it is the particular literary tradition that psychoanalysis speaks. In expressing that relation, psychoanalysis is produced by it as not-psychology: metonymically, by the temporal gap between *Oedipus Rex* and *Hamlet;* metaphorically, by the correlation of the two plays across that gap. The psychoanalytic notion of desire is represented by the metonymic difference between *Hamlet* and *Oedipus Rex:* desire, as quintessentially Oedipal desire, defines the relation of slippage and retroactive signification between the two plays. Furthermore, not only do *Hamlet* and *Oedipus* represent the desire of psychoanalysis, as the paradigmatic objects of (Oedipal) interpretation, but, in speaking the plays' metonymic relation, psychoanalysis is spoken *as their desire,* as the next text in the series, which, by promising to disclose their meaning, further displaces it. Thus, following Lacan's formula of desire, we might say, if psychoanalysis is the metonymy of literature, it is not a metonymy to say so.

By extension, the psychoanalytic notion of the symptom as

---

3. Cf. Jane Gallop, who connects the dream of the dead father to the story of Oedipus (*Reading Lacan* 158).

a metaphor motivates the correlation of *Oedipus Rex* and *Hamlet*, whereby the obsessional symptoms of Shakespeare's hero are explained by reference to Sophocles' play. *Oedipus* and *Hamlet*, moreover, together suffer psychoanalysis *as their symptom*, as the metaphor in which the two disjunct texts are violently yoked. Psychoanalytic *Verdichtung* (condensation, the mechanism of symptom formation), writes Lacan, is itself a condensation of *Dichtung*, poetry (*Écrits* E 160): the psychoanalytic symptom, then, is a metaphor of poetic metaphor, and it is, moreover, not a metaphor to say so. In the process of this condensation, psychoanalysis itself becomes *a symptom of literature*, a discourse that is neither *Dichtung* nor *Wahrheit*, neither literature nor psychology, but precisely their metaphoric condensation.[4]

What Does Psychoanalysis Want (with Shakespeare)?

In the bottom half of the second graph of desire, Lacan sketches the imaginary and symbolic modes of subjective identification implied by the signifying process (Fig. 7). In the process of its encounter with the Other (A), the battery of signifiers, the subject "fades" in its primary identification with one signifier, a single feature—for example, the father's not-knowing—that defines the Other as an ego ideal, I(A). Under the aspect of imaginary meaning, the ego is produced through its identification with a specular object, the ideal ego that the subject would like to be, labeled i(a). Note, however, that imaginary identification is logically secondary to symbolic identification, since metaphoric meaning (the imaginary model of the ego) is retroactively generated by the metonymic movement of signifiers.[5]

Within the interaction and retroaction of literature and psy-

4. *Dichtung und Wahrheit* (*Poetry and Truth*) is, of course, the title of Goethe's autobiography. Goethe is the crucial link between Shakespeare and Freud in the chain of signifiers that constitutes "literature" for Freudian discourse. See Avital Ronell, *Dictations*.

5. The bottom half of the second graph rearticulates the four positions of the "L" schema introduced by Lacan in the second year of his seminar.

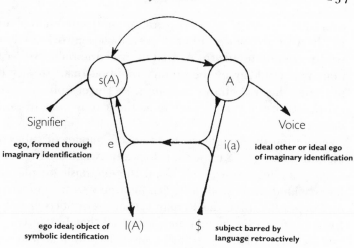

Figure 7

choanalysis, these modes of identification represent two poles in the history and prehistory of the psychoanalytic criticism of Shakespeare (Fig. 7a). The imaginary vector describes the applications of *character criticism:* the reification of *personae* into persons through the interplay of specular identifications. The vector of symbolic identification describes the project of *genre*

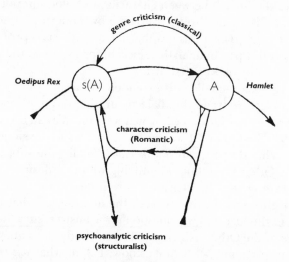

Figure 7a

criticism, from Aristotle to structuralism: the implication of texts in "the discourse of the Other," the symbolic network of literary paradigms and motifs formalized through their allusive reception. We could say of the literary tradition that "Homer did not know he was literature," since, in Hegel's phrase, art is always art of the past, becoming aesthetic only in its historical demise.

Following the imaginary and symbolic modes of subjective identification, genre criticism is logically as well as chronologically prior to character criticism; the emphasis on plot and literary kind in Aristotle's *Poetics,* in large part a commentary on *Oedipus Rex,* precedes Romantic character criticism, with its focus on Shakespeare's heroes, above all that fragile type of interiority, Hamlet. According to this dialectic of imaginary and symbolic identification, psychoanalytic Shakespeare criticism— and psychoanalysis *as* Shakespeare criticism—proceeds as a return to Classical structure from the vantage point of Romantic subjectivity, a return that invites both the subjectification of structure (Oedipus as Hamlet) and the structuration of the subject (Hamlet as Oedipus). Our graph in this second exfoliation maps Lacan's dialectic of identification onto Hegel's analysis of Shakespeare: according to Hegel, Shakespeare's drama embodies the breach between character and plot, interior and exterior, a disjunction to be overcome by modern philosophy (*Aesthetics* 1: 575ff). In this graph, such a synthesis is promised by structuralist psychoanalytic criticism, for example, the work of Paul Ricoeur or René Girard.

This Hegelian teleology is extended in Lacan's third graph (Fig. 8), which redraws the dialectic of identification into one of desire. The mythical need, which was voiced as an objectless demand to the Other ("I wanna . . . "), returns to the subject as desire: "What do you want?" *Che vuoi?* Finally, the subject returns the Other's question, identifying with that desire: "What do *you* want *of me?*" For Lacan, desire is always the *question* of desire. Desire entails, that is, both the question of what is desired, and the fact that the question *is* the answer, since desire, as desire of the Other, is structurally somebody else's question: "What do *you* want?"—"I don't know, I want what *you* want."

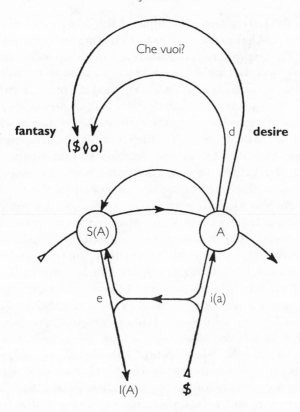

Figure 8

The response to "Che vuoi?" is filled by fantasy ($ ◊ *a*), insofar as an object is plugged in as the imaginary answer to the symbolic question of what the Other (and hence the subject) wants.[6] Thus, for the Lacan of "Seminar VI," the object is not *of* but *in* desire: not separate from, but constituted in the fantasy wherein the subject attempts to refind the enjoyment canceled by its entry into language.

6. Lacan says in the context of *Hamlet,* "The fantasy is located at the extreme tip, the end-point of the subject's question, as if it were the buttress [*butée,* lit., abutment], just as the subject tries to get control of himself in the fantasy, in the space beyond the demand. This is because he must find again in the very discourse of the Other what was lost for him, the subject, the moment he entered into this discourse" ("Desire" 16).

Lacan's Shakespearean example of this "object *in* desire" is
Hamlet's Ophelia; so too, our concern in Part One of this book
is with "Shakespeare *in* psychoanalysis," not as an independent
literary object, but rather as an object of interpretation produced by psychoanalysis as an intertextual discourse. Furthermore, Shakespeare enters into psychoanalysis precisely in the
position of fantasy object, in the dialectical narrative in which
psychoanalysis imagines itself as the synthesis of the oppositions
between Classical and Romantic, symbolic and imaginary, *Oedipus* and *Hamlet*. The subject, Lacan says, is always present in
its fantasy ($ ◊ *a*). In the fantasy described by the formula
(psychoanalysis ◊ *Shakespeare*), it is not simply that psychoanalysis "has a fantasy about Shakespeare" (Shakespeare as neurotic, perverse, etc.), since such a formulation would once again
relegate psychoanalytic criticism to either "mere" allegory or
to critical mastery of the literary object. Fantasy does not belong
to a subject, but rather instantiates a subject by fixing a scenario
that imagines a resolution to desire's endless question. Thus,
following Lacan's formula for fantasy, we could say that *psychoanalysis has a fantasy about itself and Shakespeare*, about its com-
pletion of and by Shakespeare, the dream of satisfying
Shakespeare, and of being satisfied by it. This formula describes
not only the constitution of psychoanalysis in its relationship
with literature, but also the particular enjoyment which drives
it, the *jouissance* from which, in Lacan's pun, it is de-rived.

What Do You *Really* Want?

This dialectic of desire, however, is both set into play by and
leaves over an excess quantity, the difference between desire
and demand which returns as something opaque in the discourse of the Other, indicating the Other as lacking. If the
"Che vuoi?" can be glossed as "What do you *really* want?," the
"really" here points to the *real*. The real is that which exceeds
the symbolic and imaginary, the hole in the symbolic, at once
inaugural and residual, which the imaginary function of fantasy
contains but can never quite conceal. This lack in the Other is

manifested in the temporal lag that enables but does not disappear into the retroactive production of meaning. In the statement, "He did not know he was dead," the final word not only gives meaning to the first, but also fundamentally contradicts it, since "knowing" and "being dead" are mutually exclusive. This contradiction is conserved as material non-sense in the temporal act of signification. The "Che vuoi?" signaling the excess left out by the play of imaginary and symbolic, statement and utterance, demand and desire, is the return of desire in a foreign tongue, as a foreign body marking the signifier of the lack in the Other, rendered by Lacan as S(A̸).

From this perspective, the "Che vuoi?" of the upper graph is posed as a question asked to the lower graph, a question stopped up by the fantasy of dialectics that had produced it as a question. If the critical synthesis of character and genre, *Hamlet* and *Oedipus*, comprises the bottom half of the graph, the "Che vuoi?" is the persistent question that literature continues to ask of psychoanalysis in the wake of the Classical Romance, and which prevents psychoanalysis from filling the place of philosophy in the dialectical fantasy.

The "Che vuoi?" is above all the question asked by *Lear*, the play that signals the remainder left over by the family romance of *Oedipus* and *Hamlet* in psychoanalysis, the undigestible Thing preserved in and as the motif of the three caskets. *Hamlet* dramatizes the repression of *Oedipus Rex*, while *Lear* stages the foreclosure of *Oedipus at Colonus*, becoming what Lacan calls its "derisory" repetition (Fig. 8A).

Psychoanalysis, in speaking the *Oedipus-Hamlet* sequence ("He did not know / he was dead"), comes up against something that does not slip away into the unfolding of that dialectic. This knot is the contradiction between utterance and statement, which divides the dream thought across the two stages or stories of the graph, locating *Hamlet* at the level of statement, of imaginary and symbolic signification ("he was dead"), and *Lear* at the level of utterance, where the linguistic shifter in its pure materiality deictically indicates, rather than semantically signifies, the subject ("he did not know"). *Hamlet*, as the tragedy of the obsessive neurotic, dramatizes the father as most pow-

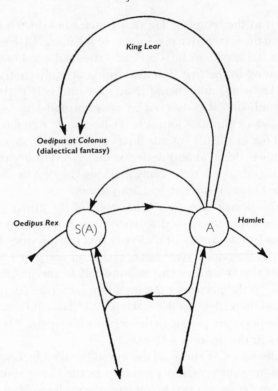

Figure 8a

erful in his return as ghost, as name. ("'What is a Father?' 'It is the dead Father', Freud replies" [*Écrits* 310].) *Lear*, as the tragedy of psychosis, the disorder characterized precisely by the absence of the father's name, points insistently as well to the real, the lack in the Other on which the symbolic order founds itself, and founders.

The Rest Is Silence

To stage *Hamlet* and *Lear* as an opposition, however, is to risk falling back into the dialectical mode whose limits *Lear* approaches. The space occupied by *Lear* in psychoanalysis is demarcated by the movement from *Oedipus* to *Hamlet* and back,

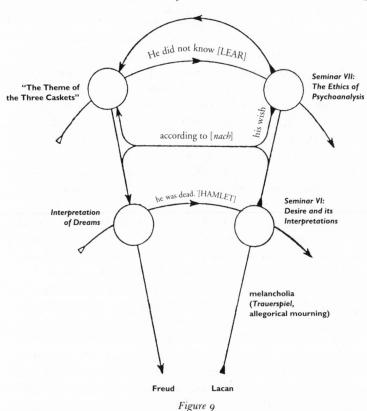

Figure 9

a movement that leaves a melancholy difference: the difference precisely of the melancholic *Hamlet,* whose signifiers of the mother in mourning, "Niobe all tears," exceed and inform the play's governing Oedipal narrative of the dead father. Thus we have placed "melancholia" in the position of "voice," the material detritus of signification, in Lacan's graph (Fig. 9). If *Hamlet* mourns *Oedipus Rex* as its literary father, *Hamlet*'s persistence as the "problem play" of the mother signals the melancholic limits of the Oedipal in the theory and history of tragedy, since the mother marks the "pre-Oedipal" excesses of the feminine as they are dramatized in the post-Sophoclean tradition of Euripides, Seneca, and Baroque drama. From the problem of too much mother, "more than kin," arises the ques-

tion-mark of not enough daughter, "less than kind"; *Hamlet*'s
melancholic identification with the mother of bad rhetoric
("Must like a whore unpack my heart with words" [*Hamlet*
II.ii.581]), is inverted and rearticulated in Lear's violent rejection of the laconic Cordelia: "Unfriended, new-adopted to our
hate, / Dower'd with our curse and stranger'd with our oath"
(*Lear* I.i.202–3). In Hamlet's last words, "The rest is silence":
the "rest" of *Hamlet*—the play's melancholic remains or residuum in psychoanalysis—gestures toward the silence of Cordelia, Freud's third leaden casket. Freud located melancholia
between obsessional neurosis and psychosis, designating what
we would call a "transitional pathology"; as a trope of intertextuality, melancholia moves from one Shakespearean text
to another, in the process shifting from a figure of inclusion
to an index of exclusion, from incorporation to foreclosure.
In the discourse of psychoanalysis, *Hamlet* and *Lear* meet at
the theoretical, textual, and intertextual borderlines of neurosis and psychosis, of feigned madness and its stormy de-
realization.

They meet, we could say, at the crossroads of the "nach
seinem Wunsch," "according to his wish," which both reconciles
and separates the two halves of the graph.[7] Lacan notes that
Freud resolves the contradiction between the two halves of the
sentence through the addition of a little phrase, "according to
his wish"; the statement makes perfect sense, Freud implies,
once explained in terms of the subject's patricidal desire. Lacan
writes the word "according to," [*selon*] on the line of fantasy,
since fantasy is fundamentally *that which accords*, that which
strives to bring demand and desire, statement and utterance,
conscious and unconscious, into a hermeneutic resolution.[8] The

7. We are relying here as much on the several versions of the graph in
"Seminar VI" (unpublished) as on those in Lacan's essay "The Subversion of
the Subject."

8. Lacan writes that the dream works through "the elision of a pure and
simple signifier, the elision of the *nach*, of the "according to," of that which
signals agreement or disagreement between enunciation and the signifier"
("Seminar VI," 10 December 1958, 84).

"according to his wish" is, of course, the interpretive formula governing *The Interpretation of Dreams*, the fantasy-phrase, "The dream is the fulfilment of a wish," which fulfills the psychoanalytic dream of interpretation. *Nach*—according to, toward, but also *after*—indicates both the dialectical fantasy of mournful recuperation and the chronic aftermath of melancholic identification.[9] In the double articulation of the "nach dem Wunsch des Ödipus"—both "according to the wish of Oedipus," and "after the Oedipal wish"—we locate the third logical moment of psychoanalytic criticism, at the nondialectical remainder of the critical agon staged between character, plot, and their structuralist resolution. This is the position of "Shakespeare the signifier"—the encounter with Shakespeare as a battery of puns, of verbal coincidences and historical accidents, and their effects in later (and earlier) literature and theory. Such criticism occurs not as "its own thing" or "the right thing" but as "the Thing," the waste product left by the necessary circulation through the symbolic and imaginary tracts of criticism.

In this sense, Walter Benjamin's *Origin of German Tragic Drama* is the exemplary critical text for our project. Benjamin reads Baroque tragedy through and as a theory and history of allegory; as such, his book reconceives genre criticism around the signifier. Yet, rather than adjudicating between generic and rhetorical criticism, Benjamin's text stages their relation, a relation conceived moreover not as a tragic agon between two distinct alternatives, but as itself a *Trauerspiel*, in which rhetorical theory appears as the melancholy sequel and supplement to tragic criticism. *Trauer* operates in Benjamin's work as a trope of intertextuality that figures intertextuality as trope, as, that is, a function of signifiers structurally implicated in mourning as a textual, historical, and psychic process. *Trauerspiel* is *nach* tragedy: not its Oedipal inheritor or specular double, but, in its desire to accord with tragedy, its insignificant afterthought. So, too, "according to its wish," the *Trauerspiel* of the psychoan-

9. See Samuel Weber's analysis of the word *nach* in Heidegger's "Die Frage nach der Technik" ("Upsetting the Set-Up" 981).

alytic encounter with Shakespeare falls "after Oedipus," as at
once the desire, the symptom, and the foreclosure of Oedipal
tragedy.

The "After" of "After Oedipus" is also the *After-* of German
polemics; used by such figures as Luther, Kant, and Schope-
hauer to signify pseudo, spurious, or secondary, *After-* also
means anal.[10] This rhetoric of the *After-* is theorized and repeated in Freud's 1908 essay "On the Sexual Theories of Children," which narrates the birth of theory in a theory of anal
birth; if theory is always a theory of origins, Freud locates that
origin in an *After,* at once an "anus" and an "afterwards." The
After-, that is, names the "hole thing": as the marker of anality,
the stage set between the oral and the genital, *After-* divides
and binds the Oedipal and the pre-Oedipal in a hole, rim, or
ring, a "Sphinx-ter," which, like the grammatical colon, knots
together the imaginary and symbolic with the real.[11] At once
the crude matter and waste product of exchange, shit is a gift
always returned unopened. In a late footnote to *The Three Essays,* Freud links primal repression (the origin of the symbol)
to foreclosure (its radical negation) via anality. The prohibitions
of toilet-training "must be the first occasion on which the infant
has a glimpse of an environment hostile to his instinctual impulses, on which he learns to separate his own entity from this
alien one and on which he carries out the first 'repression' [*erste
Verdrängung*] of his possibilities for pleasure. From then on,
what is 'anal' remains the symbol of everything that is to be
repudiated and excluded from life [*das Symbol für alles zu Ver-
werfende*]" (*SE* 7:187; *SA* 5:93). The infant's compelled and
compulsive ordering of defecation struggles to submit one of
the body's most powerful models of projective expulsion into
a token of obedient love. If the moment of "Beyond Oedipus"

10. See Walter Kaufmann, introduction to Friedrich Nietzsche, *The Birth
of Tragedy* 5–6, who analyzes Erwin Rohde's 1872 *Afterphilologie,* a defense of
Nietzsche's *Birth of Tragedy.*
11. "Sphincter" and "Sphinx" have the same root, *sphincter,* to bind or draw
tight. In Latin, *anus* means anus, ring, or old woman.

is dedicated to the symbol, to the relations of the Imaginary
and Symbolic, the moment of "After Oedipus" emphasizes the
detritus of symbolization, the horrific non-relation, which must
be repudiated or foreclosed [*Verworfen*] in order for symbolization to take place. Freud's 1920 footnote to his 1905 *Three
Essays* transposes the scene of a primary loss from the oral to
the anal stage in an addendum, *Nachtrag*, or "*After*-word," which
stages the structural rather than developmental status of the
erogenous zones in psychoanalysis. The point is not to locate
the Thing in either the oral or the anal as its legitimate origin,
but rather to see these zones as sites where psychoanalysis refinds a genealogy of the object in its different modalities. So
too, "After Oedipus" names not so much a progression as a
regression—a return, however, not to an origin but to an *After*,
an ever-repeated and always secondary encounter with the
Shakespearean Thing in its psychoanalytic figurations and
defigurations.

Works Cited

Abraham, Karl. *On Character and Libido Development*. Ed. Bertram D. Lewin. Trans. Douglas Bryan and Alix Strachey. New York: W. W. Norton, 1966.

——. *A Psychoanalytic Dialogue: The Letters of Sigmund Freud and Karl Abraham, 1907–1926*. Ed. Hilda C. Abraham and Ernst L. Freud. Trans. Bernard Marsh and Hilda C. Abraham. New York: Basic Books, 1965.

Abraham, Nicolas, and Maria Torok. *L'écorce et le noyau*. Paris: Flammarion, 1978.

——. "Introjection—Incorporation; Mourning *or* Melancholy." In *Psychoanalysis in France*, ed. Serge Lebovici and Daniel Widlocher, 3–16. New York: International Universities Press, 1980.

——. *The Wolf Man's Magic Word: A Cryptonomy*. Trans. Nicholas Rand. Introduction by Jacques Derrida. Minneapolis: University of Minnesota Press, 1986.

Adorno, Theodor. W. *Kierkegaard: Construction of the Aesthetic*. Ed., trans., and with foreword by Robert Hullot-Kentor. Minneapolis: University of Minnesota Press, 1989.

Allen, Michael J.B., and Kenneth Muir, eds. *Shakespeare's Plays in Quarto*. Berkeley and Los Angeles: University of California Press, 1981.

Allison, David B., Prado de Oliveira, Mark S. Robert, and Allen S. Weiss. *Psychosis and Sexual Identity: Toward a Post-Analytic View of the Schreber Case*. Albany: State University of New York Press, 1988.

Alpers, Paul. "*King Lear* and the Theory of the Sight Pattern." In *In Defense of Reading*, ed. Reuben Brower and Richard Poirier, 133–52. New York: Dutton, 1963.

Ansermet, François, Alain Grosrichard, and Charles Méla, eds. *La psychose dans le texte*. Paris: Navarin Éditeur, 1989.

Aparicio, Sol. "La forclusion, préhistoire d'un concept." *Ornicar?* 28 (January–March 1984): 83–105.

Aristotle. *Poetics: Classical Literary Criticism*. Trans. and ed. T. S. Dorsch. Harmondsworth, Middlesex: Penguin, 1965.

Artaud, Antonin. *The Theatre and Its Double*. Trans. Mary Caroline Richards. New York: Grove Press, 1958.

Bender, John. *Spenser and Literary Pictorialism*. Princeton: Princeton University Press, 1972.

Benjamin, Walter. "The Task of the Translator." In *Illuminations*, ed. Hannah Arendt, trans. Harry Zohn, 69–82. New York: Schocken Books, 1969.

———. *Ursprung des deutschen Trauerspiels*. Ed. Rolf Tiedemann. Frankfurt: Suhrkamp, 1955. Trans. John Osborne, under the title *The Origin of German Tragic Drama*. Introduction by George Steiner. London: NLB, 1977.

Benveniste, Emile. *Problems in General Linguistics*. Trans. Mary Elizabeth Meek. Coral Gables: University of Miami Press, 1971.

Berger, Harry, Jr. " 'Some Squeaking Cleopatra': Shakespeare, the Renaissance, and the History of Textuality." Unpublished.

Bergeron, Danielle. " 'The Letter against the Phallus': Analysis of the Masculine Position in *Fatal Attraction*." *American Journal of Semiotics* 7, no. 3 (1990): 27–34.

Besserman, Lawrence. *The Legend of Job in the Middle Ages*. Cambridge: Harvard University Press, 1979.

Bevington, David. *From Mankinde to Marlowe: Growth of Structure in the Popular Drama of Tudor England*. Cambridge, Mass.: Harvard University Press, 1962.

Bollas, Christopher. "Cutting." Paper presented to Groupe de Recherche et d'Application des Concepts Psychanalytiques à la Psychose. Paris, 3–4 June 1989.

Booth, Stephen. *"King Lear," "Macbeth," Indefinition, and Tragedy*. New Haven: Yale University Press, 1983.

Bowie, Malcolm. *Lacan*. Cambridge: Harvard University Press, 1991.

Boyer, Philippe. "Enigmatiques: Freud et Goethe." *L'Infini* 2 (Spring 1983): 90–105.

Braden, Gordon. *Renaissance Tragedy and the Senecan Tradition: Anger's Privilege*. New Haven: Yale University Press, 1985.

Braunstein, Nestor. *La Jouissance: Un concept lacanien*. Paris: Points Hors Ligne, 1992.

Bright, Timothy. *A Treatise of Melancholie*. 1586. Facsimile. Introduction by Hardin Craig. New York: Columbia University Press, 1940.

Brooks, Peter. *Reading for the Plot: Design and Intention in Narrative.* New York: Vintage Books, 1985.

Bröser, Stephen. "Kästchen, Kasten, Kastration." *Cahiers Confrontation* 8 (Autumn 1982): 87–114.

Burgin, Victor. *Between.* Oxford: Basil Blackwell, 1986.

Bushnell, Rebecca W. *Prophesying Tragedy: Sign and Voice in Sophocles' Theban Plays.* Ithaca: Cornell University Press, 1988.

Butler, Judith. *Gender Trouble: Feminism and the Subversion of Identity.* New York: Routledge, 1992.

Cameron, Alister. *Plato's Affair with Tragedy.* Cincinnati: University of Cincinnati Press, 1978.

Cantin, Lucie. "The Letter and the 'Thing' in Femininity: Analysis of the Feminine Position in *Fatal Attraction.*" *American Journal of Semiotics* 7, no. 3 (1990): 35–42.

Castanet, Hervé. *L'experience clinique des psychoses.* Nice: Z'éditions, 1988.

Cavell, Stanley. *Disowning Knowledge in Six Plays of Shakespeare.* New York: Cambridge University Press, 1987.

Charraud, Nathalie. "Topologie de *das Ding.*" In Analytica 56, *L'enfant et le semblant,* ed. Rosine Lefort and Robert Lefort, 25–30. Paris: Navarin Éditeur, 1988.

Chase, Cynthia. *Decomposing Figures.* Baltimore: Johns Hopkins University Press, 1986.

———. " 'Transference' as Trope and Persuasion." In *Discourse in Psychoanalysis and Literature,* ed. Shlomith Rimmon-Kenan, 211–32. London: Methuen, 1987.

Crewe, Jonathan. " 'Naught So Damned as Melancholy': *Hamlet* and the Future of Psychoanalytic Criticism." Unpublished.

———. *Trials of Authorship: Anterior Forms and Poetic Reconstruction from Wyatt to Shakespeare.* Berekely and Los Angeles: University of California Press, 1990.

———. "The Violence of Drama: Towards a Reading of the Senecan *Phaedra.*" *Boundary* 2 17 (Fall 1990): 95–115.

Damrosch, David. "The Politics of Ethics: Freud and Rome." In *Pragmatism's Freud: The Moral Disposition of Psychoanalysis,* ed. Joseph Smith and William Kerrigan, 102–25. Baltimore: Johns Hopkins University Press, 1986.

Dayan, Maurice. *Les relations au réel dans la psychose.* Paris: Presses Universitaires de France, 1985.

Deleuze, Gilles, and Félix Guattari. *Anti-Oedipus: Capitalism and Schizophrenia.* Trans. Robert Hurley et al. New York: Viking Press, 1977.

———. *Kafka: Toward a Minor Literature.* Trans. Dana Polan. Minneapolis: University of Minnesota Press, 1986.

de Man, Paul. *The Resistance to Theory*. Minneapolis: University of Minnesota Press, 1986.

———. "The Rhetoric of Temporality." In *Blindness and Insight: Essays in the Rhetoric of Contemporary Criticism*, 2d ed., rev., 187–228. Minneapolis: University of Minnesota Press, 1983.

———. "Semiology and Rhetoric." In *Allegories of Reading*, 3–19. New Haven: Yale University Press, 1979.

———. "Sign and Symbol in Hegel's *Aesthetics*." *Critical Inquiry* 8 (Summer 1982): 761–75.

De Quincey, Thomas. *Confessions of an English Opium Eater and Other Writings*. Ed. Aileen Ward. New York: Carroll and Graf Publishers, 1985.

Derrida, Jacques. "La Loi du genre/The Law of Genre." Trans. Avital Ronell. *Glyph* 7 (1980):172–232.

———. *Memoires for Paul de Man*. Trans. Cecile Lindsay et al. New York: Columbia University Press, 1986.

———. *The Post Card: From Socrates to Freud and Beyond*. Trans. Alan Bass. Chicago: University of Chicago Press, 1987.

———. *Of Spirit: Heidegger and the Question*. Trans. Geoffrey Bennington and Rachel Bowlby. Chicago: University of Chicago Press, 1989.

———. *Writing and Difference*. Trans. Alan Bass. Chicago: University of Chicago Press, 1978.

Drakakis, John, ed. *Alternative Shakespeares*. London: Methuen, 1985.

Eliot, T. S. "Hamlet and His Problems." In *The Sacred Wood*. 95–103.

———. *The Sacred Wood*. 1920. Reprint. London: Methuen, 1960.

———. "Shakespeare and the Stoicism of Seneca." In *Selected Essays*, 126–40. 3d Edition. London: Faber and Faber, 1951.

———. "Tradition and the Individual Talent." In *The Sacred Wood*. 47–59.

Felman, Shoshana. "Beyond Oedipus." In *Jacques Lacan and the Adventure of Insight: Psychoanalysis in Contemporary Culture*, 99–159. Cambridge: Harvard University Press, 1987.

———. "To Open the Question." In *Literature and Psychoanalysis*, 5–10. Baltimore: Johns Hopkins University Press, 1982.

Ferenczi, Sandor. "Introjektion und Übertragung." 1909. Trans. Ernest Jones as "Introjection and Transference." In *First Contributions to Psycho-analysis*, 35–93. New York: Brunner/Mazel, 1952.

Ferguson, Margaret W. "*Hamlet:* Letters and Spirits." In *Shakespeare and the Question of Theory*, ed. Patricia Parker and Geoffrey Hartman, 292–309. New York: Methuen, 1985.

———. *Trials of Desire*. New Haven: Yale University Press, 1983.

Fineman, Joel. "Fratricide and Cuckoldry: Shakespeare's Doubles." In *Representing Shakespeare: New Psychoanalytic Essays*, ed. Murray

Schwartz and Coppélia Kahn, 70–109. Baltimore: Johns Hopkins University Press, 1980.

——. *Shakespeare's Perjured Eye: The Invention of Poetic Subjectivity in the Sonnets.* Berkeley and Los Angeles: University of California Press, 1986.

——. "The Structure of Allegorical Desire." In *Allegory and Representation,* ed. Stephen J. Greenblatt, 26–60. Baltimore: Johns Hopkins University Press, 1981.

Fink, Bruce. "Alienation and Separation: Logical Moments of Lacan's Dialectic of Desire." *Newsletter of the Freudian Field* 4 (Spring/Fall 1990): 78–119.

——. "Lacan's Reading of *Hamlet.*" Unpublished.

Fowler, Alastair. *Kinds of Literature: An Introduction to the Theory of Genres and Modes.* Cambridge, Mass.: Harvard University Press, 1982.

Freedman, Barbara. *Staging the Gaze: Postmodernism, Psychoanalysis, and Shakespearean Comedy.* Ithaca: Cornell University Press, 1991.

Freud, Sigmund. *The Complete Letters of Sigmund Freud to Wilhelm Fliess, 1887–1904.* Trans. and ed. Jeffrey Moussaieff Masson. Cambridge: Harvard University Press, 1985.

——. *The Ego and the Id.* In Strachey et al., *The Standard Edition,* 19:3–66.

——. *The Standard Edition of the Complete Psychological Works.* Trans. and ed. James Strachey et al. 24 vols. London: The Hogarth Press, 1952, 1974.

——. *Studienausgabe.* 14 vols. Frankfurt: Fischer Verlag. 1975.

Friedberg, Anne. "The Punishing Other: *Fatal Attraction.*" *American Journal of Semiotics* 7, no. 3 (1990): 43–52.

Gallop, Jane. *Reading Lacan.* Ithaca: Cornell University Press, 1985.

Garber, Marjorie. *Shakespeare's Ghost Writers: Literature as Uncanny Causality.* New York: Methuen, 1987.

Garner, Shirley Nelson, et al., ed. *The (M)other Tongue: Essays in Feminist Psychoanalytic Interpretation.* Ithaca: Cornell University Press, 1985.

Goldberg, Jonathan. "Perspectives: Dover Cliffs and the Conditions of Representation." In *Shakespeare and Deconstruction,* ed. G. Douglas Atkins and David M. Bergeron, 245–265. New York: Peter Lang, 1988.

Granon-Lafont, Jeanne. *La topologie ordinaire de Jacques Lacan.* Paris: Points Hors Lignes, 1985.

Green, André. *The Tragic Effect: The Oedipus Complex in Tragedy.* Trans. Alan Sheridan. Cambridge: Cambridge University Press, 1979.

Grigg, Russell. "Metaphor and Metonymy." *Newsletter of the Freudian Field* 3, nos. 1–2 (1989): 58–79.

Grosz, Elizabeth. *Jacques Lacan: A Feminist Introduction.* London: Routledge, 1990.

Hamacher, Werner. "The Word *Wolke*—If It Is One." In *Benjamin's Ground: New Readings of Walter Benjamin,* ed., Rainer Nägele, 147–76. Detroit: Wayne State University Press, 1988.

Hegel, G. W. F. *Aesthetics: Lectures on Fine Art.* Trans. T. M. Knox. 2 vols. Oxford: Clarendon Press, 1975.

——. *Lectures on the History of Philisophy.* In Paolucci and Paolucci, eds., *Hegel on Tragedy,* 330–66.

——. *The Phenomenology of Spirit.* Trans. A. V. Miller. Oxford: Oxford University Press, 1977.

Heidegger, Martin. *Poetry, Language, Thought.* Trans. Albert Hofstadter. New York: Harper Colophon, 1971.

——. *What Is a Thing?* Trans. W. B. Barton, Jr., and Vera Deutsch. South Bend: Regnery/Gateway, 1967.

——. *What Is Called Thinking?* Trans. J. Glenn Gray. New York: Harper and Row, 1968.

Herington, C. J. "Senecan Tragedy." *Arion* 5, no. 4 (1966): 422–71.

Hertz, Neil. *The End of the Line: Essays on Psychoanalysis and the Sublime.* New York: Columbia University Press, 1985.

Hogan, Patrick Colm, and Lalita Pandit. *Criticism and Lacan: Essays and Dialogues on Language, Structure, and the Unconscious.* Athens: University of Georgia Press, 1990.

Holland, Norman. *Psychoanalysis and Shakespeare.* New York: Octagon Books, 1976.

Homer. *The Odyssey.* Trans. Richmond Lattimore. New York: Harper and Row, 1965.

Hunter, G. K. "Seneca and the Elizabethans: A Case-Study in 'Influence.'" In *Dramatic Identities and Cultural Tradition,* 159–73. Liverpool: University of Liverpool Press, 1978.

——. "Tyrant and Martyr: Religious Heroism in Elizabethan Tragedy." In *Poetic Traditions in the Renaissance.* ed. Maynard Mack and George de F. Lord, 85–102. New Haven: Yale University Press, 1982.

Irigaray, Luce. *Speculum of the Other Woman.* Trans. Gillian C. Gill. Ithaca: Cornell University Press, 1985.

Jakobson, Roman. "Why 'Mama' and 'Papa.'" In *Selected Writings,* 1:538–45. The Hague: Mouton, 1962.

Jay, Gregory S. *T. S. Eliot and the Poetics of Literary History.* Baton Rouge: University of Louisiana Press, 1983.

Jennings, Michael W. *Dialectical Images: Walter Benjamin's Theory of Literary Criticism.* Ithaca: Cornell University Press, 1987.

Jones, Emrys. *The Origins of Shakespeare.* Oxford: Clarendon Press, 1977.

Jones, Ernest. *Hamlet and Oedipus.* 1949. Reprint. New York: W. W. Norton, 1976.

Kahn, Coppélia. "The Absent Mother in *King Lear.*" In *Rewriting the Renaissance: The Discourses of Sexual Difference in Early Modern Europe,* ed. Margaret Ferguson et al., 33–49. Chicago: University of Chicago Press, 1986.

Kanzer, Mark. "The 'Passing of the Oedipus Complex' in Greek Drama." In *The Oedipus Papers,* ed. George H. Pollock and John Munder Ross, 85–96. Madison, Conn.: International Universities Press, 1988.

Keitel, Evelyne. *Reading Psychosis: Readers, Texts and Psychoanalysis.* Trans. Anthea Bell. London: Basil Blackwell, 1989.

Kiefer, Frederick. *Fortune and Elizabethan Tragedy.* San Marino: Huntington Library, 1983.

Kierkegaard, Søren. *Either/Or.* Volume 1. Trans. David F. Swenson and Lillian Marvin Swenson. Princeton: Princeton University Press, 1959.

———. *Either/Or.* Part 1. Ed. and trans. Howard V. Hong and Edna H. Hong. Princeton: Princeton University Press, 1987.

Klein, Melanie. *The Writings of Melanie Klein.* 4 vols. Ed. Roger Money-Kyrle. New York: The Free Press, 1975.

Klibansky, Raymond. Fritz Saxl, and Erwin Panofsky. *Saturn and Melancholy.* London: Nelson, 1964.

Knight, G. Wilson. *The Wheel of Fire: Essays in Interpretation of Shakespeare's Sombre Tragedies.* London: Oxford University Press, 1930.

Kowsar, Mohammad. "Lacan's 'Antigone': A Case Study in Psychoanalytical Ethics." *Theatre Journal* 42, no. 1 (March 1990): 94–106.

Kristeva, Julia. "On the Melancholic Imaginary." In *Discourse in Psychoanalysis and Literature,* ed. Shlomith Rimmon-Kenan, 104–23. London: Methuen, 1987.

———. *Powers of Horror: An Essay on Abjection.* Trans. Leon S. Roudiez. New York: Columbia University Press, 1982.

———. *Revolution in Poetic Language.* Trans. Leon S. Roudiez. New York: Columbia University Press, 1984.

———. *Soleil noir: Dépression et mélancolie.* Paris: Gallimard, 1987. Trans. Leon S. Roudiez, under the title *Black Sun: Depression and Melancholia.* New York: Columbia University Press, 1989.

———. *Tales of Love.* Trans. Leon S. Roudiez. New York: Columbia University Press, 1987.

———. "Le vréel." In *Folle vérité,* ed. Jean-Michelle Ribettes, 11–30., Paris: Editions du Seuil, 1979. Trans. Seán Hand under the title

"The True-Real" in *The Kristeva Reader,* ed. Toril Moi, 214–237. New York: Columbia University Press, 1986.

Lacan, Jacques. "Desire and the Interpretation of Desire in *Hamlet.*" In *Literature and Psychoanalysis: The Question of Reading: Otherwise,* ed. Shoshana Felman, 11–52. Baltimore: Johns Hopkins University Press, 1982.

———. *Écrits.* Paris: Éditions du Seuil, 1966.

———. *Écrits: A Selection.* Trans. Alan Sheridan. New York: Norton, 1977.

———. "L'étourdit." *Scilicet* 4 (1973): 5–52.

———. "Hamlet, par Lacan." *Ornicar?* 24 (1981): 7–31; 25 (1982): 13–25; 26–27 (1983): 7–44.

———. *The Language of the Self: The Function of Language in Psychoanalysis.* Trans. with notes by Anthony Wilden. Baltimore: Johns Hopkins University Press, 1968.

———. "Science and Truth." Trans. Bruce Fink. *Newsletter of the Freudian Field,* 3 (Spring/Fall 1989): 4-29.

———. *Le Séminaire, Livre I: Les écrits techniques de Freud, 1953–54.* Text established by Jacques-Alain Miller. Paris: Édition du Seuil, 1975. Trans. John Forrester, under the title *The Seminar of Jacques Lacan, Book I: Freud's Papers on Technique, 1953–54.* New York: W. W. Norton, 1988.

———. *Le Séminaire, Livre II: Le moi dans la théorie de Freud et dans la technique de la psychanalyse, 1954–55.* Text established by Jacques-Alain Miller. Paris: Édition du Seuil, 1978. Trans. Sylvana Tomaselli, under the title *The Seminar of Jacques Lacan, Book II: The Ego in Freud's Theory and in the Technique of Psychoanalysis, 1954–55.* New York: W. W. Norton, 1988.

———. *Le Séminaire, Livre III: Les Psychoses, 1955–1956.* Text established by Jacques-Alain Miller. Paris: Éditions du Seuil, 1981.

———. "Le Séminaire, Livre V: Les formations de l'inconscient, 1957–58." 3 vols. Unpublished.

———. "Le Séminaire, Livre VI: Le désir et son interprétation." 3 vols. Unpublished. Sections published as "Hamlet, par Lacan" in *Ornicar?* 24 (1981): 7–31; 25 (1982): 13–36; 26–27 (1983): 7–44. Abridged and trans. by James Hulbert as "Desire and the Interpretation of Desire in *Hamlet*" in Shoshana Felman, ed., *Literature and Psychoanalysis: The Question of Reading: Otherwise,* 11–52. Baltimore: Johns Hopkins University Press, 1982.

———. *Le Séminaire, Livre VII: L'éthique de la psychanalyse.* Text established by Jacques-Alain Miller. Paris: Édition du Seuil, 1986.

———. "Le Séminaire, Livre X: L'angoisse, 1962–63." 2 vols. Unpublished.

———. *Le Séminaire, Livre XI: Les quatre concepts fondamentaux de la psychanalyse, 1964.* Text established by Jacques-Alain Miller. Paris: Édition du Seuil, 1973. Trans. Alan Sheridan, under the title *Seminar XI: The Four Fundamental Concepts of Psychoanalysis.* New York: W. W. Norton, 1978.

———. "Le Séminaire, Livre XIV: Logique du fantasme, 1966–67." Unpublished.

———. "Le Séminaire, Livre XV: L'act psychanalytique, 1967–68." Unpublished.

———. *Le Séminaire, Livre XVII: L'envers de la psychanalyse, 1969–70.* Text established by Jacques-Alain Miller. Paris: Édition du Seuil, 1991.

———. *Le Séminaire, Livre XX: Encore, 1972–73.* Text established by Jacques-Alain Miller. Paris: Édition du Seuil, 1975.

———. *Le Séminaire, Livre XXII: R.S.I., 1974–75.* Text established by Jacques-Alain Miller. *Ornicar?* 2 (1975): 87–105; 3 (1975): 95–110; 4 (1975): 91–106; 5 (1975): 15–66.

———. *Le Séminaire, Livre XXIII: Le Sinthome, 1975–76.* Text established by Jacques-Alain Miller. *Ornicar?* 6 (1976): 3–20; 7 (1976): 3–18; 8 (1976): 6–20; 9 (1977) 32–40; 10 (1977) 5–12; 11 (1977): 2–9.

———. "The Subversion of the Subject and the Dialectic of Desire in the Freudian Unconscious." In *Écrits,* 292–325.

———. *Television: A Challenge to the Psychoanalytic Establishment.* Trans. Denis Hollier et al. Ed. Joan Copjec. New York: W. W. Norton, 1990.

Lacan, Jacques, and Wladimir Granoff. "Fetishism: The Symbolic, the Imaginary, and the Real." In *Perversions, Psychodynamics and Therapy,* ed. Sandor Lorand and Michael Balint, 265–76. New York: Random House, 1956.

Laplanche, Jean. *Life and Death in Psychoanalysis.* Trans. Jeffrey Mehlman. Baltimore: Johns Hopkins University Press, 1976.

Laplanche, Jean, and J.-B. Pontalis. *The Language of Psychoanalysis.* Trans. Donald Nicholson-Smith. New York: W. W. Norton, 1973.

Laurent, Éric. "Mélancholie, douleur d'exister, lâcheté morale." *Ornicar?* 47 (October–December 1988): 5–17.

———. "Structures freudiennes de la psychose infantile." *Ornicar?* 20–21 (1980): 220–24.

Lefort, Rosine. "Le S₁, le sujet et la psychose." *Analytica* 47 (1986): 51–56.

Longinus. *On the Sublime.* Trans. W. Hamilton Fyfe. In *Aristotle,* vol. 33, ed. G. P. Goold. Cambridge: Harvard University Press, Loeb Classical Library, 1927.

Lukacher, Ned. *Primal Scenes: Literature, Philosophy, Psychoanalysis.* Ithaca: Cornell University Press, 1986.

Lupton, Julia Reinhard. "Afterlives of the Saints: Hagiography in *Measure for Measure*." *Exemplaria* 2, no. 2 (October 1990): 375–401.
Lupton, Mary Jane. *Menstruation and Psychoanalysis*. Forthcoming.
MacCannell, Juliet Flower. *Figuring Lacan: Criticism and the Cultural Unconscious*. Lincoln: University of Nebraska Press, 1986.
———. "The Semiotics of *Fatal Attraction:* Preliminary Remarks." *American Journal of Semiotics* 7, no. 3 (1990): 5–12.
Miller, Dominique, and Guy Trobas, eds. *Traits de perversion dans les structures cliniques*. Paris: Navarin Éditeur, 1990.
Miller, J. Hillis. *The Ethics of Reading*. New York: Columbia University Press, 1987.
———. *Versions of Pygmalion*. Cambridge: Harvard University Press, 1990.
Miller, Jacques-Alain. "Extimité." *Prose Studies* 11 no. 3 (1988): 121–130.
———. "Lacan et psychose." In Proceedings of the colloquium held at Marseille, 12 and 13 March 1988 under the auspices of l'École de la Cause Freudienne. *L'experience clinique des psychoses*, 15–29. Nice: Z'éditions, 1988.
———. "La psychose dans le texte de Lacan." *Analytica* 58, *La psychose dans le texte*. Ed. François Ansermet, Alain Grosrichard, and Charles Méla, 131–41. Paris: Navarin Éditeur, 1989.
———. "Les réponses du réel." In *Aspects du malaise dans la civilization*, ed. Marcos Zafiropoulos, 9–22. Paris: Navarin Éditeur, 1987.
———. "To Interpret the Cause: From Freud to Lacan." *Newsletter of the Freudian Field* 3 (Spring/Fall 1989): 30–50.
Mitchell, Juliet. "Introduction." In *The Selected Melanie Klein*, 9–32. New York: The Free Press, 1986.
Mitchell, Juliet, and Jacqueline Rose, eds. *Feminine Sexuality: Jacques Lacan and l'école freudienne*. Trans. Jacqueline Rose. New York: W. W. Norton, 1982.
Mueller, Martin. *Children of Oedipus and Other Essays on the Imitation of Greek Tragedy, 1550–1880*. Toronto: University of Toronto Press, 1980.
Müller, Gerhard. *Sophokles Antigone*. Heidelberg: Carl Winter Universitätsverlag, 1967.
Muller, John. "Psychosis and Mourning in Lacan's *Hamlet*." *NLH* 12, no. 1 (1980): 147–65.
Murray, Timothy. "Drama Trauma: Psychoanalysis and the Epistemology of Tragedy, or, Weighing Statues and Stones in Shakespeare." Forthcoming.
———. "Translating Montaigne's Crypts: Melancholic Relations and the Sites of Altarbiography." In *Reconfiguring the Renaissance: Essays in*

Critical Materialism, ed. Jonathan Crewe, 121–149. Lewisburg, Pa: Bucknell University Press, 1992.

Nägele, Rainer. "Benjamin's Ground." In *Benjamin's Ground: New Readings of Walter Benjamin,* ed. Rainer Nägele, 19–38. Detroit: Wayne State University Press, 1988.

——. *Reading after Freud: Essays on Goethe, Hölderlin, Habermas, Nietzsche, Brecht, Celan, and Freud.* New York: Columbia University Press, 1987.

——. *Theater, Theory, Speculation: Walter Benjamin and the Scenes of Modernity.* Baltimore: Johns Hopkins University Press, 1991.

Nasio, J.-D. *Cinq leçons sur la théorie de Jacques Lacan.* Paris: Rivages, 1992.

Nietzsche, Friedrich. *The Birth of Tragedy.* Trans. and with introduction by Walter Kaufmann. New York: Random House, 1967.

——. *Ecce Homo.* Trans. Walter Kaufmann. New York: Random House, 1967.

——. *Werke.* 5 vols. Ed. Karl Schlechta. Frankfurt: Ullstein, 1969.

Paolucci, Anne, and Henry Paolucci, eds. *Hegel on Tragedy.* Garden City, New York: Doubleday Anchor, 1962.

Parker, Patricia, and Geoffrey Hartman. *Shakespeare and the Question of Theory.* New York: Methuen, 1985.

Pitkin, Hanna Fenichel. *Fortune Is a Woman: Gender and Politics in the Thought of Niccolò Machiavelli.* Berkeley and Los Angeles: University of California Press, 1984.

Plato. *The Last Days of Socrates.* Trans. Hugh Tredennick. Harmondsworth, Middlesex: Penguin, 1954.

——. *The Republic.* Trans. Desmond Lee. Harmondsworth, Middlesex: Penguin, 1955.

Pommier, Gerard. *Le dénouement d'une analyse.* Paris: Points Hors Ligne, 1987.

——. *D'une logique de la psychose.* Paris: Points Hors Ligne, 1983.

Pool, John. *Lid Off a Daffodil: A Book of Palindromes.* New York: Holt, Rinehart and Winston, 1982.

Ragland-Sullivan, Ellie. "*Hamlet,* Logical Time and the Structure of Obsession." *Newsletter of the Freudian Field* 2 (Fall 1988): 29–45.

Rajchman, John. *Truth and Eros: Foucault, Lacan, and the Question of Ethics.* New York: Routledge, 1991.

Ramazani, R. Jahan. "Freud and Tragic Affect: The Pleasures of Dramatic Pain." *Psychoanalytic Review* 78, no. 1 (1991): 77–101.

——. "Heidegger and the Theory of Tragedy." *Centennial Review* 32 (1988): 103–129.

——. *Yeats and the Poetry of Death: Elegy, Self-Elegy, and the Sublime.* New Haven: Yale University Press, 1990.

Rand, Nicholas. "Family Romance or Family History? Psychoanalysis and Dramatic Invention in Nicolas Abraham's 'The Phantoms of Hamlet.'" *Diacritics* 18 (Winter 1988): 20–30.

Rashkin, Esther. "Tools for a New Psychoanalytic Literary Criticism: The Work of Abraham and Torok." *Diacritics* 18 (Winter 1988): 31–52.

Reinhard, Kenneth. "Allegories of Mourning: Henry James, Psychoanalysis, and Representation." Ph.D. Johns Hopkins University, 1989.

——. "The Freudian Things: Construction and the Archaeological Metaphor." Forthcoming in *Freud/Art/History*. Ed. Stephen Barker. New York: Suny Press, 1993.

Reiss, Timothy J. *Tragedy and Truth: Studies in the Development of a Renaissance and Neo-Classical Discourse*. New Haven: Yale University Press, 1980.

Ronell, Avital. *Dictations: On Haunted Writing*. Bloomington: Indiana University Press, 1986.

Rose, Jacqueline. "Controversial Discussions: Negativity in the Work of Melanie Klein." Lecture delivered at the Johns Hopkins University, 17 April 1989.

——. "Hamlet—The 'Mona Lisa' of Literature." In *Sexuality in the Field of Vision*, 123–40.

——. "The Imaginary." In *Sexuality in the Field of Vision*, 167–97.

——. "Introduction II." In *Feminine Sexuality: Jacques Lacan and l'école freudienne*, ed. Juliet Mitchell and Jacqueline Rose, trans. Jacqueline Rose, 28–57.

——. *Sexuality in the Field of Vision*. London: Verso, 1986.

Rose, Louis, trans. and ed. "Freud and Fetishism: Previously Unpublished Minutes of the Vienna Psychoanalytic Society." *Psychoanalytic Quarterly* 57, no. 2 (1988): 147–66.

Rosenberg, John D., ed. *The Genius of John Ruskin*. 1963. Reprint. Boston: Routledge and Kegan Paul, 1979.

Rudat, Wolfgang E.H. "Ernest Jones' *Hamlet* Interpretation and Nevile's Translation of Seneca's *Oedipus*." *American Imago* 38, no. 4 (1981): 369–387.

Rudnytsky, Peter L. *Freud and Oedipus*. New York: Columbia University Press, 1987.

Sacks, Peter. *The English Elegy: Studies in the Genre from Spenser to Yeats*. Baltimore: Johns Hopkins University Press, 1985.

Sade, Marquis de. *Juliette*. Trans. Austryn Wainhouse. New York: Grove Weidenfeld, 1968.

Schneiderman, Stuart. *Jacques Lacan: The Death of an Intellectual Hero*. Cambridge: Harvard University Press, 1983.

Schwartz, Murray, and Coppélia Kahn, eds. *Representing Shakespeare: New Psychoanalytic Essays.* Baltimore: Johns Hopkins University Press, 1980.

Segal, Charles. *Language and Desire in Seneca's "Phaedra."* Princeton: Princeton University Press, 1986.

Seneca. *Seneca: His Tenne Tragedies.* Ed. Thomas Newton. Introduction by T. S. Eliot. Bloomington: Indiana University Press, 1966.

———. *Three Tragedies: Trojan Women, Medea, Phaedra.* Trans. Frederick Ahl. Ithaca: Cornell University Press, 1986.

———. *Tragedies.* Trans. Frank Justus Miller. 2 vols. London: William Heinemann, Loeb Editions, 1953.

Shakespeare, William. *Arden Hamlet.* Ed. Harold Jenkins. London: Methuen, 1982.

———. *Arden Lear.* Ed. Kenneth Muir. London: Methuen, 1972.

———. *The Riverside Shakespeare.* Ed. G. Blakemore Evans et al. Boston: Houghton Mifflin, 1974.

Shaw, George Bernard. *Misalliance, The Dark Lady of the Sonnets, and Fanny's First Play.* New York: Brentano's, 1914.

Shell, Marc. *The End of Kinship: "Measure for Measure," Incest, and the Ideal of Universal Siblinghood.* Stanford: Stanford University Press, 1988.

Showalter, Elaine. "Representing Ophelia: Women, Madness, and the Responsibilities of Feminist Criticism." In *Shakespeare and the Question of Theory,* ed. Patricia Parker and Geoffrey Hartman, 77–94. New York: Methuen, 1985.

Silverman, Kaja. *The Acoustic Mirror: The Female Voice in Psychoanalysis and Cinema.* Bloomington: Indiana University Press, 1988.

———. *The Subject of Semiotics.* New York: Oxford University Press, 1983.

Smith, Joseph. "On the Work of Mourning." In *Bereavement: Its Psychosocial Aspects,* ed. Bernard Schoenberg et al., 18–25. New York: Columbia University Press, 1975.

Sophocles. *Antigone.* Trans. Elizabeth Wyckoff. In *Sophocles I: The Complete Greek Tragedies,* ed. David Grene and Richmond Lattimore. Chicago: University of Chicago Press, 1954.

Spackman, Barbara. *Decadent Genealogies.* Ithaca: Cornell University Press, 1989.

Sprengnether, Madelon. *The Spectral Mother: Freud, Feminism, and Psychoanalysis.* Ithaca: Cornell University Press, 1990.

Steiner, George. *Antigones.* Oxford: Clarendon Press, 1986.

"Le sujet et l'acte sexuel: Une affaire de réel." *Scilicet* 5 (1975): 29–43.

Swan, Jim. "*Mater* and Nannie: Freud's Two Mothers and the Discovery of the Oedipus Complex." *American Imago* 31, no. 1 (1974): 1–64.

Taylor, Gary, and Michael Warren, eds. *The Division of the Kingdoms: Shakespeare's Two Versions of "King Lear."* Oxford: Clarendon Press, 1983.

Taylor, Mark. *Altarity.* Chicago: University of Chicago Press, 1987.

Vasari, Giorgio. *Lives of the Artists.* Trans. George Bull. London: Pengnin Books, 1965.

Vernant, Jean-Pierre. "Ambiguity and Reversal: On the Enigmatic Structure of *Oedipus Rex.*" In *Tragedy and Myth in Ancient Greece,* ed. Jean-Pierre Vernant and Pierre Vidal-Naquet, trans. Janet Lloyd, 87–119. Brighton, Sussex: Harvester Press, 1981.

Walsh, Michael. "Reading the Real in the Seminar on the Psychoses." In *Criticism and Lacan,* ed. Patrik Colm Hogan and Palita Pandit, 64–83.

Warminski, Andrzej. *Readings in Interpretation: Hölderlin, Hegel, Heidegger.* Minneapolis: University of Minnesota Press, 1987.

Warner, William Beatty. *Chance and the Text of Experience: Freud, Nietzsche, and Shakespeare's "Hamlet."* Ithaca: Cornell University Press, 1986.

Weber, Samuel. "Genealogy of Modernity: History, Myth, and Allegory in Benjamin's *Origin of the German Mourning Play.*" *MLN* 106, no. 3 (1991): 465–500.

——. *The Legend of Freud.* Minneapolis: University of Minnesota Press, 1982.

——. "Upsetting the Set-Up: Remarks on Heidegger's Questing after Technics." *MLN* 104, no. 5 (1989): 976–991.

White, Hayden. *Metahistory.* Baltimore: Johns Hopkins University Press, 1973.

Willbern, David. "Shakespeare's Nothing." In *Representing Shakespeare,* ed. Murray M. Schwartz and Coppélia Kahn, 224–63. Baltimore: Johns Hopkins University Press, 1980.

Winnicott, D. W. "Transitional Objects and Transitional Phenomena." In *Playing and Reality,* 1–25. London: Routledge, 1971.

Zeitlin, Froma. "Playing the Other: Theater, Theatricality, and the Feminine in Greek Drama." *Representations* 11 (Summer 1985): 63–94.

Zizek, Slavoj. "The King Is a Thing." In *For They Know Not What They Do: Enjoyment as a Political Factor,* 253–77. London: Verso, 1991.

——. "Looking Awry." *October* 50 (Fall 1989): 30–55.

——. *Looking Awry: An Introduction to Jacques Lacan through Popular Culture.* Cambridge: MIT Press, 1991.

——. *The Sublime Object of Ideology.* London: Verso, 1989.

——. "With an Eye to Our Gaze: How to Do a Totality with Failures." *Newsletter of the Freudian Field* 4 (Spring/Fall 1990): 49–68.

Index

Abraham, Nicholas, and Maria
    Torok, 5, 12n, 20n, 23n, 32,
    106
Achilles, 36, 40–44
alienation, 57–58, 72, 81, 124–25,
    232–33
Allegory, 14, 17, 33, 41, 231–32
    and autobiography, 16–17
    and criticism, 88
    and desire, 70–71
    and the mother, 61–67
    and mourning, 80–81, 96
Aristotelian categories, 163
Aristotle's *Poetics*, 35, 53, 96, 129n
    anagnorisis in, 55, 90–91, 214,
        223–29
    catharsis in, 64
    mythos in, 58, 100–101, 104, 238
    mythos and *ethos* in, 122–24, 128,
        133, 162, 213
    spectacle in, 127, 213
Artaud, Antonin, 127–31, 213,
    221–22
autobiography, 14–17, 33

Benjamin, Walter
    and the mother, 61–67
    and Nietzsche, 45–46
    Origin of German Tragic Drama,
        34–59, 80, 61–67, 95–98, 101,
        245–56
    and *Ursprung*, concept of, 34, 45–
        46, 63

Benveniste, Emile, 182
"between two deaths," 85, 137, 141,
    221–22, 228
Booth, Stephen, 227
Braden, Gordon, 99–100, 105, 111,
    116, 117n
breast, the, 23, 54, 59, 72
Bröser, Stephen, 17, 155n
Bushnell, Rebecca, 139

canon, literary, 41, 133–36
    and construction, 214–18
    and intertextuality, 120, 214–18
character criticism, 3–4, 86, 118,
    162, 237–38
construction, 203–8, 215–16, 218–
    23
Crewe, Jonathan, 15, 12n, 94, 98n,
    102n, 107n

de casibus tradition, 101
deixis, 179–83
Deleuze, Gilles, and Felix Guattari,
    5, 200, 213n, 216–18
de Man, Paul, 32, 61–62n, 180–81
de Quincey, Thomas, 224–45
Derrida, Jacques, 28n, 30n, 31–32,
    61–62n, 130–31
Diana and Actaeon, 175–76
drives, 73, 85, 195

ego, 122
    ideal ego and ego ideal, 47, 50,
        85, 128, 236–37

ego (*cont.*)
and mirror stage, 42n
elegy, 22, 82
Eliot, T. S.
    "Hamlet and His Problems," 65–
        66, 87–88, 112
    "Shakespeare and the Stoicism of
        Seneca," 97–98
    "Tradition and the Individual
        Talent," 87, 132–35
Erinnerung, 27–28, 32, 114n
Euripides, 34, 43, 90–92, 102, 243
    The Bacchae, 114
    Hecuba, 102
    Trojan Women, 102
extimité, 4–6, 141, 158, 190

fantasy, 68–73, 86, 239–40
    traversing the, 206–8, 226–29
Fatal Attraction (Adrian Lyne), 84–85
father
    as ghost, 48, 57, 90, 118
    name of, 22–24, 70, 190
    primal, 76
Felman, Shoshana, 3, 24, 125n, 193,
    196
Ferenczi, Sandor, 21
fetish, 80, 154–58, 159–60, 169
Fineman, Joel, 70–71, 177, 231
Fink, Bruce, 72n, 74–75, 81, 207n
foreclosure (*Verwerfung*), 78, 146,
    190–91, 244
    and disavowal (*Verleugnung*), 171
    and repression (*Verdrängung*), 171,
        199–202, 227, 246–47
    of tragedy, 7, 209–18
fort-da game, 28–32, 234
Freud, Sigmund
    "Analysis Terminable and
        Interminable," 56–57
    Beyond the Pleasure Principle, 28–32
    "Case of Schreber, The," 199,
        202, 227
    "Constructions in Analysis," 203–8
    "Dissolution of the Oedipus
        Complex," 23n, 34, 55–59
    "Dostoevsky and Parricide," 169–
        71
    The Ego and the Id, 20n, 23n, 30n
    "Fetishism," 155
    "Fetishism: Remarks to the

        Vienna Psychoanalytic Society,"
            156–57
    Inhibitions, Symptoms, and Anxiety,
        171n
    "Instincts and Their Vicissitudes,"
        20
    The Interpretation of Dreams, 14–16,
        26–28, 67, 167
    Letters to Fliess, 12–19, 151
    "Loss of Reality in Neurosis and
        Psychosis," 205
    "Medusa's Head," 155n, 169–70
    Moses and Monotheism, 50
    "Mourning and Melancholia," 16,
        19–26, 29, 170–71
    "Negation," 20n, 21n, 178–79,
        202, 204–5
    "Project for a Scientific
        Psychology," 178–79
    "Psychopathology of Everyday
        Life," 18
    "Sexual Theories of Children,"
        246
    Studies on Hysteria, 23
    "Theme of the Three Caskets,"
        145–62, 164, 166–67, 189,
        193n–94n, 194, 198–99
    Three Essays on Sexuality, 246–47
    "Two Principles of Mental
        Functioning," 233–34
    Wolf-Man, The, 200

Garber, Marjorie, 26, 106n, 114n
gaze, the, 219–21
genre, 36–37, 45–53, 94
    and character, 237–38
    and genus, 101, 137
    and rhetoric, 58
Goethe, Johann Wolfgang, 17, 107,
    236
Goldberg, Jonathan, 219, 227
grammar and rhetoric, 179–80

hallucination, 80, 207–8, 212n, 213,
    223–29
Hamlet
    Claudius, 74–76, 81, 121
    first soliloquy, 60–61, 75, 82, 110–
        12, 117, 119–25
    Gertrude, 65–66, 74–76, 81–87,
        111–14
    the Ghost, 107–8
    Glenn Close as Gertrude, 82–87

"More than kin and less than
    kind," 1–3, 58
Olivier's film of, 82–86, 140
Ophelia, 76–82, 240
Player's speech, 43–44, 97n, 100–
    103
play within a play, 105, 117
Polonius, 44–45, 79, 112, 203
as satyr-play, 112–13, 123
soliloquy as form in, 109
"The rest is silence," 51–52, 242
third soliloquy, 115–17, 244
"To be or not to be," 28, 77n–
    78n, 105
"tragical-comical-historical-
    pastoral," 112–13, 123
Zeffirelli's film of, 82–87, 140
Hegel, G. W. F., 35–41, 53, 238
on Antigone, 39, 131, 134
and Lacan, 174–75, 180–83
Heidegger, Martin, 150, 182–85,
    193
Hitchcock, Alfred, 84, 85n, 123
Homer, 36, 238
Iliad, 42–43
Odyssey, 39–40, 138–39
Hyppolite, Jean, 201

imaginary, 124, 153
incorporation, 32, 139, 244
intertextuality
and canonicity, 120, 132, 191,
    215–18
and influence, 98, 120
and mourning, 43, 139
and the real, 162
introjection, 18–31, 94, 103–5, 113–
    14, 133, 139

Jakobson, Roman, 233
Job, Book of, 147–48, 158–62, 215–
    17
Jocasta, 140, 209, 222, 229
jouissance, 69–70, 74–77, 113, 125–
    26, 177
and ethics, 193–94, 197
and loss, 150–53
Judaism
and Benjamin, 50–51
and literary history, 158–62
and psychoanalysis, 217–18
and Shakespeare, 147–48

Kasten
and castration, 155, 209–10, 223
Freud's memory of, 17–19, 24–25,
    153
and Thing, 153, 157–58, 186
Kierkegaard, Søren, 53, 123, 132–
    36
Klein, Melanie, 21–22, 30n, 97n,
    114, 200, 212n
Kristeva, Julia, 24n, 64n, 184n
and abjection, 21n, 94, 106
Kyd, Thomas, 103

Lacan, Jacques
"Agency of the letter," 189
Che vuoi? diagrams, 75, 232–46
"La chose freudienne," 164, 172–
    92
Les complexes familiaux, 229
"Direction of the Treatment,"
    155n
"Fetishism," 156, 169–70
L-Schema, 120–28, 236n
objet a, 4, 68–74, 128–29, 172,
    178, 207, 211, 221, 231
point de capiton, 199, 211–12
"Remarque sur le rapport de
    Daniel Lagache," 175n, 184n
"Rome Discourse," 174
R-Schema, 120, 128–31
S_1 and S_2, 185, 209–11, 219–23,
    231
"Science and Truth," 196, 228n
Seminar I, 24, 184n, 199, 201
Seminar II, 78n, 121–22, 166–69,
    172, 195–96, 199
Seminar III, 199–202, 207n
"Seminar V," 199n, 232
"Seminar VI," 34, 55–56, 67–88,
    104–6, 125–26, 232, 240, 244–
    45
Seminar VII, 125–26, 138, 163–89,
    191–99, 200, 221
"Seminar X," 79, 171n
Seminar XI, 77, 129n, 150n, 171–
    72, 184n, 196, 219–21, 225
"Seminar XIV," 150n, 200n, 206
"Seminar XV," 196, 206
Seminar XX, 175–78, 188n
Seminar XXII, 188
Seminar XXIII, 189n

Lacan (*cont.*)
    "Subversion of the Subject," 73,
        81, 232–46
    Television, 155
Lear
    and *Antigone*, 140–41, 148
    beard of, 128
    blindness in, 210–14
    Cordelia as Thing, 145–46, 198
    Cordelia recognized by Lear, 223–
        26
    Cordelia's "bond," 148–50
    "darker purpose," 152
    Dover Cliffs, 170, 218–23
    ending of, 226–29
    and Job, 158–62
    "Nothing" in, 150–51, 186–89,
        209, 212, 224
    "plague-sore," 159–60
    storm scene, 128
    Tom o' Bedlam, 159–60
Longinus, 43–44, 53
loss versus lack, 149–50, 154–56,
    170, 188
Lynch, David, 77

melancholia
    and gender, 23, 54–58
    history of, 49–50
    and identification, 36, 117
    and narcissism, 20–22, 31, 52, 63,
        123
    and orality, 23, 114
    and the pre-Oedipal, 13–26
menstruation, 85n
metaphor, 189
    literalization of, 160, 212–13
    and metonymy, 58–59, 70–71, 79,
        230–36
Miller, Jacques-Alain, 4, 72n, 190–
    91, 212n, 229
mother, 48
    and allegory, 61–67
    and demand, 58, 71–86, 103–5,
        109, 116, 130
    flesh of, 57, 74–76
    and mourning, 17–19, 27
mourning
    intertextual, 42, 95
    and melancholia, 13, 19–20, 57
    and periodization, 52
Murray, Timothy, 146n, 212n, 226

Nachträglichkeit, 7, 23n, 27, 55, 150–
    51, 235
Nägele, Rainer, 12n, 48n, 50–52,
    62, 97n, 105n
neurosis
    obsessional, 77–78, 85, 241–42
    and psychosis, 190, 202–3, 228
Nietzsche, Friedrich
    Birth of Tragedy, 35–38, 41–45
    Ecce Homo, 44
Niobe, 111–16, 119–25, 243

object
    as cause of desire, 3–4, 134–36,
        150, 164, 171
    in desire, 3, 38, 63, 68–71, 86,
        239
    of loss, 57, 154, 197, 207
    transitional, 155, 171
Oedipus, name of, 44, 211–14
Oedipus complex
    dissolution of, 55–56, 76, 94–96,
        99, 104, 114
    and gender, 55–56
    and historical narration, 28, 87–
        88
    and interpretation, 25, 235
    and the pre-Oedipal, 19–26, 31,
        94, 114
    and tragedy, 34, 122, 190, 208–9
Oedipus Rex. See Sophocles
Orpheus and Eurydice, 171–72,
    175–76
Other
    and alienation, 57–58
    barred, 72–73, 75, 79, 81, 240–41
Ovid, 110, 115, 127

phallus
    and the breast, 23, 54, 59
    as real, 75–77, 81, 125
    as signifier, 69–70
Plato, 36, 40–41
Pommier, Gerard, 206–8, 211, 222
projection, 19–31, 103–6
Prosopopoeia, 22, 177
psychosis, 199–208
    and construction, 202–6
    and mourning, 78
    See also Foreclosure

real, 4–5, 75–79
    and trauma, 129, 136, 151, 164–
        65
Rose, Jacqueline, 12n, 65–66, 109,
    116, 153n
Ruskin, John, 22

Sade, Marquis de, 221
Schneiderman, Stuart, 194, 218n
secret, 135–36
Segal, Charles, 110
Seneca
    Hercules Furens, 93, 95n
    Medea, 93, 95n
    Oedipus, 91–93, 101–3, 114
    Phaedra, 93–94, 102, 105–6, 110
    Phoenician Women, 102, 104
    Thyestes, 93, 103
    tradition of, 58, 88, 98–99, 243
    Trojan Women, 93, 95n, 96, 97n,
        102
Shakespeare, William
    Macbeth, 224–25
    The Merchant of Venice, 69, 151,
        158, 161
    The Tempest, 230–31
    See also Hamlet; Lear
Shelley, Percy Bysshe, 131
Socrates, death of, 36–40, 47, 51–52
Sophocles, 35, 57
    Antigone, 39, 119–20, 125–27,
        131–41, 148–51, 194–95, 198
    Oedipus at Colonus, 91, 104, 127,
        141, 192–98, 211–12, 228–29,
        241
    Oedipus Rex, 55, 91–92, 100–101,
        104, 127, 140–41
Sphinx, 152, 246
structuralism, 175, 238
sublime, 43, 188
symbolic
    and the imaginary, 24, 79, 84,
        113, 121, 124, 178, 247
    and the real, 178, 188
symptom, 189, 230–32, 235–36

Thing
    and femininity, 85n, 128–29, 131,
        166–68, 175–78
    in Heidegger, 182–84
    and loss, 154, 172
    murder of, 70, 174–75
    and nothing, 149–50
    and object, 76, 145
    as sign and signifier, 174–75, 185,
        211
topology, 131, 140, 153, 158–59,
    223
tragedy
    bad, 35, 98
    Baroque, 95–96, 104–5
    Christian, 38–41, 131, 161–62
    and gender, 54–59, 102, 118
    post-classical, 35–36, 88
    revenge, 118
    translation, 14–15, 28, 37, 54, 57–
        59, 95–96
    Trauerspiel, 34–59
    and gender, 54–59
    and historicism, 95–97, 113
    and melancholia, 36
    and tragedy, 37–38, 62, 95
    trauma. See real.

underworld, descent to, 40–43, 92–
    93
Unheimlichkeit, 64, 155
Untergang,
    of Oedipus complex, 34, 55–56,
        94–96
    of tragedy, 42, 46–54

Virgil, 96n–97n, 100

Weber, Samuel, 35n, 45, 46n, 167n
Winnicott, D. W., 155
Wo Es war, soll Ich werden, 195–97,
    206, 228–29

Zeitlin, Froma, 139
Zizek, Slavoj, 4, 73n, 137, 161–62,
    189n, 195, 228n

Library of Congress Cataloging-in-Publication Data

Lupton, Julia Reinhard, 1963–
After Oedipus : Shakespeare in psychoanalysis / Julia Reinhard Lupton
and Kenneth Reinhard.
    p.   cm.
Includes bibliographical references and index.
ISBN 0-8014-2407-0 (alk. paper).—ISBN 0-8014-9687-X (alk. paper)
    1. Shakespeare, William, 1564–1616—Knowledge—Psychology. 2. Shake-
speare, William, 1564–1616. King Lear.   3. Shakespeare, William, 1564–
1616. Hamlet.   4. Oedipus complex in literature.   5. Psychoanalysis and literature.   6. Psychology in literature.   7. Benjamin, Walter, 1892–1940.
8. Lacan, Jacques, 1901– .
PR3065.L86 1993
822.3'3—dc20   92-54975